Only So Many Tides

Ray
To will away
the winter
evenings.
with love
M xxoo
Jan 2002.

Dedicated to Mum and Dad

Only So Many Tides
The Story of a Man's Lifelong Association With a Small Boat Called *Deva*

Jon Wainwright

ILLUSTRATED

SEAFARER BOOKS
2001

This edition published in 2001 in the UK by

Seafarer Books
102 Redwald Road, Rendlesham
Woodbridge
Suffolk IP12 2TE

UK ISBN 0 9538180 3 9
.

Typesetting and design by Julie Beadle
Cover design by Louis Mackay

Illustrations:
Boat plans and maps by Jon Wainwright
Drawings by Walter Kemsley and Jon Wainwright

Printed in Finland by WS Bookwell OY

Foreword

What is it that we all find so appealing about old things? Old boats, antique furniture, old books, the old familiar places. Like all creatures we humans are most comfortable with what we know and are used to. But I think there is more to it than that especially with the human relationship with old wooden boats. The essence of it is surely that they are human scale. With a few simple tools and the trees in the nearby wood you can build a boat that could take you across oceans. Whereas steel and fibreglass vessels imply foundries, vast petrochemical complexes, money, industrial society. Add to our wooden boat builder's know-how, the record of a few hundred years of human experience, a rope walk, a weaver and enough helpers and they could turn their human scale crafts into a *Victory* or a Grand Banks schooner like *Bluenose*. On his own he would be quite capable of building a humble "nobby", a north-west prawner like Jon Wainwright's *Deva*, originally built about 1914 for a workaday life of fishing.

But discerning yachtsmen soon appreciated the sea-kindly lines, sailing qualities and sturdy build of *Deva*'s traditional hull and gaff rig. Jon Wainwright's lifelong ownership started in 1962 and his intimate relationship with her has resulted here in a deeply considered assessment of these traditional craft and the "mysterie of their waye in the sea". His descriptions of a Liverpool boyhood and his early fascination with boats surely chime with the similar boyhood interests of innumerable boat lovers. The later accounts of races and old gaffer events which have meant so much to him recall my own seminal meeting with sailing and gaff rig long ago in the 1930s, in our Sea Scout ex-Bristol Channel pilot cutter *Bonaventure*. The year 1962, when he acquired *Deva*, was a landmark for me too; I joined the Port of London Authority that year and began my longtime love of London River's rich shipping and maritime history. Jon's book has thus dusted off a lot of my nautical memories too, so I take this opportunity of thanking him for a jolly good nostalgic and very informative read, which I commend to all lovers of old boats, everywhere.

Alan Cameron

Contents

In The Beginning

I was not always interested in boats and the sea.

In fact my memories of my first visit age four to the Liverpool Pierhead to go on the Ferries in 1950, then steam driven, only recall the trams. There seemed hundreds of tram tracks with Green Goddesses swaying, screeching and switching all over the place. The scene was a giant-size dodgem park.

I do remember on a trip on the Overhead Railway seeing the Liverpool Docks and all the huge liners and cargo ships towering above the warehouses. However, I was more interested in the little tank engines pulling their trucks so perilously close to the water's edge. On one Bank Holiday in 1954 my dad managed to talk one of the engine drivers into letting me into the cab. He let me handle the regulator, and we nearly ran a taxi down!

Liverpool Waterfront 1950s

Dingle

Toxteth

Liverpool

LIVERPOOL OVERHEAD RLY.

Pierhead

1 = Stanley
2 = Collingwood
3 = Trafalgar
4 = Waterloo
5 = Prince's
6 = Canning
7 = Albert
8 = Salthouse
9 = Duke's
10 = Wapping
11 = Queens
12 = Coburg
13 = Brunswick

My interest in boats actually developed from comics. Boys' comics in those days had four basic themes. Space, cowboys and Indians, Yanks winning W.W.II and pirates. Space travel was too far off, the Wild West had been won, I was not a Yank, so my only aspiration was piracy, or the prevention thereof. The pirate galleons fascinated me. They always had fair winds, they sailed amongst all these beautiful islands, and although most of their crews had lost an eye, an arm or a leg, they all seemed very happy, healthy and wealthy.

My first boat was therefore a galleon, made out of a piece of offcut timber five inches by two inches and two feet long. I sawed a rough bow, and two little chunks off the other end to make rudimentary quarters for a stern. On this I fixed three six-inch nails crossed with lollipop sticks for yards. Some old rags formed the basis for three square sails, and we were ready to launch.

Where I lived in Hale, on the north bank of the Mersey, there were several "pits". Possibly they had been dug out for clay hundreds of years ago, because they were deep. They all had names. There were the Blackwater, the Clodymore, the Dog Kennel, the Ice House and one with a

name something to do with rabbits. There was sometimes a conflict with the sport of coarse fishing, but generally we did try to keep clear. Indeed I used to fish myself and had a little sideline selling eels, or "snigs" in Lancashire, to one or two locals.

The galleon, despite tank trials in the bath, sailed very badly. She made more leeway than headway, and this has been my problem for half a century. However, more research material came to hand. A new comic came out, based on classic stories. There was a story about "Mutiny on the Bounty". The illustrations were much more realistic and detailed on the ships. The crews were less handicapped by war wounds, but they did suffer an awful lot of lashing with a cat-of-nine tails, keel hauling and swinging from the yardarms. However, they still sailed in beautiful waters and had lots of fun. In Tahiti the mutineers met up with these lovely ladies in grass skirts, who appeared to be a great improvement on my sister. Not only did they spend the whole time ashore cooking and waiting on the matelots, but they played boats with them too.

My galleon thus developed considerably over the years. The six-inch nails were replaced with dowels, which in turn sprouted topmasts and topgallants. We crossed four yards on the main, three on the fore and two on the mizzen. Hornblower came on the reading list, and the old galleon became *HMS Victorious*. By this time she had had another piece of wood nailed on her bottom to increase the draft, and some flattened lead piping for ballast to counteract the lead hamper. The ship kept evolving through the centuries until she ended her days as a brigantine. By that time I was writing my own sea stories basically to myself, and *Victorious*, now decommissioned, was sailing a lot faster in fiction than in fact. I remember writing about her leaving port "leaving a tug boat rolling in her wash".

In those days little boys sailed boats on ponds very seriously, often encouraged by dads. My mother was rather embarrassed by *Victorious* being eclipsed by shop-made boats, and pestered my father to buy me a new yacht. She was called *Endeavour IV*. She was quite advanced with Bermudan sloop rig, self-acting headsail, hollow with a massive fin keel. She sailed quite well, and, with the temporary loss of interest, *Victorious* was consigned to the bin by my mother.

Plastic was then appearing in the hobby shops. I remember being given a "Penguin Ocean Racer", which was a marvellous moulding of a 40 foot sloop with classic underwater lines and counter stern, moulded cabin top and cockpit. It also had a little dinghy which could be towed astern or stowed on the foredeck. She saw relatively short service before suffering a serious attack by some yobs with catapults. After that she was converted to gaff rig before following the fate of *Victorious*. I also had a plastic model of a lugsail dinghy. She was a real beauty, but was too realistic. In those days buoyancy was not universal, and one day she sank on the Dog Kennel in a squall. I wrote a poem in lament.

3 Lugsail Dingys

1st Verse When I had a fourteen foot dingy
I was over joyed by the sight
Of a fourteen foot dingy
My friend did envy and he said
My Birthday's soon and so I'll have one
Soon when we reached the lake
And when we hoisted the sail
It began to flap and shake
We had a race and mine won first
And another race his came first
Then the wind began to blow
And we had to spill the wind out of the sail
But that did good
Luggers feeling in a beam wind
Always defying and never surrendering
To the mighty sea
My friends sank first and mine last;
And they bravely sank to the bottom
of the sea

2nd Verse I bought another lugger dingy
And sailed her in a race;
But the currents were too strong;
And wired her to
The mighty ocean wave
She managed it and did it,
And gave us a hope
Of beating the doggy sea
When she failed in that bloody sea;
Which had taken two luggers down;
She clipped along, at the speed of the wind
And she did it well and beat all the dangers
The second time, she sailed in the Dog Kennel
There was a mighty gale
She gapered before the wind
As fast as you could say
The gale got up and the waves high;
But she always defied the winds and the waves,
Never losing never winning
Half a foot of freeboard on the lee

Five foot on the weather
Always defying, making leeway.
Always defying the sea.
Always losing but never surrendering.
Under reefed sail she skidded along
Always defying the sea
Always fighting with all her strength
Always being beaten but never surrendering
She pounded herself on a mighty rock
She she was being washed over it
And her fate was near.
She lifted her lee gunvale,
And her mast waved to me;
"Goodbye, I shall see you in heaven"
And she sank to the bottom of the
sea

5th Verse A fourth lugsail dingy will rule
the doggy sea
With the phantom fleet
Never surrendering always defying
There's always a hope that one'll win
And beat the bloody Doggy

I had several other little boats. There were a Broads cruiser, *Tugboat Annie*, a drifter and a clockwork lifeboat, which was lost in the darkest part of the Lleyn peninsula, despite a search by most of the village. However my last and best boat was the re-rigged *Endeavour IV*. Her Bermudan rig was replaced with a cutter-headed schooner rig, with gaff foresail and topsail, plus a Marconi main - which was the original sloop mainsail. She could also set a spinnaker.

Her performance was astounding. By that time I had graduated from pits to proper boating lakes. Sefton Park had a super lake, over half a mile long. In the winter it was given over to yachting, and they even had a model yacht clubhouse. The old gents (they were probably about 25 years old) had these magnificent yachts with wind vanes, sloop rig and a length up to five feet long. They used to tack up the lake and reach down it. They were very snooty about my toy yacht, but had to eat their words when *Endeavour* ran wing and wing with a spinnaker set the length of Sefton Park. That was without any rudder either, and by trimming the sails I could make that boat sail like an arrow at speed on any point of sailing in virtually any wind. I wish I had recorded both the lines of the boat and the rig for future reference. I do remember she had a spoon bow with a very long fine run aft, a streamlined cod's head and mackerel stern.

I was getting on in years by now, nearly ten years old and starting to look seaward. My mother, when visiting her aunt in Wallasey, used to take me and *Endeavour* down to the boating lake at New Brighton. There was always plenty to see on the water then, especially at high tide when ships used to take the tidal Rock Channel out of the Mersey. The *Kathleen and May*, the last British schooner, used to sail past there sometimes. She was by then basically a motor sailer, but she still had three masts with gaffs. There were also the nobby fishing boats, again setting sail on occasions, punching out into the Irish Sea.

My reading on sailing boats was by now quite prolific. The comics had gone, Hornblower was hull down and I was reading proper sailing books. Dad had an old manual of seamanship from his Navy days, and that had all sorts of useful information in it, including several pages on full-rigged ships and barques. We had an etching of *HMS Victory* in the hall. Bearing in mind that the books I was reading were all very second-hand and old, I might have been forgiven for thinking I could have a career in the fighting navy under sail. After all I had had a thorough grounding in square rig as well as fore and aft, and knew the name of every halliard sheet and stay there was to be had on a ship. I could dispense with the midshipman bit, given a bit of training in the use of a sextant and wearing uniforms, and go straight in as a first lieutenant or higher.

However, I was short of sea time for myself, although my miniature navy had had plenty on its own. The first real boat trip I remember was on holiday in North Wales. We used to go to a place called Nevin (Nefyn in Welsh) quite frequently, where they used to do fishing trips early morning and evening. One of the most memorable days in my young life was a trip on Will Evans's cutter. She was a cabin yacht with a big cockpit which he had built himself, pretty basic mind, and on which he used to take groups out fishing for mackerel. Not only did I get the best catch of mackerel, but Will Evans let me steer, nearly all the way back. And he was so impressed he did not charge for me. I was hooked as badly as the mackerel on real boating.

The next holiday I rushed down to the beach again and scoured the sea for sight of Will Evans's boat. I asked around. Tragedy. Will Evans had sold his boat out of the area. There was no hire sailing to be had. However, there was a little lugsail dinghy for sale, £45. I worked on Mum and convinced her that rather than all this hiring of dinghies (about £3.00 per day even then) Dad could buy this boat and get his money back in saved hire fees in two holidays. Mum worked on Dad, Dad worked on the vendor and *Kaieda* was ours for £30!

Kaieda was a Twinkle 10 lugsail dinghy, built by Wright's of Ipswich. She was exceptionally heavily built and had a big iron centre plate. She needed the combined efforts of half the holidaymakers on the beach to launch her. With sister in the bows, Dad rowing in the midships and me on the helm, all wearing bulky kapok lifejackets, we somehow got out to sea. The boat was dreadfully slow to windward, but was very safe. It is probably a good job she was so stiff, because she only had a tractor inner tube as buoyancy.

When we got back to Lancashire, we showed our new boat to everyone. A very interesting visitor was old Sam Kirby. People in the village had told me that he had sailed a schooner single-handed up the Mersey. Apparently the engine was not working and the crew refused to sail the ship up to Widnes. I quizzed him about this, but he did not boast of his achievement to a small boy. In fact the memory rather depressed him. After a lifetime in sail, that was the end of an era. He had chucked the crew ashore and sailed the ship up a crowded and tidal river with shoals and fierce currents. That I believe was the last time he worked under sail. I seem to remember that the boat's name was *Protection*, but I could be wrong. We lads used to look up to old Pop Kirkby with a great deal of respect. Even in old age he had great stature and a deep booming voice, and the ability not only to chew Thick Twist or old War-Horse tobacco, but to smoke it as well really did impress.

Dad decided to base *Kaieda* on Winsford Flash, at the head of the River Weaver in Cheshire and that was the site of my first confirmed sighting of *Deva*. Looking rather out of place so far from the sea, there was a man in a flat hat on this waterlogged old boat trying to sort out a heap of wood on deck.

I also saw *Deva*, on occasions, at The Mersey Estuary at Hale. After the opening of the Manchester Ship Canal, there was very little shipping up the Mersey above Garston Docks. What there was attracted my attention as I took the dog for a walk. However, the Ship Canal did cost money, so a small number of vessels continued to navigate the treacherous tidal waters, within one or two hours of high water. Ships were headed either for West Bank Docks in Widnes, or the lock into the Ship Canal at Frodsham for access to the River Weaver. It was very rare to see a yacht, but at that time some nobbies used to work out of Widnes. They tended only to go out on an early morning tide, rushing down the river on the ebb, generally under engine, although they were still rigged for sailing. Their catches of shrimps were boiled and potted and sold round the pubs. I recall seeing one of these boats missing the tide off Hale Head by the lighthouse and her catch coming ashore in large sacks. I thought they were smuggling!

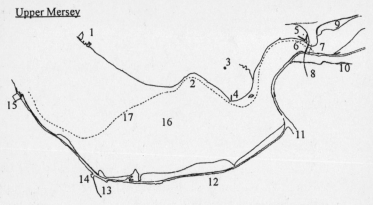

Upper Mersey

1 = Garston; 2 = Dungeon; 3 = Hale; 4 = Hale Lighthouse; 5 = Wset Bank Docks Widnes;
6 = Runcorn Bridge; 7 = Transporter; 8 = Runcorn; 9 = St Helens Canal; 10 = Bridgewater Canal;
11 = River Weaver to Winsford; 12 = Manchester Ship Canal; 13 = Shropshire Union Canal;
14 = Ellesmere Port; 15 = Eastham; 16 = River Mersey; 17 = Approx. Line of Channel.

Deva (I did not know her name as yet) looked similar in shape to the nobbies, but she seemed daintier and more colourful in her red sails. She anchored on occasions in the channel off the Dungeon at Speke to await the turn of the tide.

About that time, Dad managed to obtain some tickets for the Royal Mersey Yacht Club Regatta on the Mersey. We travelled on the committee boat after being picked up from the Liverpool Landing Stage. This was memorable with all sorts of craft taking part, all of which by today's standard would be considered classic. The lovely Mylnes took pride of place. These were about 26 feet long with a good freeboard but the lines of a metre boat. The ship itself was a museum piece, being a coal burner, and there was a problem in weighing the anchor at the end of the day, which needed the services of a tug.

After a season or two with *Kaieda*, during which she gained a staysail, we sold her for a GP14 kit. At that time there was a tremendous expansion in kit building of boats.

Locally, the preferred classes were the GP14 and the Enterprise, the latter being preferred for more sheltered waters. Dad made a very strong job of the GP14, my help being limited to painting and finishing. Opportunities for sailing were fairly limited at that time with school, rugby and Dad's busy job in Liverpool, not to mention girls. However, we still took holidays at Nevin, where we did a little racing. I made great friends with a lad in much the same position, an architect's son called Graham Maclaren. His dad was quite an expert GP14 helm, with much experience in lake sailing on Bassenthwaite. Graham and I used to sneak off in our GP on our own to enjoy the freedom of the seas and an illicit smoke.

Out of holiday season, we used to sail from Hoylake, on the Wirral. The Hoyle bank used to stretch to kingdom come, and the potential for sailing seemed very limited. However, at high water the whole place seemed to come alive. There were some very interesting local classes, with origins in antiquity. The Sea Bird Half Rater was one-some 17ft long, of heavy carvel construction (planks with cotton caulking between them fastened to ribs), drawing about 18 inches with a centre plate and gaff rig. The Hoylake Opera class was even more antiquated with its lug sloop rig and beamy clinker hull (like Viking construction, with overlapping planks clenched together). Nevertheless they were superbly suited to the boisterous local conditions in the days when otherwise capsize could mean disaster. As the tide went out the half-deckers and working nobbies made for their moorings. Within half an hour they could walk ashore dry shod on the hard sand.

In complete contrast to the old yachts and fishing boats, another vessel, which was to influence commercial and military thinking greatly, made her appearance at Hoylake. She was the first working hovercraft, the SRN2. She was incredibly noisy, her sound reaching us long before we saw her spray as she skimmed across the flats.

As something of a change to Hoylake, word came about that they were going to try and start a sailing club at Speke, by the airport. For us, faced with the problems of trailing a boat through the Mersey Tunnel to get to Hoylake, this was worth investigating. About twenty boats on trailers were convoyed through the airport grounds to the bank of the Mersey, where there was a rudimentary slipway. The plan was to sail up the river to Hale on the flood tide and return on the ebb. The breeze was a close fetch up the river, and the fleet set off at a cracking pace. However, heads began to turn as a gaff rigger ploughed her way through the fleet. It was *Deva*. It was the first time I saw her at close quarters. Remember, it was very unusual to see any sailing boats on that part of the Mersey. By the time our fleet reached Hale, *Deva* was sailing "under the arches" of the Widnes-Runcorn bridge, to Fiddlers Ferry and beyond.

This was not the last time I came across a *Deva* "connection" in my early days. In Knowsley Park my school was kindly given the opportunity to sail the lake in the summer. One on occasion we met the owner, Lord Derby. Lord Derby had sailed at one time on *Deva* before the War.

Sailing the GP14 on Merseyside was very limiting in some ways, unless you went racing. Racing One Designs meant honing the boat down till it met the rules, using the latest gadgetry you could get away with and being very nasty and lawyerish with fellow boaters. The alternative of cruising those rough and polluted waters was limited. So we started to look for something with a lid.

In those days the concept of the "pocket" cruiser had just arrived. These were boats of a size that previously would have only been considered for day sailing. However, by craftily sliding the legs of berths either under the foredeck or under the cockpit seat, designers were able to save several feet off the length of the older style minimal cruiser. The Caprice, Lysander and the Silhouette had come on the market, offering plywood kits not much bigger than dinghies. The yachting press were full of reports about such vessels, including accounts of major voyages being made by some of their skippers.

Dad and I decided to go to the Earl's Court Boatshow, then sponsored by the *Daily Express*. Unlike today's glitzy affair, the show was full of exhibits for the ordinary man. There were one or two posh yachts, but classics like the Folkboat tended to be no less than middle range. Also you were able to talk to the chaps who built or designed the boats, rather than a sales representative or executive director. You could crawl all over the boat at will, taking measurements; indeed half the visitors at the show were equipped with notebooks and rules.

We came away full of ideas and laden with brochures and boarded the train at Euston. Euston had connections with Hale, for it was being modernised at the time, and one of our richer villagers Peter Fleetwood-Hesketh was in the news trying to buy the Euston Arch from British Railways. The train journey itself was interesting in that it was one of the last London - Liverpool trains to be hauled by steam, the line having been electrified in 1961. The poor loco was in very bad condition, leaking water so much that it had to make several unscheduled stops to take on water. But it was determined to show it could still do its job, going absolutely flat out, blasting sparks, smoke and steam in profusion. Experts were advising that the speed at which the telegraph poles were going by showed that we were going well over a hundred miles per hour. Everyone on the train was taking a great interest in proceedings, the guard walking up and down the coaches keeping up a running commentary. The train was very nearly on time and everyone congratulated the driver for his efforts. But there was to be no reprieve for the loco or its crew, worked till they dropped then cast aside. Little did I know then that this was to be my fate in life too!

We looked at several boats of various types in this period. We came quite close to buying a pretty little boat called the *Sapphire* at Harlech. She was advertised as a nobby 21 feet long, and had a Bermudan rig. She was actually a Jewel class, built by Crossfield of Arnside. She had a very small cabin over the front end of the original cockpit, and a Coventry Victor engine. Her rig was in fact a neat Dragon rig, mast and all, a by-product of the change to alloy and terylene by the elite class at Abersoch. I prepared lots of plans for enlarging the cabin with a dog-house over the winter. We almost bought her, but the owner was sticking at £475, not reckoning on my Dad's frugality.

The sale of the GP14 and trailer had brought in £185, and with some scrimping and begging we hoped to raise this to £350 or so. This would buy a kit for a Silhouette, but not the delivery. The second-hand market at that price would deliver very little that was useable. We looked at some hamfisted home building efforts, we looked at converted lifeboats. The nobby conversions looked very tempting, as they appeared to be plenty of proper boat for the money. There was one big one for sale in Liverpool, straight off the fishing grounds. She looked very knocked about, but she had sail and a massive truck engine. She had six berths in the forepeak, so she must have been forty-five or fifty feet long. She clearly needed much work, but what a vessel! Regrettably we were beaten to it by some other buyers, who sailed her straight out of the dock to the bottom of the Mersey in a gale. A 32 foot converted nobby came on the market, and we rushed up to Fleetwood to see her. She looked quite a nice boat until we studied some of the repair work. She had had a bad collision recently, which had knocked half her bow off. The trouble was that the planking butts had not been staggered, and the timber used was very poor deal. Further north we went to Glasson Dock to look at a bigger, chunkier nobby called the *J.B.W.* She had a wheel-house as well, but hard times had mis-shapen her prawner lines.

The search was becoming impossible. We just did not have enough money for anything that was remotely seaworthy. Just then a friend at Tranmere Sailing Club passed over details of two boats for sale on the club notice board. One was the *Styx*, the other was the *Deva*, both advertised as nobbies. We went to look at *Deva*, where she was ashore at Bromborough Dock. Her owner, Harry Williams, worked there as foreman shipwright for Westminster Dredging Co.

Deva was a refreshing sight after most of the old "tore outs" we had looked at. Harry was in the middle of replacing part of the horn timber up to the eliptical counter stern, common to the nobby type. It was so nice to be on a boat that smelt sweet and felt so sound. She looked well built too, with timbers the same size as some 32 foot nobbies we had seen. Harry had taken all the original deck off, and replaced it with ply, reusing some of the old deckbeams forward and aft. The cabin went the full width of the boat, but was nicely styled and not too obtrusive. In the bilges lurked a 4hp engine which we shall refer to as Stuart.

Deva 1960 Conversion

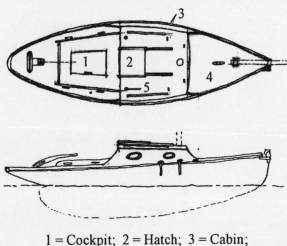

1 = Cockpit; 2 = Hatch; 3 = Cabin;
4 = Mooring cleat; 5 = Winch

Harry was blunt to deal with, but intrinsically honest. He made no great claims for the boat, but explained some of her background and the sailing he had done in her. He had indeed carried out the ditch crawling I had witnessed earlier, and also taken her on holiday to North Wales and Nevin. Coincidence indeed. *Deva*, he explained, had raced with the Rivers class with Royal Mersey Yacht Club (RMYC). All the class were named after rivers. The class had been abandoned when the RMYC brought in the Mylne class before the war. Harry had done some handicap racing with the cruiser class at Tranmere Sailing Club, but was finding it difficult to compete with contemporary boats. He had designs on a Hilbre Island One Design, now a classic boat, but then quite a modern design. The Hilbre was about 20 foot long, with centreboard, lofty rig and a cuddy up forward.

We went back to his house to look at the sails. Her main was originally almost a gunter, but he had had the angle increased to aid its setting. The jib was fairly new. I had some disagreement over the title of the rig. To me she was a sloop, setting just one headsail off an unusual bent bowsprit. He insisted she was a gaff cutter. Harry then showed us photographs taken by the *Liverpool Echo* for an article they had done about the *Deva*. Harry's forays up the Mersey had not gone unnoticed.

Whilst we were far from committed at this stage, we were certainly very interested. We did have a look at *Styx*, but her conversion was not as good and her sails were not one hundred per cent. She was cutter rigged however, with a 4hp Brit auxiliary.

Talking to members of Tranmere Sailing Club, we began to find out more about *Deva*. The reason it appeared that Harry could not compete with contemporary yachts was the boat's extraordinary speed potential for her size on a reach. The boat was average on other points of sailing, but in certain conditions she would suddenly leave the whole fleet standing still. With a fair handicap rating for her size and type she raced with an average performance for average conditions. But there was a certain rare combination of weather and sea situations that made a mockery of the handicap. Unfortunately these occasions were not rare enough for the other competitors, and the handicap committee was made to react accordingly. This meant that for most of the time she was badly handicapped for her normal performance, which took much of the fun away for Harry.

This situation is the same several years later, to the consternation of handicappers up and down the coast. I find from a racing point of view that it is fascinating to sail a boat with such a strange psyche. I always feel that if the boat decides she wants to win she will suddenly find this special speed from nowhere. It mostly does not happen, but thinking it might is a great morale booster for the crew when doing badly on a race.

Harry Williams also had a bit of a reputation himself. Every year the club ran a "Midnight Race" to the Isle of Man. One year, when the wind was north-west and strong on the nose, Harry's crew was very sick and wanted to go back. The rumour was that Harry shoved him down below, locked the hatch and then beat single-handed for seventeen hours to windward, to take third place. I would guess that the crew, if he survived, would have taken the ferry back, probably to receive emergency psychiatric treatment on landing. The big mental home in Chester is called the "Deva" hospital. I wonder why.

The boat was certainly worth going for, so the long period of haggling began. Harry wanted £450 or so, Dad was quite a few quid short of that. The "other buyer" came on the scene. A couple of chaps wanted to convert her back to fishing with a big engine, and take the sailing gear out of her. Harry did not want that to happen any more than we did. Mum intervened, insisted Dad stopped torturing Harry or me, put in some money herself; we closed the deal at £412 10s, subject to sea trials.

Deva 1960 - 1980

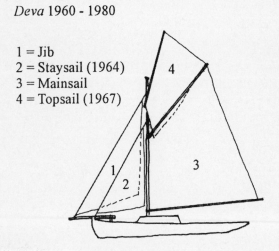

1 = Jib
2 = Staysail (1964)
3 = Mainsail
4 = Topsail (1967)

Liverpool Days

1962 – 1964

The trial sail happened to coincide with a rip-roaring north-westerly up the Mersey. *Deva* was based on swinging moorings at Tranmere, adjacent to the oil tanker terminals, but somewhat exposed to onshore winds. Harry had not sailed the boat since she had been launched, and was concerned about setting the main in the conditions. One mistake in bending it on, and it might rip. I was not too pleased about this, so it was agreed that we might try her just on the jib. Harry wanted his money after all!

It was quite a change after dinghy sailing to be on a boat which was judged to be self-righting. It was also fascinating for me to sit in the cabin and look out of the ports, sheltered from the hostile environment. The cabin had two slatted berths and a place for the cooker with the gas underneath. As far as the sailing went, it was pretty rough. The boat manoeuvred fine on just the jib. When we went to go about, I made preparations to wear ship, rather than risk stalling her without the main, to drive her through the wind. Harry was cross about that; "She's not a bloody lifeboat, you know!" he said.

We sailed her up to the mooring, flattening the jib to take the drive out of it. In the clubhouse Dad reluctantly wrote the cheque, on the understanding that Harry would take us out for a second trial sail and show us how everything worked. The second trial sail was held on a much nicer day, with a nice little breeze which made *Deva* zip along.

The gaff sail for all its antiquity certainly gave a splendid drive. We also studied the operation of the Stuart. Harry explained that it had an impulse magneto, and only needed a gentle swing to start. That was to be the last time the little brute was to start gently over the next twenty-five years.

It was lovely sailing on the river, for it was so bustling with trade then, especially going up to Eastham Locks and the Ship Canal. All the ships seemed to know *Deva*, tooting at Harry as he put his special top hat on! We sailed up to an island just above Eastham and went ashore for a picnic. This was the life, this was the boat. Then suddenly it was all taken away from us. We received a phone call that *Deva* had sunk!

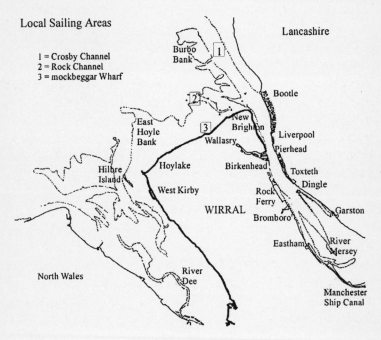

Local Sailing Areas

1 = Crosby Channel
2 = Rock Channel
3 = mockbeggar Wharf

Lancashire
Burbo Bank
1
Bootle
2
East Hoyle Bank
3
New Brighton
Wallasry
Liverpool
Pierhead
Hoylake
Birkenhead
Toxteth
Hilbre Island
West Kirby
Dingle
Rock Ferry
WIRRAL
Bromboro
Garston
Eastham
River Mersey
River Dee
North Wales
Manchester Ship Canal

Apparently someone who lived in one of the houses overlooking the moorings had noted that *Deva* was missing.

There had been thick fog in the night, and possibly a ship or fishing boat had become lost amongst the moorings.

We rushed over to Tranmere to find the entire waterfront in action with Harry directing salvage operations. *Deva* was completely submerged in about 30 feet of water at low tide. Harry was fishing round for the mooring tackle. A big tender from the Mersey Docks and Harbour Board (MDHB) had been "arranged" to just happen to be in the vicinity. The mooring tackle was winched aboard, then the tender opened up her powerful engines and *Deva* arose from the murky depths like some sea monster. Increasing speed to the point of plane, the tender headed for the shallows. She then turned hard about, simultaneously dumping the mooring tackle, leaving *Deva* to surf on to the bank. As she grounded we all leapt aboard and bailed hell for leather.

The next morning we came down to find that the boat had been moved opposite Sammy Bond's slipway. Two lads had been left aboard with buckets, but no dinghy to get ashore. It was explained to me that it was a means of ensuring the boat did not sink through crew stoppage! Unfortunately Bond's could not take us on the slip, as they had a whole load of Mylnes to launch for the RMYC. We would have to put a temporary patch over the hole. *Deva* was towed into shallow water just by the slip, and a couple of anchors were laid out. As she took the ground she sunk into the most vile mud I have ever seen or smelt. Not only was there the natural mud of the river, not only was there the sewage of the foulest river in Europe, but also the whole stinking mess was bonded by treacle-like oil from the tanker terminal.

I had to jump into this lot armed with hammer, nails, canvas and battens to try and stop the leak. The damage was strange in that nothing was seriously broken. A couple

27

of planks had been pushed right in then sprung out again jamming against the plank above. This had caused a linear gap to form which had gradually let in enough water for the boat to sink. Having fixed the leak I struggled back to terra firma and saw Harry and thanked him. "No problem, but you didn't buy me with the boat, you know!"

After a couple of weeks, *Deva* was slipped into Sammy Bond's Yard. Bond's was typical of many small boatbuilders around the coast in pre-fibreglass days. I think there were about ten men employed throughout the year building new boats, maintaining the yachts and repairing fishing boats. Bond's were building wooden motor cruisers, and although there were two working nobbies on the slip, they had not built any fishing boats for some time. Had the impending expansion in yachting stayed in timber, such yards would have expanded and kept several men in employment. But this was not to be. Fibreglass would turn the industry from a craft based one into mass production. The low maintenance factor would take away many man days of regular work from the waterfront, the rich man's wealth being diverted into imported electronic gadgets and bigger Japanese diesels.

Although the boat had only been down a tide, she was absolutely filthy inside and stank to high heaven. We spent several hours removing ruined and waterlogged gear from the boat, to leave the damaged planking accessible from the inside. Just as we were finishing, a man came aboard, unshipped the boom crutches, and rested the boom end on deck. That was the way they always stowed the gaff and boom on nobbies, he explained. To this day I do not know why fishing boats stow their booms on deck; it still seems very inconvenient to me, and more work on the topping lift.

Although *Deva* had apparently been one of the Royal Mersey Rivers Class, local fishermen and other longshoremen always referred to her as a nobby. At the time I thought it was a bit of an insult to have her referred to as a workboat, when she had indulged in such aristocratic pastimes in her youth. Why, even the Earl of Derby had sailed her! However, all the time we kept her in the North, in both England and Wales, she was referred to as a nobby. This was all to change with the rise in interest in ex-working sailing vessels, and by the 1980s people started saying to me and spitting, "That's no work boat, that's 'only' a yacht". The reality is that *Deva* was built by Crossfield of Arnside to almost exactly the same specification and design as the working nobbies. The only difference was the absence of the rubbing strake along the topsides, to minimize damage from trawl irons, but even this practice was far from universal. Subsequently on the East Coast, Maldon author and fisherman, Mike Emmett told me he had come across an 1895 reference whilst doing his research to the "Nobby Deva" in a paragraph on the setting and design of topsails. Certainly her appearance and performance is different to other Rivers Class boats I have sailed. She is beamier and heavier than the class rules require.

Motorized Fishing Nobby 1960s

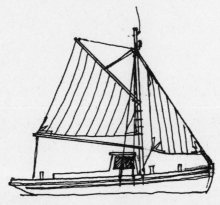

Thus the poor old girl has always been a bit of a maritime outcast, too scruffy to fit in with proper yachts, too flashy for the elitist workboat brigade. This could be due to subconscious envy of her all-round ability. Certainly few yachts can match her simultaneous versatility for shoal-water cruising and seagoing capability. Certainly few workboats can match her speed size for size on a race course. She is an excellent all-rounder for her size, and gives pleasure racing, cruising and trawling.

However, such pleasure was still in the future for me. The yard was awaiting the go-ahead from the insurance company; like most boatbuilders they had always something more urgent to do. Meanwhile the summer began to slip away. Eventually work did start, and almost in a blink *Deva* had two new planks and a rotten piece of deadwood replaced. The little Stuart was re-installed, with a new lick of paint. Indeed the whole boat had received a complete coat of "Harry Slappers" from a communal drum of paint kept for all Bondy's repairs. Grey blue for topsides, red sludge for the bottom.

The launch was fun as *Deva* hurtled precariously down the marine railway on a bogie with just a few blocks of wood supporting her. With the rudder well lashed amidships she ploughed stern first into the river again, and she was afloat!

One of the yard men went below to start the motor. It would be no problem, it had been started several times ashore, it just needed a gentle swing! An hour later, we gave up trying as the tide was going. The yard launch towed us to the mooring.

Dad got the bill the next day. Seventy pounds for the two planks and stripping down/rebuilding the engine, plus of course all the legitimate extras. The yardman spent a whole day trying to start the Stuart without success. Rude words were said about the magneto, a new one was tried, but still no joy. There was petrol in the cylinder, there was a big spark to light it. We tried hot plugs, we tried cold plugs, we tried no plugs. The laws of internal combustion remained sullied.

The only decent thing which had happened was that the new dinghy we had bought was a great success. A firm in Speke had just started making these new fibreglass dinghies. They were selling mouldings for 9 foot dinghies for twenty-five pounds each, about a third of the cost of wooden boats. The man jumped up and down on one; he picked it up and threw it against a steel stanchion. We were impressed and took it. Mother was horrified to see it. It looked like cardboard according to her. However, with a hardwood gunwale, oak thwarts and elm floorboards, it began to look like a proper boat. It performed exceptionally well under oars or Seagull outboard, and proved an excellent seaboat.

I had a short break that summer in 1963 to help a friend's father, Richard Warburton, take a narrow boat from Paddington to Stoke Bruerne on the Grand Union canal. Richard was a highly respected railway enthusiast, but he had spent many years sailing a 12 square metre Sharpie at Fiddlers Ferry on the Mersey. He was certainly no novice on the water. Richard also had the added skills of giving a continuous commentary on the steam locomotives snorting up and down the lines that criss-crossed the canal. Indeed, on the way down to Paddington, we had managed to arrange a trip on the Welshpool to Llanfair Light Railway, which had just been handed over to enthusiasts by British Railways. The journey was remarkable for the way the little loco hauled us through the side streets of Welshpool, almost in people's back gardens, before emerging into the rich green countryside of the Welsh borders, thrashing through the high grass which covered the rails. The railway still runs today, although the section through the Welshpool streets has long been lifted.

That experience on the canals was to prove most informative, especially on lock work. It was to stand me in good stead for a major inland voyage in the future.

For no reason at all the engine decided to start on occasions, so we began to venture out on *Deva*. With the swift currents and all the shipping about in those days, the Mersey was no place for a novice, especially one without an engine.

The Liverpool weather was fairly predictable. The morning would normally break with a force five from the North-West, laden with rain and squalls, blowing straight into the river. Many was the time we would arrive at Rock Ferry, only to be put off going out. The moorings were quite exposed, and the trip out in the tender would have been dangerous. If we did decide to risk it, there would be a brisk wind-over-tide beat down river through Rock Channel into Liverpool Bay - going out via the main bar seemed a very long way round. The Rock Channel was a half tide channel in those days, but with plenty of north in the wind, we could lay through it reasonably easily and reach deep water.

One of the first times we attempted it we grounded. Within half an hour we could hardly see the sea, just a thin line on the horizon. There were several depressions in the bank containing large flashes of water. I did hear of a power boat which found itself stranded within one, and spent the afternoon tearing around like a demented creature, ramming the sand to force a way through till her bottom had been ripped out. Then the tide did come in and sank her.

Typically the afternoon would turn out sunny. The fishing nobbies could be seen trawling for shrimp and sole. They all carried and used sail then, while fishing. However, by that time their mainsails had been cut down to a triple reefed size, and none ran out a bowsprit. You could still see their fine sailing boat pedigree. Their low hulls had beautiful lines with a rounded bow and eliptical counter stern. The relative lack of sheer, the roughly maintained hulls and the black tarred sails tended to make them a bit workaday, but they were really more classic yacht than anything else. It was rather sad to see these magnificent beasts brutalised with big engines and cut down sailing gear.

The nobbies used to follow the young flood tide up the Rock Channel, just using sail as there was no point in rushing until there was enough water. *Deva* felt very superior with her full sailing rig as her defrocked sisters drifted along under pathetic scraps of steadying sail. Now the tables have turned considerably as thirty-five years on the nobby owners have their own prestigious race in craft restored to full sail again. Yachty creatures like *Deva*, even if she is the same shape and pulls a trawl, definitely have to stay in the background now.

Most of our sails took us out past Hilbre before the flood set in to take us back into the Mersey. Occasionally we sailed a short way up the Mersey on a midday tide, up past Garston Docks, but the real pleasure was to escape the industrial filth. The vigour of the sea breeze was a real tonic.

The Stuart did not improve its behaviour, and several times we were forced to use the dinghy lashed alongside to pull us out of trouble. Rarely did the engine choose a safe place to have a tantrum. As the season drew to a close - it was as early as mid September in those days - we began to have thoughts on where we might lay up, and what needed to be done.

In Hale there were no secure places to lay up, either ashore or afloat. Local sailing centres were either to the north of Liverpool, or on the Wirral, quite some distance away. However, there were several miles of Liverpool Docks where there might be a quiet corner for a little boat. Some local research revealed that because the Docks had been built out into the Mersey, local fishermen had lost their ability to land their catches and access the river generally. To compensate for this, the Mersey Docks and Harbour Board used to allow such boats free berthing and locking in and out.

Dukes Dock was one of the docks used by small craft. This was originally built for the Duke of Bridgewater, and was originally used by canal boats that had made their way across the Mersey from the Bridgewater Canal from Manchester. The Duke had been a very powerful man in those parts, and there are still many references to him on old buildings and street names in Liverpool. However, the dock was hardly the place for the discerning yachtsman. There were all sorts of old "tore-outs" in various states of hopelessness. There were several lifeboats, ex-services craft and old nobbies berthed there, not always afloat. It was like a pre-classic boat festival. Instead of the varnish and glistening paint of today's vessels, it was green paint stolen from the city council tram shed and gas works tar. Instead of the fine grained cedar, teak and mahogany in today's restoration, old driftwood and bottom boards out of railway wagons would be nailed over the gaps. The people at this pre-classic boat festival would not be the learned middle class enthusiasts whom we see today; they would be poor men, often unemployed, trying to fight the relentless rot of yesterday's navy in wretched conditions. To make ends meet, it was not unheard of to have boats offered to you at very low price, only for you to realise that the chap offering the bargain did not even own the boat!

Deva was given a much more select dock to rest in, the now famous Albert Dock. The dock was no longer used for commercial traffic, but the magnificent Napoleonic warehouses were stashed full of wine. This gave the place a marvellous aroma, but it was very quiet, almost ghostly, in the dock with *Deva* the only boat. You would be hard put to imagine this situation nowadays, Albert Dock being a major activity centre with pubs, restaurants, night clubs and shops, as well as the museum.

Our free stay in Albert Dock was relatively short as we were craned out at Canning Dock a few weeks later. We then had to pay the MDHB for ground rental!

The sinking in the Mersey had left *Deva* stinking of horrible things. Notwithstanding the swilling out she had had in the boatyard, the smell remained. With all those massive timbers and frames to lurk behind, the nasties had kept in business. The major task then, apart from the outside work, was to clean and paint every nook and cranny in the bilges, which was not an easy job in the extremely cramped conditions on such a small boat.

One advantage of such a task was that we were able to examine in minute detail every single part of *Deva*. We found one cracked frame up forward to port, which Dad doubled with a laminated one. The worst we found were one broken grown frame and one broken steamed rib amidships. This damage had probably happened in the collision. *Deva*'s construction was typical of quite a few prawners which had a rib cage of both heavy grown oak frames and steamed timbers. The planks were spiked to the grown frames with iron nails, and clenched to the steamed timbers with copper nails. Any naval architect will tell you that there is enough electrolysis with such an arrangement to light a 200 watt bulb, but the fact was that she had already lasted half a century without any serious signs of problems, and has survived thirty-plus years since.

The success of this practice was due to the heavy grown frames resisting impact and point loading, such as drying out on hard grounds, or taking a bash from trawl heads. The steamed ribs however would be better at strapping the planks together, and keeping the overall shape of the boat sound. The construction compared to that of proper yachts was very basic, with hardly a sophisticated timber joint in the whole structure. But the design was very good, enabling a strong boat to be produced quickly using basic materials. Four men would build a 32 foot prawner in six weeks, working a seventy-hour week. In modern terminology, that is equivalent to 1680 man hours, which together with materials would have given a total cost without sails but including everything else of under £30,000 at today's prices. This would be very competitive with fibreglass, and indeed if you take the 1912 price of £70 and add inflation, the story is much the same. If you were to add the cost of paying for the unemployment created by going to fibreglass, we might well have been better off all round staying with wood. But that is history.

However, in the early sixties, there was very little unemployment and the problem was finding skilled labour. With a booming building industry, many shipwrights were making a far better living on carpentry on the massive housing estates sweeping across post-war Britain. We needed a shipwright for the midship frames, and fortunately found one in a youngish chap called Jimmy. He used to spend part of every week sifting through the various bits of driftwood floating around the river and the docks. Indeed it was said he could fish the stuff out to order better than a timber merchant. At least you could be sure it was properly seasoned.

Jimmy came and looked at the boat to measure up the frames for timber, and returned next day with two pieces exactly the right size. He said he would take them back home to let them dry out. My dad was very impressed with this frugality! A couple of weeks later he returned, hacked out the old frame and formed the shape of a new one with a series of longitudinal cuts in the salvaged timber. He put glue between the cuts then pulled the frame against the planks. Similarly he did the steamed timber, although he retained the old one and just used it as a doubler. This early form of laminating has stood the test of time, although the quality of the glue may not have been up to it.

There were two other yachts nearby on the quayside. One was a modern cold moulded sloop, the other was a 30 foot Hillyard. The 30 foot Hillyard looked quite a monster out of water, and attracted attention from passers by. By contrast *Deva* was the same as the ubiquitous nobby fishing boats, still very common in those parts. Regularly we would be asked what the various boats would cost. The Hillyard would be the first one they would enquire about; we would say about two thousand. The next would be the cold moulded; we would say about twelve hundred. This still being too much for their pockets, they would then come out with the ultimate insult "And how much for an old fishing boat like this one?"

But having a nobby type of boat did help us in many ways to be absorbed into the local waterfront community. Although in those days pilfering was rife, we had not one item stolen during our stay in Liverpool. Indeed, we used to gain various items such as rope and so on, just dropped in our cockpit anonymously. I was often invited to have a look round other nobbies in various states of repair. I was told of a "new" one being built at Duke's, but this turned out to be an old one suffering major surgery in terms of new frames and several planks. She was not being converted to a yacht however, but going to resume a fishing career for commercial purposes. I often wonder where she ended up. Another one of the interesting boats passing through the docks was a Rivers class sister to *Deva* called *Dart*. She had been totally transformed from the "old fishing boat" style. Her owner, a naval architect had really gone to town in her modernisation. The elliptical counter had been cut off to form a transom stern. The rig had been made into a modern Bermudan sloop. She had a long coachroof running up to forward of the mast. Although today's traditionalists would have thrown fits at such a major modernisation, it was actually very well done. For the size of boat the accommodation was good and well thought out, and little had been done to compromise her sea-keeping qualities.

Internal *Deva* 1960 - 79

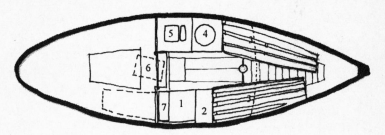

1 = Quarter berth; 2 = Storage; 3 = Slatted bunks;
4 = Thunder box / chemical toilet; 5 = Sink;
6 = Engine; 7 = Fold down cooker

I remember looking at another *Deva* sized nobby type in Duke's. This was a working boat. She had just completed a thorough refit. She had just had some new sails made as well, a mainsail and staysail. She was essentially a motor boat, but these sails, equivalent to a double reefed main on a sailing boat, would help push her along in a breeze. To me at the time it seemed such a shame that a boat like *Deva* should be deprived of a full set of sail, but I was not to know that within a decade or so the commonplace working nobby setting any sail would have become a rarity.

During our stay in Liverpool working nobbies bought up cheaply by amateurs for conversion would arrive in the docks. I remember looking over one brought in to Canning Half Tide Dock. Her owner had only paid £400 for her, all 38 feet long. She had the narrow cockpit with a small cuddy forward, and a big engine. The sailing mast was still in her, but no bowsprit. She was apparently sound as a bell below the waterline, and just needed a little bit of work on the gunwales, which could be done while she was afloat. Several years later I returned to Liverpool. I think it was she, ashore, in the last stages of restoration. She had not been for a sail since I had first seen her.

There was also an old racing yacht, said to be a twelve metre, which was being converted to a ketch for a boys' club. Whether this project ever came off I do not know. The racing yacht seemed to be short of her ballast keel, and floated high above her marks. Coupled with the coachroof and dog-house, she did not look as pretty as she should have done. She needed a tremendous amount of work on her.

When we look at boats for restoration we tend to concentrate on the hull. As long as that is sound, we are not too bothered about the rest. But really the deck is the most problematical part of a traditional boat. It is often more complicated in its construction than the hull, has openings and hatches which always leak, and is subject to damage from use. Invariably it lets water in at its junction with the topsides, the gunwales, and on boats which spend much time unused, like yachts, that water will be fresh and dangerous.

Harry had totally redecked *Deva* when he had bought her. The old planked deck had been taken right off. The original thwart had been removed, together with the old narrow cockpit and carlines. Using the original deck beams fore and aft, and with new beams amidships, he laid half-inch ply. The new cockpit was just a footwell, and a full width cabin was constructed, with mahogany sides. It sounds horrible, but actually it did not look unattractive, serving its purpose for many years. However, the old canvas was starting to go a bit, the sinking in the Mersey not helping particularly. Dad knew someone in Dunlop's at Speke, who could get hold of some Trakmark very cheaply. Trakmark was a ribbed rubber product on a nylon fabric backing, which at the time was the very best for covering decks. Everything had to be stripped off. We took off cockpit coamings, hatches, cleats, fittings, handrails, toerails and other pieces. These were items that could all be taken back into the garage to be worked on and refurbished. The Trakmark was laid over the decks, and taken over the gunwales, to be held firm by beading as well as glue.

Back home we worked on all the pieces we had taken off. The timber parts were treated with many applications of linseed oil. They were allowed to dry out before varnishing and looked absolutely splendid. Meanwhile, the outside of the boat was being worked on, specifically the bottom, which was being burnt off. We were anxious to ensure that all was sound before she went into the water again.

Buying the paint was quite fun. Locally there was a wholesaler of British Paints, then the leader on quality marine paints. If I went in wearing my work clothes, the practice was to search out any damaged tins (one or two of which could get damaged in the search). These if purchased with cash could command a very serious discount. I once made the mistake of turning up with a collar and tie, and was well and truly fleeced with full retail price.

The boat looked a bit of a mess at this time, but really much useful work was being carried out. The disreputable Stuart was now back with its creators in the south for a full works overhaul. This had enabled the engine beds to be replaced, and me to clean out and paint the bilges underneath. The whole hull internally had received a full two coat decoration service. The pigs of ballast were chipped clear of rust and given a good black leading. These were pigs indeed, nicely shaped to sit between keelson and grown frames; some weighed over a hundredweight each. Externally, all the iron work such as the keelband, rudder straps and external ballast had been red-leaded. The bottom had also received three coats of primer paint. Topside, suspect patches had been dubbed in undercoat.

Consideration was also being given to the installation of a thunder box or chemical toilet and an additional quarterberth. This was the first of many designer decisions which were to tax us over the next 30 years, how to get that quart into a pint pot. The "pocket" cruisers were now all the vogue, and magazine write-ups kept talking about boats even smaller than *Deva* packing in four berths, toilet, galley, dinette; the list went on. I don't think many were actually put to the test, for had they been successful their designers would have had a very lucrative future in designing space capsule interiors. The fact is that a combination of low freeboard, short waterline length, pinched-in ends and an interior cluttered by oversized timber structural components made comfortable living aboard a "pocket" cruiser a technical impossibility.

For *Deva*, it gradually all came together. The decking was covered in the Trakmark. All the fittings were bolted or screwed down, bedded in copious quantities of white lead. There were the usual problems with the weather, finding the appropriate window in the normally rain-laden sky to apply the marine gloss. But we were nearing fruition, and the imagination ran riot with visions of a glistening boat slicing through a sparkling summer sea. Even the little Stuart, looked immaculate with green, grey and red paint, just like the boatshow versions, was being gently lifted in - Jimmy being on hand to align the engine on its new bearers. The anti-fouling undercoat went on and we were ready for the next stage.

The next problem was the lift-in. As we were in a commercial dock, there were of course several mobile cranes in the vicinity, but few had experience of boat lifting. The Mersey Docks and Harbour Board caused us some trouble. Quite reasonably they could see a potential deal for a lift-in, and were after about seven pounds or so for arranging a crane and driver. The problem with that, we were told, was that we might not get the right crane driver. It would be far better to slip ten bob to the right driver, who, when he had a spare moment in his employer's time, could come over and drop the boat in.

Strangely enough we found the right driver, plus about six unofficial helpers. The MDHB may have fumed in the background, but that was in the days of strong union representation. No one would dare interfere with a member's traditional perks. Generally though, I do not recall anything but help and co-operation from all sides, they were just much more easy-going days then. The lift-in attracted much attention, and as the boat looked so good as she was swung into the Canning Half Tide Dock many spectators thought she was a new boat.

There was general surprise that the boat did not leak a drop. There were lots of stories about converted lifeboats having to be left sunk for three weeks before the timber would take up. But *Deva* bobbed in the grimy dock waters oblivious to tradition. Clearly the several layers of paint made a difference, but the hull itself was obviously very tight. I think much goes back to her original construction. Basically Crossfield had been into mass production, and used wherever possible standard timber sections and fastenings. Bearing in mind that the most prolific output would have been in the 28/32 foot prawner range, the very small ones like *Deva* would have had the same specification as the larger boats. Most proper yachts of *Deva's* size would have thinner planking, smaller frames and thinner fastenings. They would have been built to a much higher standard, it is true, but they would never have stood the rough and tumble of a varied career over eighty years in the same way.

The fully works-reconditioned Stuart was swung. Not a sausage!

We returned home, speculating that there must be an air lock in the fuel line that needed purging. It could not possibly be the engine. We had a £25 bill from the manufacturer to prove it. However, the fact was that several days of cursing and mouths full of free flowing petrol were to no avail. It must be something else, and the man from Stuart was summoned. I met him at Canning Half Tide Dock, and took away the casing to expose the engine. He appeared baffled too. There was a spark, there was fuel. He took the magneto to pieces, and something sprang out and with uncanny accuracy shot through a tiny finger hole used for lifting the floorboards. There was a tinkle, we looked at each other, and realised what had happened to this critical electrical component. I had no compunction in lifting the floorboards to expose glistening bilges fit to eat off, with the microscopic electrical component clearly visible as the only loose particle in sight. I was very proud of those bilges.

The engineer fiddled about with the engine to no avail, then decided it must be a faulty magneto, and replaced it with another new one. The engine started, and ran sweetly. Was this the problem solved?

Within a few days the rigging was set up and the boat was in commission. Because of the difficulty of getting a suitable mooring, the boat continued to be based at Liverpool, in the Canning Half Tide Dock. There we made friends with George Altcar and the motor vessel *MV Warrior*. George had been a tug skipper, but force of circumstance, Liverpool shipping was in decline by then, had caused him to become a taxi driver. He lived on his boat, and worked unusual hours as a taxi driver; it was very useful to have someone about the area. We had no pilfering or damage done to the boat as a consequence, I am sure. George ran his motor cruiser like a proper ship, and had all the best equipment aboard. One item was the "Beme Loop", a radio direction finder to pinpoint position, which was very impressive. He was also a very good person to learn from, his experience with ship handling, knots and splices being very much as one might expect from a skilled professional.

Canning Half Tide Dock was one of Liverpool's older docks, and many years ago it formed the national datum for charts and maps, before it was displaced by Newlyn. Unfortunately, sailing from the Half Tide Dock was not without its problems. The locks into the Mersey, which gave the dock its name were no longer operational, and to go out of the docks we had to make a protracted journey through the system. This involved the MDHB opening several bridges, including one or two railway ones, before we found ourselves in a huge ship lock. Whilst we tried to time things so that we went out on a level, sometimes we had to tie up in the lock chamber. Fortunately we had all the "donated" heaving lines, for the sides of the lock seemed about fifty foot up!

I hate to think what this service must have cost in labour terms. There would have been several bridge keepers, plus three or four men on the lock, not to mention harbour control. All this was for a tiny sailing boat, for hardly any ships were using the south docks by then. It is hard to believe it now, but we had the same service on the way back after our day's sail, coming back on the evening flood. The huge ship lock opened on our return, men would take our lines as if we were a Blue Funnel liner, and the process through the dock system would be repeated. This service did not cost us a penny, apparently because of the old fishermen's right of access to the shore.

It was a good job that we had a stout tender and a powerful outboard. Although the large tender we towed must have looked out of scale and dragged us back on a beat, it was very useful. It would carry all our old motor car tyre fenders for a start. As our engine had no astern gear, the only way we could stop was to skid along the dock walls until we stopped. Also the engine had not given up its bad old tricks. Several times it would stop, choosing a special moment such as when a massive swing bridge was being held open for us. The dinghy would come to our rescue again and again as we would tie her alongside and start the Seagull outboard.

On more than one occasion the *MV Warrior* would give us a tow in. Indeed the camaraderie in Liverpool Docks was very comforting, something we were not to see again in Wales or the South. I am not sure that it still exists in Liverpool either. I went back several years later to find many of the docks we used to traverse filled in. All the old boats in Duke's and Canning Half Tide had gone, perhaps buried in the rubble. There were some rather snooty restored boats in Canning for both purist and tourist to look at, part of the Albert Dock redevelopment. An exclusive nobby owners' association had set up in the North Docks, where the old fishing nobbies were rebuilt into racers for the annual Nobby Race, a bit like the smacks on the Blackwater. The old pump house where we moored had been converted to a "designer" pub, where a docker or fisherman in overalls would not be welcome amongst the "suits" and tourists.

It was not the Liverpool I remembered, but it was good to see what had been preserved and valued. Gone was the old Scouse sense of humour, and gone, perhaps, was the old Scouser's willingness to help out. We had all been in it together, to have fun and to make something out of nothing, because that is all we really had. There is more money about now, and the Maritime Heritage is valued by the establishment there. I often wonder what happened to George and the *Warrior* and all the other lads in Duke's; they were real characters.

However, times were about to change for *Deva* as well as we began to think about our first summer cruise.

Welsh Experience

1964 – 1966

Before the days of package holidays and cheap flights had really got going the main place for a holiday for Lancastrians was North Wales. It was a beautiful mountainous country, in total contrast to the flat plains of industrial Lancashire, the people were different and it was relatively accessible. It was small wonder that the "Menai Straits Fortnight" featured so heavily in the local yachting calendar.

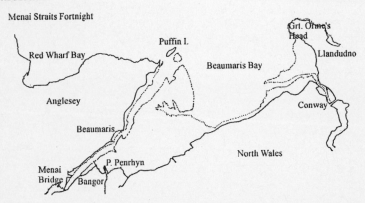

This Lancastrian wake took all the recognised One Design classes from the Mersey and Dee areas, including some of the real specials indigenous to the waters. Most of these classes still exist. At the larger end of the scale are the Mersey Mylnes, fine classic sloop rigged boats 26ft LOA first produced in the 1930s to replace the unsuccessful

48

Rivers Class. The Rivers Class, whilst they must have given good sport and were well suited to local waters, were never a proper racing boat. They were fishing boats with over heavy construction and shoal draft, too slow at a racing turn, too slow to windward. However, traditional rigs were still well represented lower down the scale. The Seabird Half Rater was a sleek gunter rigged ballasted centreboard sloop, designed nearly a hundred years ago in Belfast. They could be seen off Hoylake, in the Dee and in several locations in Wales. The most elderly looking local One Design was the Hoylake Opera Class. These craft, many of which are nearly a hundred years old, are 16 feet long and heavy clinker built and they set a standing lugsail rig with a small headsail. They are ideal for the boisterous waters off the Wirral, and are strong enough to lie on exposed local moorings. Around the corner at West Kirby, they had their own One Design as well, the West Kirby Star. This was only slightly less antique than the Opera, and was of similar size with a gunter rig. A regatta with these and other classics like Fifes and Dragons gave all the appearance of the well organised classic boat festival one occasionally sees today at Shotley in Suffolk or Hellevoetsluis in Holland. The difference was that this was for real.

Deva, being an outclassed boat, was never going to be invited to such a prestigious event. However, it was an excuse to go to the Menai Strait and watch. Furthermore friends at the Riversdale Technical College which trained people for the Merchant Navy were planning to take a squadron of Hilbre One Designs to the Strait, and one of the instructors would come with us.

Dad pressed ahead with the final fitting of the "thunderbox" and the quarter berth. I concentrated on the rigging. It was time *Deva* became a cutter! George showed me how to make a strop, then we pulled *Deva*'s mast against a high part of the quay to fit it and the halliard. Down below I laid some carpet and "made the beds". Sleeping bags were quite a rarity in those days, so we made do with conventional sheets and blankets. With the oil lamps giving out their soft light, it really was quite a cosy scene on *Deva*. I looked forward to my first night aboard.

It was arranged to bring *Deva* through the dock complex close to the sea lock the evening of the day before we were due to depart. My sister Gillian had decided to come with us, infected by the excitement about the voyage, or perhaps by a misconceived concept about a fortnight of regatta balls! I look at the chart now, and wonder why we were so worked up about the voyage. The distance from Liverpool to Llandudno is less than 40 miles. This is no greater than from Mistley to Burnham or Maldon, which we regularly have to do today, and be expected to organise a gaffers' rally on arrival. However, *Deva* now carries a powerful diesel and a wardrobe of sails for any conditions. She is probably much more suitable for coastal passages than she used to be. The idea of a day-sailer going such a distance without escort was quite rare in those days.

My sister and I stayed aboard while Dad went back with the car, ready for someone else to bring him back - there were the logistic problems of car placings even in those days! Dougie, the instructor from Riversdale, was going to meet us at daybreak. Dad returned with the bad news that the weather forecast was giving gales. We had a council of war in the cabin with someone else from Riversdale, while the rain sheeted down outside. The pipe smoke and the fumes from the oil lamps nearly suffocated my sister, but she was wedged in the fore-peak with no prospect of escape. It was decided to wait for the next forecast at 0500 hours, just before we were meant to lock out.

Dawn broke with the wind having gone down considerably, but with the prospect of coming up later to force six from the south-west. However we reckoned we should be at least within spitting distance of Llandudno when it happened. Dougie arrived, and we locked out into a grey damp Mersey. The Stuart seemed to be working for once, which we mistakenly thought was a good omen!

The wind was calm, so we motored down the Mersey, setting sail as we took the ebb out through Rock Channel. The wind was full and bye from the south, and we could just lay our course along the coast. It was still very misty, and we could see no further than the Point of Ayr at the nearest corner of the Welsh coast. The staysail, which was really just a smaller jib, was set with some success. We sailed with the favourable ebb tide under us, watching Hoylake pass by, and then the mouth of the Dee estuary.

It was not midday when the mist suddenly cleared exposing the Great Orme on the horizon. The Great Orme is a huge rock mountain guarding the entrance to the Menai Strait. It is quite a feature, and attracts many visitors, who use a unique cable tramway to climb its steep slopes. Whilst it was good in some ways to be able to see the destination at such an early stage, it did present a psychological problem to us. We were looking at that mountain for hours without any apparent sign of it getting any closer. This was distressing as the day wore on and we became tired.

The early sighting of the Great Orme heralded something else - a blow from the south-west, right on our nose. With the tide about to turn against us, we decided to put the engine on to maintain headway. However, the little Stuart was no match for the increasing wind and waves, so it was up sails again and tack.

One of the skills I had yet to learn was that of reefing. My formative years had been dinghy sailing in unballasted boats, or sailing model boats on ponds, where reefing is rare. Sailing a boat with a keel and ballast that was self-righting was a novelty, but from my point of view, why reef? *Deva* was thus to be seen on occasions with her gunwale well beneath the seas and the crew perched on the topsides. I did try reefing once, but the sail began to tear. It was much easier to feather the mainsail or let the boat heel. The idea that an overpressed boat just slides to leeward had not dawned on me.

The result of my ignorance was that *Deva* was incapable of being efficiently reefed, and was careering along on her ear. This was great sport, if it was only going to last an hour or two, but against wind and tide the passage time was going to be a great deal longer than that! Dougie was really enjoying himself, but the rest of us were cold, wet and scared. The boat tacked right in to the shallows off Prestatyn before sailing off over the horizon on the other tack. And where were we when we tacked for land again - Prestatyn! We considered putting into Rhyl, where there is a little harbour at Foryd. However, the pilot book kindly donated by George did not reckon much of it at low water or in anything of a sea, especially for the first time. So we tacked out to sea yet again.

The seas were breaking heavily in the shallows, thumping against the bilge. Pulling a tender laden with an outboard, several fenders and a considerable amount of bilge water must have put a great deal of strain on the boat too. The boat was certainly taking quite a lot of water on board, through several hatchway leaks and the spindrift sweeping across her. The pump was brought into action to try to clear the bilges, and it was then that we realised the limitations of the design. The pump was a semi-rotary type which required priming. Its outlet was also onto the deck.

The result was that at least two buckets of water had to be poured down the beast before anything came out. And when it did come out, the odds were that a fair percentage found its way back into the bilges again! If the boat really had sprung a seam we would have been in very serious trouble.

The day wore on and on, and still the Great Orme came no nearer. It was like that for the best part of five hours. Then imperceptibly the Orme started to become larger and more menacing. Now it was a case of how long could it keep on growing! *Deva* with feathered main sailed along with her cockpit coamings dragging through the water, a foot of water sloshing up the topsides inside the cabin. Dougie seemed impervious to my fear of becoming the Flying Lancastrian, my boat spirit destined to sail to eternity round the Orme in a gale of headwind, as the Dutchman does round Cape Horn. "Och, she sails like witch!" he kept saying. He had anticipated a rather boring sail in a slow old crate, but this was much nearer to dinghy sailing without the rescue boat on hand!

The Orme seemed to glower over us as we tacked into Llandudno Bay, and anchored in the lee of the promenade. The sails were just dumped, and "Old Coldnose" (the anchor) heaved over the side. We made rapidly for the shore, and looked for a hotel for Gillian. Like Dad and myself, she was in a pretty bad way. We had not made Beaumaris as intended, so Dougie needed her berth. The hotel management could not believe how we had put a girl through such an ordeal. They gave us all a big meal, and in a comatose state we staggered back to the boat. We crashed out in all our boots and oilskins - they were proper oilskins in those days, ex-War Department - on the sodden blankets, with water sloshing over the cabin sole.

I awoke next morning feeling awful, and stuck my head out of the hatch. The Orme had disappeared! Perhaps it was more likely though that we had dragged our anchor into the Irish Sea. When I thought of all the rocks around the entrance to the Menai Strait, it seemed a miracle that we were not wrecked. Instead Providence had taken us gently out to sea without even disturbing our sleep.

The way the wind was set meant it would be another dead noser to get back to Llandudno. We would be quicker getting into the Strait. The mainland side at low water would only give us Conway, again a beat against wind and tide, so we set a course to take us up to Menai Bridge. After the previous day's blow, the wind was dropping away nicely, and indeed towards the afternoon it came gently from the east.

It is a beautiful entry into the Menai Strait, past Puffin Island with its rocks and birdlife. On the mainland side there are the drying banks of Dutchman and Lavan, but it is all very impressive. Beaumaris is the principal yachting centre, and it was very crowded with sailing dinghies and dayboats, as well as some massive motor yachts for the gentry. Further up the Strait, on the mainland side were Port Penrhyn and Bangor. Port Penrhyn was the port for the big slate quarries, and in those days still had a little steam narrow gauge railway to bring the slate down the mountains.

We were soon at Menai Bridge, and tied up to St George's Pier. We had a line ashore and an anchor out into the

Strait. Now was the time to dry everything out, while Dad
went to find Gillian. Poor girl, she had been abandoned in
Llandudno without any money and *Deva* gone. Dad
eventually found her and put her on a train to Liverpool.

We spent a few days at Menai Bridge, watching the coming
and going of all the very snooty yachts for the Straits
Fortnight. It was a change to have such clear water about
us after the mud of the River Mersey. However, boredom
eventually set in, and I was anxious to move on. George's
pilot book was studied and the sailing directions read very
carefully, for we were about to attempt a passage through
the dreaded Swellies.

The Swellies had a very bad name. People in Liverpool used
to shake their heads about going through them. The Swellies
is the expression used to describe the stretch of Strait
between the road bridge and the rail bridge. It is both
narrow and rocky, and tides rush through at eight knots and
create big whirlpools which can be dangerous to a small
boat. As a very small boy I was taken to see the wreck of
H.M.S. Conway in the Swellies. She was towing up to
Liverpool, a bit late on the tide when the ebb set in. The
tugs could not control her and the ebb washed her over the
rocks. Her back was broken as she came to rest in a cove. I
had seen this in my Hornblower phase, and I thought it
was an absolute tragedy that a frigate which had kept the
"Frenchies" at bay was wrecked not just by a broadside but
by a cheapskate penny-pinching admiralty taking a short
cut. I had had every intention, when I became Admiral of
the Fleet, to find the person responsible for the decision,
and have him flogged round the fleet.

We intended to start our attempt about an hour before
high water, and were just in the process of casting off from
Menai Bridge Pier when the anchor fouled. We could not
work out what it was. Try as we might, nothing would

shift it. We followed the tide down, missing our tide gate through the Swellies. Eventually the obstruction showed itself. It was a massive anchor, good enough for a coaster, just lying loose. Had we been better equipped, it would have been a marvellous piece of salvage. As it was, the only way we could free our own cable was to consign the beauty back to the deep. Every time I have laid a mooring since I have always thought "if only" I could have had that beast to hand.

The next day our passage down the Swellies was more successful. It really is a beautiful stretch of water, with magnificent engineering achievements in the bridges either end. The tubular railway bridge and the suspension road bridge contrast with the wild and wonderful waters swirling round the rocks. However, from a yachtsman's point of view, it is all very sinister.

We passed under the suspension bridge just to the north of the centre span, taking the boat to the north of Platter Rocks. We then held to the south shore, passing to the south of Swellie and Cribbin, before coming out under the southern span of the tubular bridge. The Strait made a broad sweep between the wooded slope of Vaynol Park to the south and Plas Newydd on the island and we were through!

There was still plenty of water about so we thought we would have a look at Port Dinorwic, or Y-Felinheli to give it its Welsh village name. Compared with Beaumaris and Menai Bridge, this was ever so quiet. There was a small basin formed in slatework with a few local boats tied alongside. Ashore it was dereliction. In the grass there were remains of a narrow gauge railway and slate wagons, together with various sheds and buildings. We tied alongside, and as we did so we were met by the harbourmaster. As *Deva* was a local type of boat, he greeted us initially in Welsh, but was none the less friendly when he found we were English. The last commercial ship had loaded slate sixth months back, and now there was nothing. He would probably have to retire, but was being kept on while the company decided whether they would sell up for conversion to one of these newfangled luxury marinas.

As you might expect, he had many interesting memories of the port. The Dinorwic quarries about ten miles inland, up in the mountains, sent their slate down by rail to the port. An unusual aspect of the journey was that the little slate wagons were loaded four at a time on to a larger wagon on a larger gauge railway. The train then ran down to the coast, where it stopped on the cliff edge. The little wagons were then sent down a large incline to the quayside. The harbourmaster also had memories of the little schooners, which had used the port until the 1930s, before the steamers took over. Before long he was showing me how to do a long splice to run through blocks, a regular task in the days when natural fibre ropes used to wear out at the turn of the block on halliards. He did one for us on a jib halliard.

We asked about staying. No problem he said, but he did not know how long it would be before things changed. The harbour was not geared up to take small boats. The charge was only about £7.00 for the year. My father signed up on the spot, and *Deva*'s last northern mooring was to be Welsh until we went south. The harbourmaster showed us how to tie alongside, and how to ensure that the boat always leaned against the quayside when the tide went out. This was done quite cleverly by the use of chain as well as rope. Apart from the usual head rope, stern rope and springs, a long length of chain was taken from a line from the shroud chainplate to a point on shore. The chain's weight acted at nearly the widest point of the hull, but, more importantly, its weight also kept the boat against the quay with the bowsprit out. When she dried out the "give" in the rubber tyre fenders let her lean gently but firmly. In all the time we were based at Dinorwic we had but one "leaning" the wrong way. This was caused by wash from a passing ship at a critical stage of tide bouncing off the quay wall.

Port Dinorwic at that time was ideal for us. It had not been "discovered" by the yachting fraternity, yet had some facilities from the commercial days. Its location, for Wales, was good in terms of access from Lancashire, better than some of the more fashionable yachting centres. The village had shops and pubs for supplies, and as it was not a tourist resort the locals did not exploit the gullible English too badly!

There were some interesting boats in the little harbour, all by today's standard very "classic". There were two nobby type craft, one a 28ft or thereabouts, *Elidir*, and another 30/32ft craft whose name I forget. Both were now converted to pleasure craft. *Elidir* still set occasionally a cutter rig, but swung a big prop and rarely sailed. She had rather a neat set of davits for her tender, built out over her counter. The larger nobby was of very shallow draft, no more than 3 feet. She carried steadying sail on two short masts, and was very much a motor vessel, but with beautiful lines. Another old fishing vessel in the harbour was a Polperro gaffer or Plymouth Hooker. She was not in good condition, and her owner was fighting a losing battle. In those days people bought big old gaffers because they could not afford anything better. In such hostile waters these craft regularly came to grief, towed in by local fishing boats, their owners cutting their losses by leaving their craft to fall to pieces in an unfavourable part of the anchorage.

However there were still rich people about who had big classic yachts with professional crews. Convenient flights to the Mediterranean had not been established at that time, and there were several really big yachts in the Menai of "ship" size. Some berthed in the wet dock at Dinorwic, but one huge Dutch Boier yacht took the mud in the tidal basin. Her accommodation was palatial, and she had two full-time crew.

There were also some state of the art vessels, for those days. I remember a centre cockpit Hillyard, and an East Anglian a long way from home. They had good headroom, good equipment and engines which worked. These were craft I would like to have when we sold *Deva*, but even then I was becoming rather attached to her. Sentimentality was already starting to take over from common sense. Strangely enough both vessels belonged to people we knew in Liverpool, the Gouldons owning the Hillyard, the MacClarens owning the East Anglian. Graham MacClaren, a school friend of mine, used to visit *Deva* quite a lot. He found the oil lamps and the cramped cabin quite characterful!

It was an idyllic location for sailing, but the opportunities for sailing were limited for most of us. In my case studies, exams, rugby and the normal young person's social life in Liverpool took their toll. With the tide restrictions and the journey out to North Wales as well, I doubt if the boat sailed more than twenty times a year. However, most of my memories are of quite nice weather, surprising for the Welsh Coast. The Stuart also features highly, as it could be relied on to make a crisis out of any drama. The trouble was that the boat could not always be relied on to go to windward very well. The worn sails and probably a lack of technique made beating a bore. Matters were not helped either, with a heavy dinghy astern, loaded with rubber tyre fenders. Even now with good sails, the boat needs a lot of understanding to make her sail to windward. The secret is to keep her moving fast with a goodly lee bow wave. She rests on this, keeps the heel of her keel down and her head high, and makes reasonable ground up wind. However, in close quarter situations, such as in racing or in a narrow channel, she hates being pinched to weather a mark or respond to a luff. She heels and goes leeways. The same in a lumpy sea, if she is not moving forward fast, she is certainly sliding to leeward at a great rate of knots! So, with the narrow channels and the sluicing tide, it felt safer to use the engine, however unreliable it was.

Compared with the East Coast or the Mersey, the Menai banks were generally hard sand, scoured by fierce currents. Grounding on them could be quite hard, and with the current piling up as well the boat would heel heavily. However it did teach me about "club hauling". More of a square rigger wheeze, this technique involved putting the anchor out over the weather side of the boat as she started to bounce on the sand. We would sail on, until much of the chain had been let out, then let the boat snub against the cable. Her snout would pull round, through the eye of the wind, and then by hauling in furiously as the boat bounced back over the bank we could sail back over the anchor. The old timers would even slip the cable if it lay too far to windward. But better to lose the anchor and save the ship!

After one winter in the harbour we decided to put the boat in the local boatshed. This still stands, quite a large structure, with slipway as well as a substantial area under cover. There I learned about boatyards. Normally there is no problem in getting lifted out or slipped, because the boatyard has now entrapped the craft, for fees and other sundry income. But returning the boat to her element is a different situation altogether! Grif, the boatyard owner, would promise faithfully that the boat would be slipped back by Easter. Jones the farmer would bring his tractor down, Grif would put the "nobby" on the bogie, and Jones could get her to the slip.

Needless to say it did not happen. Jones was behind with the spring wheat. Next fortnight OK - so very sorry. Fortnight later, no launch, Jones was behind with the hay. The weather had been terrible, not his fault, he was normally very reliable. Another fortnight came and went. No launch. Enraged, we went to find Grif. We found him eventually in a terrible state. His slate privy, sewers had not arrived in the Principality by then, had collapsed about him. It had probably been run into by Jones's tractor, because the next excuse to coincide with a suitable tide was that the "diff" had gone on the tractor!

We had gone from Easter to Whitsun by now, and the holiday was running out. Grif said he could get a crane from Bangor to do the job. This was summoned immediately, and this huge Iron Fairy of a mobile crane came along. The crane driver took one look at the boat and shook his head. Couldn't lift that, wrong position. He went all the way back to Bangor, and we had a bill for his advice!

It was not until the summer that progress could be made. Having finished exams, I went down to Dinorwic and plagued Grif. I slept on the boat by night, kept track of his movements by the local pub network by evening, and pestered him by the day. Jones's tractor never materialised, so the new plan was to move the boat to a position where the crane could get a decent lift. To give Grif his due, he was very skilled at moving the boat sideways on to the bogie from its position leaning on a column. There was one horrible time when he left me propping *Deva* on my back while he went to find a suitable timber prop. Finally we levered her out into the open air and waited for the crane. Eventually it turned up and dropped her in. Without her ballast, without her heavy spars, the boat weighed over 2.5 tons. I would guess that in sailing trim she would have been about 3.7 tons or so, probably nearer 4 tons now with all the additions she has had since then.

Having rigged her, I then gave thought to starting the engine. There was not a sausage, so the "nobby" as she was known was towed round to the wet dock. The locals never referred to the boat by her name, *Deva*. She was just called "the nobby". The other two nobbies were not considered as such. It was something to do with the fact that she was very much a full sailing boat still. Most of the other nobby types had very cut down rigs, even the yacht conversions, and they all used engines. *Deva*, flaunting her big gaff main brought back memories of the real days of sail, when most of the local boats were these lovely elegant prawners with towering cutter rigs. Whereas most working sailing boats were work boats adjusted to sail, the nobby was a sailing boat adjusted to work. Certainly, all the old salts used to say how lovely it was to see a nobby under sail. Despite my protestations about the Rivers Class, she was always a "nobby" in North Wales.

That season, 1965, was when I learned more about handling the boat than at any other time. A college friend, Philip, had come down for a couple of weeks. He was the ideal crew on *Deva*, short, sprightly but very strong. Stuart, lurking in the bilges, however, refused point blank to start. I could not let Philip down, so we decided to do it all under sail. We had a good anchor and a big dinghy, and as long as we did not clout another boat we could not come to much harm. Despite being tied up alongside in a harbour, we found it actually quite possible to sail *Deva* out. With the wind often in the west, we could set sail, back the jib and sail her right out. Similarly coming in, we would round up and glide into our berth, again backing the jib to use it like a bow thruster. Some hefty tyres obviously helped, but it all seemed to work fine. With easterly breezes though we would swing her on her berth, and she could normally slip by the pierhead without too much effort. The tide could be used to give a lee bow effect.

We made some little cruises to Trevor, a little slating port which was still in use then. The harbourmaster was very friendly to us and complimentary about our "nobby". We also went along to Nevin and other places along the coast. However, our confidence with engineless sailing in tricky waters was soon to turn to foolhardiness. We thought we would do some evening fishing.

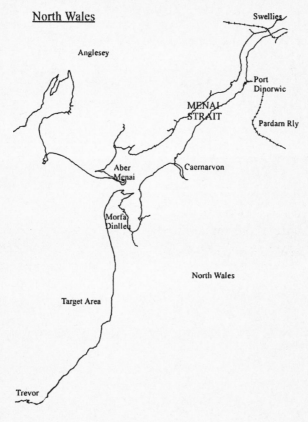

Unusually, it had been a blazing hot day with a gentle offshore breeze. We wafted down the Strait past Aber Menai out to sea and set our trolling lines. We felt lazy, and so did the fish. The light breeze started to drop, so we hauled our lines and headed back to the Strait with a little bit of flood under us.

A brilliant red sun lit up the skies and the slate mountains into molten lead. We tacked slowly towards the entrance of the Strait. Unfortunately the wind dropped just as the favourable tide slackened. The tide went on the ebb and darkness fell. The entrance to the Strait was not lit in those days, so we stood off the shore and hove to, reconciled to a night at sea.

However the wind that had deserted us so cruelly in the evening returned with a vengeance. The hot slate mountains cooled down while the water stayed warm, generating one hell of an offshore gale. The weak cotton main was lowered for its own safety as much as ours, and we ran terrified to the west under jib ahead of building seas. All night we ran. Philip was as sick as a dog. The skiff kept rising up on our stern, joining us in the cockpit on several occasions with sickening crunches.

The first signs of daybreak brought ink black seas breaking blood-red foam. Philip was comatose below and a waterlogged skiff continued to smash into *Deva*'s counter. But the wind was starting to ease. Ahead I could see land on the horizon, which must have been Ireland. Wearily I set the mainsail and started the long haul back. We had a compass, but no chart or idea of position. I set *Deva* on a full and bye course and just hoped we would find mainland Britain somehow. All day we sailed, *Deva* often sailing herself while I bailed out the sinking skiff.

Later in the morning we sighted the tops of mountains on the horizon. A misspent boyhood of tramping round disused slate railways such as the Ffestiniog, Welsh Highland, Pardarn, meant that I could tell one mountain from another, and as we closed the land I recognised Bardsey Island and the Lleyn Peninsula. Towards the end of the afternoon we could just make out the entrance to the Strait. *Deva* had found her own way back, guided by an unknown hand; there had been no help from the crew - one a zombie 36 hours without sleep, the other very ill. We had no water or food. Yet, despite *Deva's* navigational feat, the wind dropped again, and we feared a repeat of last night's performance.

Out of the haze a trawler came upon us, and circled round the becalmed *Deva*, "as idle as a painted ship upon a painted ocean". Her skipper offered us a tow. I replied in my best Welsh that I had no money. Whether he thought I was Welsh, or whether he took sympathy on a boat from a past tradition on this coast, I do not know. However, he towed us back at 8 knots to the mouth of Port Dinorwic. A planned three hour fishing trip had taken ten times as long!

With Isopon and fibreglass cloth I repaired the skiff. Dad came down and had another look at the engine. We realised that the spark/ignition sequence was completely out of timing, and we eventually located a nut that lurked behind the magneto drive coupling. It was one of those nuts which is never meant to move in the life of an engine! The engine roared, as much as a Stuart could ever roar, into life.

The next time we went fishing, we went out early morning. We found some real killing grounds, but unfortunately they were in a military practice area. We had the fright of our lives when a Lightning fighterjet buzzed us several times, and skig-aggled out of the way, and even the Stuart was panicked into life. Never mind - we had a cockpit full of fish and a rip-roaring sail up the Strait, doing over ten knots with the tide under us! We swept into the Dinorwic harbour under sail, displaying our catch to a crowd of onlookers. I bet some of my smackie friends must have envied us. We were after all doing what inshore fishing boats used to do - get a good catch and race back to sell the fish for the best price. We had to give our black fish away! What a pose!

This was to be our last season in Welsh waters. Commercial interests were taking over the old slating port, with huge rises in mooring fees. Everywhere else in the Strait and North Wales was already too expensive. Furthermore my studies were taking me to London. We laid the boat up afloat in the Wet Dock, wondering what the future would bring for *Deva*. How could we take her with us down south? Would we have to sell her, and forget about boating for a while?

I knew very little about sailing from a Londoner's point of view. I understood most of them sailed in the Solent area, and that was probably nearly as expensive as North Wales. But on the other hand there were some muddy places at the top of Portsmouth Harbour which might be within reach - I had seen them in my Navy cadet days. As for the East Coast, it was on the wrong side of London, and I gave it very little consideration.

Getting *Deva* down to the South Coast or London was going to be a problem. Sailing her round Land's End seemed out of the question then - nowadays with her diesel engine and better gear I would consider it. Road transport was far too expensive. Although rail was a lot cheaper then, finding a boat lifting crane on a rail accessed quay at both ends was very difficult.

My dad and I then gave the canal network a thorough study. If a route could be found, we could do the passage in easy stages, without worrying about the weather. The problem was the Birmingham Canal Navigations - seven feet maximum width and *Deva* was just a bit more! Nevertheless the seed of an idea grew, and we worked out that we could get to Boston on the Wash, and only have to do the relatively short trip round East Anglia to the Thames. There were also a number of possible havens for overnight staying. Some of these we inspected in the winter. As for a temporary base, we could get a cheap mooring in the Thames Young Mariners basin at Ham.

About that time I joined the Old Gaffers Association, having seen Secretary, John Scarlett's address in one of the yachting magazines. I later wrote an account of the voyage for the Association Newsletter. Part of this is reproduced in the next chapter. You may notice a slight change in writing style, but I was only 20 at the time!

Y-Felinheli To Richmond
– Via Wigan

1966

It was in 1966 that *Deva* was to follow the rest of the family to the wicked South – she was getting fed up with the increasing number of rude motor-boats and floating gin palaces which appear to dominate the Menai Strait these days and force harbour dues and other expenses to Solent heights. Luckily, being a student, I was able to spare a month and a bit to take her round, but additional labour was difficult to get hold of. However, in the last weeks of the summer term a college friend from "Gin & Jaguar", Claygate in Surrey, signed on for a month. In the end we set off from London in a very heavily laden estate car with all the gear required for fitting out.

Within thirty-six hours *Deva* was ready to start her fifty-fourth season on a beautiful sunny day – a good introduction to sailing for Nick. I swung the handle of the not so faithful Stuart P5MC auxiliary. The sound of machine-gun fire and a Welsh valley full of smoke indicated one of a number of possibilities, including an actual explosion of petrol vapour in the Stuart.

After an all-too-rare thanksgiving ceremony, *Deva* motored out under a lift bridge into the sea-lock – twenty minutes later the old gaff was sliding up the mast with a faded mainsail in the light north-easterly. Up staysail and flying jib and she swung away from the breeze and ghosted down the Strait – past Caernarfon and Aber Menai. Thus began one of those all too rare days where everything goes perfectly – the sort of day one can tell one's grandchildren about in thirty years' time but no grandchildren 34 years later. Nick enjoyed himself immensely and quickly learnt the ways and means of the *Deva* over the next few days while I had the satisfaction of seeing the beautiful Lleyn Peninsular and the west coast of Anglesey for the last time for many years. The weather was fantastic, although the wind was beginning to blow a bit more.

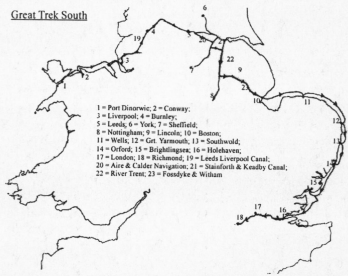

Great Trek South

1 = Port Dinorwic; 2 = Conway;
3 = Liverpool; 4 = Burnley;
5 = Leeds; 6 = York; 7 = Sheffield;
8 = Nottingham; 9 = Lincoln; 10 = Boston;
11 = Wells; 12 = Grt. Yarmouth; 13 = Southwold;
14 = Orford; 15 = Brightlingsea; 16 = Holehaven;
17 = London; 18 = Richmond; 19 = Leeds Liverpool Canal;
20 = Aire & Calder Navigation; 21 = Stainforth & Keadby Canal;
22 = River Trent; 23 = Fossdyke & Witham

However, while we were eating breakfast in the tidal basin at Y-Felinheli, the new harbourmaster came along and told us we couldn't stay in the basin because some posh motor yacht was due in. I pointed out that this berth was the one we had had for years, and paid for, and had checked for this season with the authorities. This made no difference with this particular official. Obviously the expected gin palace was worth a couple more bob in tips and dues, and we had to leave on the high tide for somewhere else. As we knew well that there wasn't another space to the west before Ireland, our only recourse was to go to the east – via the dreadful Swellies.

All went well until we came under the Menai Suspension Bridge. We were just looking at some girls on the bridge and it struck us that we were getting a longer look than we ought to be getting. Speed through the water four and a half knots – speed over ground nil!

I made a dash for the dinghy, lashed it alongside and started the outboard engine. Speed through water five knots: speed over ground – still zero! After ten minutes of this we began to lose ground badly. This was embarrassing to say the least.

"Well," I said to myself, "if I am going to be wrecked, I might as well be wrecked in style!" So, I swung old *Deva* round and ran before the tide at a tremendous pace. The wind was freshing and fair too. And I tell the truth when I say that *Deva* did the measured mile at a speed of twelve knots. What took her half-an-hour coming took her less than ten minutes going!

However, having been swept west by the tide from the Swellies, we decided to carry on out to sea and try and round Anglesey the other way to the north, via Holyhead instead. The wind was quite strong now, force five and gusts of six – what a beautiful sense of wind speed I have! - but we clung to all plain sail, the old lady fairly bucketing along, her cut-away forefoot rising to the occasion. We must have been making seven knots. A time check between two buoys gave us over ten, so, allowing for three knots tide, we were going like a racing dinghy. Nobbies have a tremendous speed potential down-wind with a fairly flat after-section and beautiful tugboat counters.

We were gaining rapidly on a motor fishing vessel (MFV) so, despite the rising wind, we kept her going on full sail, just to get the honour of showing up a powerboat. They say pride comes before a fall. Another final boost to our pride was a modern Bermudan sloop beating and taking a beating to windward. Pointing with the stem of a dry, burning pipe, I said to Nick "You see, Nick, these modern Bermudan jobs can't take it – too much freeboard and mast-height."

At that point the fishing vessel ahead of us turned about – too much sea running for him, for the waves were quite brutal now that we were well into the midst of the Irish Sea. Ten minutes later I turned chicken too. I didn't fancy entering Holyhead in what might turn out to be a gale. So we swung round into wind and the sluicing ebb. I should have taken a reef in, but in those days I was a bit of a driver of gaff-rigged hell ships and we had the tide to contend with, not to mention a chance of notching up another taking-of-a-Bermudan-job-to-windward.

So old *Deva* started bashing to windward. Her sheets were pinned down till the sails were as flat as boards. Over she heeled, putting her lee gunwale right under the water. Her bowsprit seemed to claw through waves, a tusk heralding the arrival of savage teeth as her knife-edge bows sliced every wave to spray, which was cast forty feet to leeward. We weren't pointing as high as the Bermudan chap but we were sailing faster through the water and gaining slowly. At this point I said to Nick "Give me a tops'l and we'd take that b-----d twice as fast!"

Then came the fall! I looked up at the leech of the mainsail and saw that a moth hole had grown by a foot. Down came the gaff and I jumped below and gave the Stuart such a curse that it started first time. But, even with the engine and two headsails, progress was very slow against the tide.

At long last we managed to reach the entrance to the Strait but the tide was too strong to let us through the narrows. The Bermudan vessel couldn't make it either, so we both anchored in the lee of Morfa Dinlleu. Then it was a matter of food and shut-eye.

At the turn of the tide we motored through the narrows and anchored at Aber Menai to listen to the World Cup in company with twenty other craft, all with their radios tuned to Wembley. A hearty cheer from all the English vessels indicated that another foreign team had fallen to the wrath of St. George. This was the signal for a good booze up so *Deva* weighed anchor and motored up to Y-Felinheli, making closing time with ten minutes to spare.

The next morning it was a matter of making good any damage. I also wanted to fit a forestay – it was a little silly just to have a fore-topmast stay bearing on the end of a flexible bowsprit! So, with sail and strop specification we took a bus into Bangor. The sailmaker was at first rather hostile to the two Englishmen. It was three days to the Strait's Regatta etc. Then I muttered something about a nobby; his eyes lit up. Everything was different now.

He had owned one of *Deva*'s sisters. The best craft ever made, he said. He then proceeded to run down every breed of modern craft – what rotten sea boats they were, nobbies were twice the sea boats and just as fast. He told me all about the Rivers Class nobby – they were originally shrimpers, but they sailed so well that many were built for the Royal Mersey Yacht Club. They were all built at Crossfield's, both at Arnside and Conway. I have never heard so much praise about a single breed of sailing craft.

The long and the short of it all was that he would go through the mainsail completely, renew all the eyes, which all needed re-doing, mend the tear and any other holes of which there were plenty. We could collect the mainsail and strop in three days' time and the cost wouldn't be more than three or four pounds. So, having seen to all the repairs and sunk a gallon of ale apiece, we slouched into our bunks, when amid my drunken stupor I thought "Where's the dinghy?".

I poked my head through the hatch and saw no dinghy. "Hey Nick, some b.... has whipped the launch!"

I went out on deck and saw the dinghy trapped under the counter, full of water. With a super-alcoholic effort we freed her and paddled to the slip, where I baled her out.

The following morning we decided to actually start the journey to London. A couple of choice four letter words and a boot, which I normally reserve for the rugby field, started the engine. It had taken me three years to realise that Stuart does not respond to the tender loving care the handbook suggests, but to brute force and imperialist domination.

So, with headsails and motor, we raced up to the Swellies on the flood tide, determined not to come back. Unfortunately, the appropriate page had blown out of the sailing directions, so a good guess and plenty of water over the rocks would have to take the place of navigation.

By hook or by crook we shot through the Swellies and relaxed to savour the magnificent view of the Menai Strait. It really is a beautiful stretch of water. The landscapes and the blue water are too strong for man to ruin significantly. We passed many craft, every one of them £50,000 (a lot of money in 1966!) company yachts. We saw just one prawner at anchor – she was in a rotten state. Nail sickness was almost pox-like.

It rather amuses me that so many luxury yachts spend all their time at anchor – the cost of motoring or sailing must work out at hundreds of pounds an hour. I reckon that the more old-fashioned and out-of-date the craft, the more she is appreciated and sailed. I can visualise a time in the computer age when people will buy boats for fantastic sums of money and specify flax sails and gaff with jackyard topsail and bowsprit every time, just to escape the soul destroying, bureaucratical, mechanised rat race which civilisation is heading for. The Old Gaffers Association is the beginning of the backlash.

After all this ideology, we decided to try the seamy side of life in Beaumaris. We picked up a mooring and rowed ashore. After going through all the low dives and pubs, we failed to even see any female talent – just lots of louts and aristocratic "in"-type yachtsmen. We settled for six pints of bitter and a fish and chip supper.

Next morning, feeling like death, we were awakened by a club launch and told to vacate the mooring. I didn't even argue! I was hardened to the fact that it is more difficult to get a mooring in North Wales than a parking space in London. It was a filthy day too, with gale force wind and horizontal sheets of rain. So up No. 1 jib and Conway lookout!

We fled before the gale and set a course for Conway and Deganwy. The sea was quite bad – the dinghy twice joined us in the cockpit. The trouble with *Deva* when running at speed is that her stern settles right down as the bow lifts and, although no sea has ever come over, the dinghy could ride right over the stern. One spends more time steering *Deva*'s stern away from the dinghy than looking out for the broach.

We made Conway in a couple of hours, missing shipwreck by inches. We went the wrong side of the Mussel Hill beacon, which marks some rocks, and scraped over a sandbank in the middle of the fairway. We asked a local where a spare mooring was – we had just passed it. We turned about to face the wind and a four-knot tide. Even the last word in sailing craft could not have beaten that lot.

So, with a roar, I jumped below, swore once, kicked twice and the Stuart replied with a bang and a puff of smoke, thereupon it started to strangle itself. As we surged down on a craft at anchor we prayed. We prayed to Mr. b......

Stuart, the mechanics down south - even Neptune might help!

I don't know which god answered but there was a sudden peace in the air. There was much smoke and it came to pass that the Angel of Petroleum came down and smote the carburettor... To say the least, the engine picked up at the last moment - our boom was a foot from the anchored craft - and gave its best for a couple of minutes, sufficient for Nick to grab the mooring buoy. When we had made fast, the engine gave a death cry and passed away.

Conway was no better than Beaumaris. Thousands of tourists but absolutely no available girls. Nick was very disappointed. I wrote a letter to my "steady" in Plymouth, in frustration. Compensation came in the form of a quayside pub – Liverpool Arms – and TV shop at which to watch the World Cup.

We went to Bangor by bus next day to collect the sail. The sailmaker had done an excellent job. He then muttered something about ten pounds – he'd spent hours on the job – then with a Celtic wink said "Well for you, boy, thirty bob will be fine!"

We lay in Conway for a few days, making arrangements with Dad in London, rigging the forestay and bending the mainsail. We also drank a fair quantity of ale and slept more than anything else. After one alcoholic session we were flat out asleep for eighteen hours.

One of the days was spent in taking the dinghy twelve miles up the Conway River, a disused navigation that wanders up a beautiful valley. We also knocked the propeller out of gear while shooting a weir; this was repaired by the string in Nick's anorak!

On one of our meanderings round the harbour, we came across my first boat *Kaieda*. It was a depressing sight. She used to be so spick and span when we had her. Now she was lying neglected on the beach, half full of water. Her sailing gear had been removed, and a rough old piece of timber nailed over her centre board case. There is a bond which develops between man and boat, possibly because of all the adventures and calamities they survive together. It is probably more so with a wooden boat, where the owner has to nurture the vessel through the tribulations of maintenance too. To watch such a vessel suffer in the hands of a neglectful new owner is a terrible sight.

Eventually my dad arrived – complete with radio direction finder and our college reports. We passed. With the car we could now visit Liverpool and see the "lie" of the land and spread our socializing over a wider range. This ended when I crashed the car into a stone-faced Yorkshire man who had me booked by the police, and we didn't have much success with the girls either – poor Nick!

At long last the weather abated and the second attempt to beat out of Conway was successful. We were glad to be at sea again – I believe it was Lord Nelson who said that Harbour rots good men and ships! Very true. See my section on maintenance or lack of it!

The sea was still confused but the wind was dying so it took some time to double the Orme. On rounding, we eased the sheets, set the spinnaker and headed for the West Constable buoy. Then a terrible thing happened – Dad dropped the "gents" over the side. That bucket was the maid of all purposes – tea (originally), brush cleaning, boiling of underwear, bailing the dinghy – an endless list. Although we laugh about it now, it was a savage blow at the time. It was the "Elsan" or nothing now – there's no pulpit on the *Deva*.

The wind had dropped to nothing, so the Stuart came into action again. The tide eased against us. We had another four hours of ebb to plug and when the North Constable came abeam *Deva* was making a mere three knots.

The weather was very strange now. Ugly black clouds were hanging over the Menai Strait and were dotted all around the horizon. *Deva* seemed to be sailing along in a tiny patch of sunlight all on her own, like an actress on stage in a spotlight. With conditions as they were we decided to haul down the spinnaker. It was only a matter of time before the gale struck.

This peculiar phenomenon hung over us for hours while *Deva* motored through a sea of molten lead. West Hoyle came abeam, the tide changed, but under power alone we were still only making a good four and half knots. Far out on the horizon we could see a prawner at work, under sail and power. Still the wind did not come. We had cut our timing rather fine by not leaving Conway till half past two and at our present speed we wouldn't hit the unlit Rock Channel until dark.

The Rock Channel is as dangerous as it sounds with reference to rocks, but it is reported to be silted up at the moment. Merchant ships use the Queen's Channel which is about fourteen miles to the north. When sailing out of Liverpool we found it almost impossible to get through at half-tide. In fact I had always made a point of running aground in the Rock. However on this occasion, in darkness and with a gale imminent, it was vital that we did not run aground. We passed the Horse buoy on dusk and headed for the last two lit buoys, which mark the entrance to the channel. By the time we reached them it was pitch-black darkness, although there were many dazzling lights on the shore in New Brighton.

The Stuart then decided to call it a day. No night shift tonight. Then the wind came - offshore force five in our teeth.

This succession of calamities completely threw us off balance. There we were lee gunwale under, haring into unknown sandbanks and shipwrecks. We did have a fighting chance though. The channel is about fifty yards wide!

Then the old knowledge of three years ago came back. Some of those lights in New Brighton belonged to a series of multi-storey flats, which I remembered from the days of sailing in Liverpool Bay. I guessed the distance we were from the shore and set a course for where I reckoned the dip in the sandbanks would be. *Deva* tacked and tacked at a furious rate. I've never seen those headsails brought round so quickly. It was turning into a terrifying night – heavy rain was starting to descend. How much longer could we keep this up? We weren't more than ten yards from the banks every time we tacked.

Providence again smiled on *Deva*. The Rock Light appeared through the murk and came abeam. Rock Ferry pier came by. We were through! The only time I have ever navigated the Rock Channel without running aground!

Providence smiled again. As we tacked inshore a mooring buoy, a good stout one, popped under our bows. Heroically Nick and Dad grabbed it. Within ten minutes all sail was stowed and supper was on the calor stove. Sometimes you get yer luck, sometimes yer don't!

However there was one danger left, shipping. In the 1960s the River Mersey at this point was one of the busiest rivers in the world. It served four ports, Liverpool, Birkenhead, Garston and Manchester. This being so, an anchor watch was set up, armed with a Very pistol to fire a flare at any ship which came near! It was a horrible night. Rolling gunwales under, bitterly cold and everything happening which could make life more miserable. Tempers flared, tea spilt, sausages burnt and we were forever being thrown on each other by the violent motion.

Daybreak eventually arrived and a shore party took the dinghy through the hair-raising seas to land at New Brighton. After re-fagging and re-victualling we set the storm-jib and made our way slowly across the Mersey to Liverpool.

Off the Waterloo Dock entrance, we hove to, to wait for the tide to make a level. But we were seen by the dock superintendent, who said we could lock in after a freighter came out. Ten minutes later we locked in, in company with a floating crane and a couple of tug boats. Little *Deva* felt very important in this huge lock for ocean liners. Three men took our lines and kept the strain on while the lock filled up. Even the sluice operator was courteous and he let the lock fill ever so slowly so as not to damage *Deva*.

The little nobby chugged out of the lock into the placid waters of Waterloo Dock. We were just mooring when a couple of officials came along, not to fire questions at us, but to admire *Deva*. They had remembered seeing her when she sailed from Canning Half Tide Dock some two years previously. Only out of politeness did they ask our plans. We told them we were making for Boston. No, not the Boston USA, we were going via Wigan and Leeds to the original Boston in Lincolnshire! Did they mind if we used the high quay side to get the mast out? They had a much better idea – why not use a little hand-crane in Princess Half-Tide Dock? If we didn't mind waiting five minutes, they would open the swing bridge and send a man along to help us!

To cut a long story of courteousness short, *Deva* was de-rigged and ready for the inland passage in less than an hour. I must at this point pay a tribute to the Liverpool dock personnel. With a service, which cost us not one penny, we were made more welcome than in any other port *Deva* had ever visited. Considering the amount of sea-going trade that Liverpool handled at that time, it was wonderful to see a little "nobby" from North Wales receive the same attention as a Blue Funnel liner inbound from the Far East.

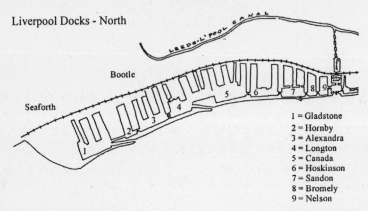

Liverpool Docks - North

Bootle

Seaforth

1 = Gladstone
2 = Hornby
3 = Alexandra
4 = Longton
5 = Canada
6 = Hoskinson
7 = Sandon
8 = Bromely
9 = Nelson

We spent the rest of that day consulting the insurance company about my car crash and *Deva*'s cover for the inland voyage. This, and the fetching of the car from Conway to take the dinghy back to London, meant we had to spend a night in Liverpool. Much as Nick and I would have liked to spend a civilised night in the right clubs in Liverpool, we were just about well dressed enough to get drunk in a dockside pub – so that's what we did.

However, Liverpool dockside pubs had changed since I had last been in one. We were the only customers not in suits! Chromium plate, Formica surfaces and upholstered furniture were the general decor, but I think crime was obviously still part of the scene. While we were shifting our keg bitters down our throats the police burst into the pub, and while they were looking around we noticed a pathetic little man under our table with his finger to his lips. Well, rather than risk a razor fight with the locals, we kept quiet!

Eight days to Boston!

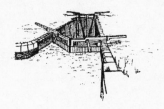

We slept a horrible sleep until mid-day next day, when we decided to find out where the Leeds-Liverpool Canal began. It was supposed to begin at Stanley Dock where we were berthed, but all we could see was a hole in the dock wall, which looked like a sewer outlet. They reckon every Liverpool dock has one of those!

However, there was always a chance that the sewer might have come via the Canal, so we decided to take the dinghy *Devette* – later to be lost off the Goodwin Sands in a westerly gale. We came to a rusty old ladder under the outlet, which we scaled to find daylight.

The sight, which presented itself to us, was not pretty. Nick said that we must have been plastered last night to have slept through World War Three. The landscape around consisted of crumbling buildings surrounded by three feet of rubble divided by a narrow strip of liquid mud. We walked along for a hundred yards or so, and we came to some ruins, which originally had been a small dwelling.

"Hey Nick!" I said. "That must have been your actual lock-keeper's cottage before the bomb dropped!"

Sure enough there was an old nameplate lying in the rubble with "Leeds and Liverpool Canal Co." etc., written on it. We came to a part of the ruin that was still standing and peered through a broken-down door.

"Look Jon, there's one of yer actual survivors!" said Nick, indicating with amazement a weather-beaten old man in a dirty old raincoat eating chips out of the News of the World.

We found out that he was the actual lock keeper. He had been notified about our arrival by British Waterways in London. The chief lengths man George would be along at four o'clock to give us a hand to get the locks going – apparently the last vessel to come through had locked in some months previously.

Without more ado *Deva* was ready to cast off. Steam had been raised about the Stuart, the mast and ancillary spare had been laid on two sets of supports and, to top it all, the lavatory seat covered the mast hole.

What follows now is a first hand account of the Battle of Stanley Dock Cut A.D. 1966.

Deva steamed into the sewer outlet and entered the No. 1 lock of the Leeds-Liverpool Canal. The lock gates banged behind us. Water swirled as the paddles of the upper gates were opened and the lock filled up rapidly. When all was calm, the top gates creaked open on the level. Our first canal lock – now for the other one hundred and fifteen locks to Boston. Full steam ahead all! As *Deva* quickly gathered speed, there was a horrible grating sound and her prow reared up in the air, like a stallion stepping on a snake. This had me worried. The canal authorities reckoned that three feet six was the maximum draft on the Leeds-Liverpool Canal, *Deva*'s is three feet in normal trim and I had told British Waterways that she drew two feet eleven! However, all was not lost. More water was let down from the next pound and *Deva* returned to a more lady-like horizontal position.

Then the enemy, in the form of local hooligans, attacked from behind the wall alongside the road. Brickbats, bones and jagged stones whistled through the air, churning the green waters into boiling pea soup. I have never felt more helpless. Nothing to throw back, no visible enemy to return fire to. It was difficult enough to steer *Deva* out of the lock without having to dodge half bricks, any one of them capable of putting us out for the count. Miraculously not one missile hit *Deva*, even though her decks were drenched with the spray thrown up. As soon as *Deva* was sheltered in the next lock we returned fire with pieces of the ruined lock keeper's hut – I hope no bystanders were struck, but it was nice to hear the little b…..s appreciating their own medicine.

Finally we emerged at the top of Stanley Dock cut to join the Leeds-Liverpool Canal. We asked the lengths man where we could moor for the night, out of range from urchins. He suggested Litherland Lift Bridge, which had a handy pub. He also lent us a key to unlock the barriers, as the cut at Liverpool was locked up at all times to prevent vandalism.

So with Nick and myself aboard *Deva* steamed on to the Leeds-Liverpool Canal. We swung round the first bend to be greeted by another broadside, although they fired too soon, for we were still some distance away. There was only one tactic left, brute force and butchery. I handed Nick the monkey wrench for him to clear the bridges while I took *Deva* through at full speed, five knots! Bravely Nick set off amidst a hail of stones – one of them struck him and that was it! Nick's temper is a bit variable at the best of times if the pubs aren't open, and with a horrible Claygate oath, which probably the Scousers did not understand, he charged at them, brandishing fifteen inches of precision steel. It was rather cruel of him although understandable; I believe he's got some Irish blood in him. A couple of wild swipes sent them running.

We followed the counter-action through, with Nick staying on land and clearing the next few bridges of louts while I took *Deva* through. The system was as follows. I would take *Deva* up the cut at about half throttle, then suddenly stop engine about fifty yards from the next bridge. The same urchins, loaded with ammunition and hiding behind the bridge parapet, would look up to see what was going on. Then Nick, having sneaked round the back streets,

 would hurl himself on them and as soon as the monkey wrench made contact *Deva* would steam at full speed through the bridge in the confusion. This worked so well that after three bridges the enemy had had enough. We could then settle down to some peaceful ditch crawling.

Our draft was rather worrying. *Deva*, under power with her mast unstepped and laid along the deck, was sitting very low at the stern, thus drawing nearly four feet. The canal although dredged to more than four feet six at its conception had silted up in the last hundred years and was full of rubbish. However, *Deva*'s iron keel didn't seem to mind, so we pushed on slowly to Litherland Bridge to begin the marathon ditch crawl the next day.

On the way it was evident that not many craft had passed that way in recent years. Wherever we passed people stopped work and lined the security fence to watch us. One middle-aged man came out of his office exclaiming "Glory be to God! A boat! I haven't seen one pass for years! God bless you!" A slightly more pious attitude than the first locals to see *Deva* on the cut!

Within an hour we made the lift bridge and moored for the night. My Dad came to see us off, before he went back to London. That night we drank to victory and returned at half past eleven with a crate of light ale, which we drank with our supper. We kept the bottles for ammunition.

At 09.00 the next morning, two hungover architectural students steered *Deva* under the hydraulic lift bridge into a typical summer's day – rain. The lift bridge really was a work of engineering art. At that time it used to let craft through only about twice in a blue moon, yet it was still in perfect working order, manned six days a week from 09.00 till 16:30 every working day. Four hydraulic rams lifted fifty tons of steel roadway up ten feet, within a substantial steel frame, a tribute to Waterway's engineering. The Stanley Dock Cut has since been filled in, and I doubt whether the bridge is there any more.

Once we were through the bridge industrial Liverpool became suburban Liverpool. We passed the scene of the Grand National, the racecourse at Aintree. The Stuart was exploding nicely, the throttle being wide open, for the canal appeared to be quite deep. We did not worry too much about striking submerged articles, for, unlike most river craft, *Deva* had a rockered keel slightly deeper than the rudder, and the screw was much too high to catch any bedsteads. Besides, the weather was raining and we wanted to arrive in time for a lunchtime booze up at the next canal pub.

We came upon our first swing bridge. Luckily for us we saw it coming, for to stop *Deva* without any astern gear takes some effort. Nick had to leap for the bank at five knots with a three-inch hawser between his teeth. Lo and behold if the rope did not uncoil quickly enough he would either lose his teeth or wouldn't make the bank. However, if we cut off the power well in advance and took *Deva* near enough to the bank so that she just grounded, we could stop in fifty yards. Unfortunately the first bridge was heavily barred from opening. Even with our monkey wrench we couldn't make the nuts turn. The bridge carried a cart track to a farm, so, smelling a rat, I went up to the farmer and told him what I thought of him and he came down to the bridge with two huge spanners, each over three feet long, and with considerable effort, undid the bolts. Apparently the local yobs used to leave the gate open so that he was trapped on his farm. Soon after passing through the bridge we came upon a complete cart in the middle of the canal – four wheels, shafts and all. All we could do was to pass to one side of it – seven feet beam through a seven-foot gap at five knots. We didn't touch the cart but we surely touched the bottom. *Deva* reared into the air like a bucking bronco, then nose-dived into deep water again.

The next bridge was a road bridge, typical of many to come on the waterway. *Deva* grounded to a halt, as I hopped ashore up to the bridge, monkey wrench at the ready. Being my usual polite self, I waited patiently for the cars to stop, but after five minutes of nose to tail traffic I decided that the loss of five minutes' drinking time was enough, so I opened the bridge.

A car screeched to a halt, its front bumper overhanging the canal bank. A stream of Scouse abuse poured through an opened window. I left the bridge half open, signalled to Nick, strolled over to the car with the monkey wrench and asked if anything was wrong. One glance at the two of us, unshaven, unwashed and positively ugly, suggested that the driver had a choice of braining – beer bottle or wrench

- if he didn't control his filthy tongue. He smiled meekly and shut the window, and I opened and shut the bridge in my own good time.

As one can see from the above script, ditch crawling is far from dull - barely five miles of fresh water under her keel and a navigation hazard every mile!

As we progressed the natives became much more friendly. Small boys didn't throw stones. They followed us along the tow path on bicycles, demanding to know where we were bound, how far we had come and how fast we were going. I lied and said *Deva* was only on third throttle - she would go three times faster, but the "law" might get on to us.

Once we were clear of Liverpool the Lancashire plain expanded before our eyes, huge fields of cabbages and corn, all looking extremely fertile. The canal wound its way along the contours of the slight swells in the landscape while the Stuart pop-popped merrily away. Soon we came to the village of Lydiate where the road bridge was very stiff. Nick and I together weren't strong enough to move it, but the local urchins came to our rescue and some twenty straining pairs of legs soon had the bridge open and shut. Unluckily *Deva's* propeller was jammed by a polythene bag, so the local young wives gathered to watch me do a strip-tease. The offending obstruction was removed from the propeller to the tune of comments about my beautiful body. Suggestions of "come back to my place and I'll give you a rub down" nearly had Nick diving into the canal too, but I thought that we had had enough trouble with the natives without having two enraged husbands and their friends chasing us all the way to Boston.

Leaving Lydiate astern, *Deva* plugged on up the canal. The next bridge was opened well in advance for us by two small boys, whom we tipped voluntarily - it was nice to be able to keep going for the Stuart does not like ticking over nor does the keel like being rust-scaled. By 13.00 we had steamed into the Ship Inn to down a few pints of beer. Half past two saw the crew of *Deva* stagger across the pub's lawn and flowerbed. The engine started first time, no doubt due to the alcoholic vapour in the engineer's breath.

The canal began to wind into hilly territory and brought us to our first lock for twenty miles. This took us some ten minutes to negotiate with the help of two young anglers, but the process included some stories about my four-pound roach and advice on bait etc. Incidentally, nearly all the locks on the Leeds-Liverpool Canal are padlocked in five places, so any craft which can pass the lock in less than five minutes must be manned by professionals or provided with a vertical take-off version of the Stuart.

The scenery began to get much bleaker. The grass began to look greyer, a sure sign that Wigan was not far away. We passed lock number ninety, which is just under the huge motorway viaduct of the M6 Motorway. Again this lock was a slow lock. So far all the locks were double locks, with one of the pair derelict, a sad reminder of the days when the canal carried over two million tons of cargo a year. We ourselves had not passed any other craft under way all day.

Thinking about the wonders of the commercial canal reminded me of the way narrow boats used to negotiate locks. The narrow boat under power used to run right into the lock, bashing the gates slightly apart. Whilst the gates were apart the skipper's wife used to bang a wedge in the slight opening and the level of the water in the lock used to drain through the gap. When the level was made the narrow boat would bash its way through the lock gates, by which time the top paddles or sluices would have been opened and the bottom gates slammed shut.

With this method the professionals could climb a lock in little more than two minutes. Needless to say the authorities did not approve of such habits, but no one was around so I decided to try the method out. Lock number eighty-nine hove into sight. I took *Deva* to within a few feet of the gates at slow speed then gave her full throttle. Four tons of pitchpine on grown oak crunched into the gates. There was an almighty shudder with splintering sounds as I rushed forward with a timber wedge in a lancing attack. Needless to say the gates opened a couple of inches and a blast of green canal water put me on my backside and sent *Deva* running back whence she came! So unless you are navigating a coal barge with fifty tons of cargo aboard, do as British Waterways recommend!

As we came into Wigan the scenery was desolate – acres and acres of waste industrial ground. A couple of urchins came running up to the canal armed to the teeth with missiles. We let them have it with the beer bottles at fifty paces.

We moored for the night ahead of a converted lifeboat with a family aboard at the waterways depot at Wigan Pier – what a place to go to for one's holidays!

As well as for its pier, Wigan is famous for rugby league, fish, chips and cheap beer. Nick tried to arrange for some women to come from Manchester – he has girl friends in most big cities – but without much luck. I decided that fish and chips and a gallon of ale were more reliable forms of vice in Wigan so we headed for the nearest boozer. With the prospect of twenty locks next day we needed plenty of beer guts to open those gates.

Next morning in our usual state we set off prepared for the worst. Within fifty yards we were booked for speeding. I pleaded with an officious Waterways clerk that we had a mere four horsepower to move four tons of nobby. I said *Deva* could not do more than the speed limit, four m.p.h., in deep water, never mind dredging the bottom! After being let off with a caution, *Deva* chugged up to the next lock, to be lifted up into the view of the first commercial waterways vehicles we had seen so far. Thanks to the clerk wasting our time we were too late to get to the next lock before a tug and two lighters. After the lighters had locked out, we went in with the tug. She was a strange craft, a craft with a hull of the same shape and size as *Deva's*, but with a shunting engine superstructure.

The tugboat and barges turned off for Leigh and Manchester while we sailed on past a power station, where a score of lighters were being unloaded of their coal. A working waterway at last!

However, the next lock showed the typical signs of lack of use - rusty gear, stiff lock gates and the usual five padlocks. On the ground on either bank were ruins and old foundations poking up above thistles and weeds, and rows of workers' terraced houses – typical Coronation Streets. To compensate for this, there were scores of healthy children playing around – useful lock labour! The next rise pictured *Deva* loaded right down to the gunwales with little boys and girls soaked to the skin in a Lancastrian cloudburst, enjoying every minute of their short ride. Irate parents were shouting from every door, telling their kids to come inside, but to no avail. Each lock we came to was opened by a score of little arms. I felt like an explorer on the Amazon, with hundreds of slaves making a passage whilst I rode on in state, smoking a peaceful pipe.

We passed another pleasure boat that had just come down the Wigan flight, so at least the water was at the right level in the locks. We stopped once for another strip-tease session with the propeller then started the next stage in earnest. We had two Waterways fellows to help us, British Waterways staff were nearly always exceptionally helpful, and to complement a contingent of other lads. By 16.00 hours *Deva* had emerged at the summit of the Wigan locks; the engine had behaved marvellously, and, despite ticking over for most of the afternoon, she had only smoked a little and had not conked out. I gave the lads a few shillings tip. Even though they were from poor families and could do with some luxury, they were embarrassed to take any money; apparently many of the richer cabin cruiser types don't even thank them for helping. Anyway they did accept eventually and bolted to the nearest tobacconist for five Woodbines and a couple of bottles of Tizer!

At the top of the locks were a couple of men who were intending to take their craft down the flight. After the Wigan Flight we felt like case hardened canal folk and told them about the dangers and generally put the fear of God into them! We compared the two craft. *Deva* was less than a foot of freeboard astern, fine lined and low in superstructure. The cabin cruiser with twice the power, three times the freeboard and four times the superstructure appeared to her owners to be far safer; they couldn't believe that freeboard at sea is like a chin held up to a punch.

We sailed on through the canal, the Stuart burning all the oil in the crankcase, which had collected in the afternoon. The canal was tremendously high up now. The chimneys of the factories, which had towered over us previously were now below us astern. To starboard the hills were becoming mountains. To port the valleys were hundreds of feet below. *Deva* might have been having trouble with the altitude - no wonder the Stuart was smoking a bit. Below us stretched acres of open-cast mining, interspaced with valleys of rural Lancashire. The view was magnificent.

Other people must have realised the magnificence of the canal as we passed quite a few pleasure craft.

At 1900 hours we made Chorley, passing "Botany Bay", and after mooring to a barge converted to a ferry we cooked a meal. If any reader ever passes through Chorley, drop in at the Railway Inn for first class beer and company. Nick and I put back a very happy gallon apiece there in very pleasant company. We met one chap who used to work the canal in the days of horse drawn barges. He used to start work at two in the morning to reach Liverpool by sunset! In addition to yarning with him we must have talked and drunk with everyone in the pub. Nick is a little sceptical of northern taverns as a rule, but even he was impressed with the beer and clientele.

The next day, a Friday, we sailed for Nelson, passing through several small villages and industrial towns, but mainly through countryside. Canals, contrary to popular belief, do not connect gasworks with glue factories in straight lines. They spend about nine tenths of their time in rural surroundings.

That day was uneventful except for a genuine compliment on the speed of our locking from an experienced canal enthusiast. He wondered why we came into locks so fast until I told him that we had no astern gear to slow us down! Nelson was a poor drinking place, but we could have done with a drink after literally sailing over the top of Burnley on a magnificent aqueduct. The view from this engineering masterpiece is magnificent as is the feeling of drama. After being hemmed in by warehouses, tunnels and cuttings, we came into a huge sense of open space, almost airborne like a gliding bird.

After victualling we set off for the summit. The Pennines were about us now as we came through the last lock up to the highest navigation in Britain. Not many sea-going craft have been nearly five hundred feet above sea level.

On reaching the top pound *Deva* oozed with pride as she was praised by the lock keeper and his wife. They said they had seen one similar to her, but not as nice, come through several months before. I thought this was strange - not many nobbies pop over the Pennines for a spot of fishing! But I found out that they were right when we sailed into Boston.

A few miles further on we salvaged a beautiful tyre. I gleefully made a lanyard and fastened my new found possession over the topsides. The fender quota was plus one for barely ten seconds before *Deva* plunged into darkness with a sickening crash and lost another fender! We had hit the Foulridge tunnel with a vengeance. I dived below for a torch while Nick throttled her down. The torch was not powerful enough to pierce the misty gloom. The end of the tunnel was not visible. The only guess to our position was a beam thrown on the side of the tunnel, so with the torch aimed abeam we steered *Deva* a foot from the starboard side, set the throttle at half speed and prayed no other craft came the other way. We wouldn't have been able to see them on account of the glare from our own torch; even if we could, we couldn't stop to avoid a collision - the canal was a mere fourteen feet wide. Luckily with the lack of commercial traffic on the summit level, the only craft we might have collided with would not have been so strong as *Deva*. Historically this canal tunnel was known locally for the time when a cow fell into the cut and swam the length of the tunnel, to be rewarded with a bottle of brandy. She later gave birth to two fine calves!

It was about twenty minutes before we saw the pinprick of light in the distance, heralding England's largest and most stubborn county, Yorkshire. *Deva* finally emerged from the tunnel in bright sunshine, pushing a fair standard of driftwood. She had no sooner shaken this off when she ran aground in what should have been the deepest part of the cut.

So this was Yorkshire!

Swearing, we hurled the anchor astern and kedged off, Nick went ashore with a line and, with *Deva* at full throttle and the mate heaving for all he was worth, the old lady of Lancashire reared over the mud bank into deeper water. I took Nick aboard, then set the throttle wide open and kept it there. I still reckon that the Ministry of Agriculture owes me a grant for ploughing the infertile mud of Yorkshire. For six miles *Deva* slid and cut through the highest waterway in Britain, through Barnoldswick and Salterforth until we hit Greenbarthfield locks. Then followed a very weedy stretch of canal to Thornton in Craven where I discovered that Nick's arm was long enough to reach the propeller without diving over the side.

The countryside was bleak, but beautiful as *Deva* descended the Pennines. As it was a Saturday people were out in their hundreds fishing the canal. We passed several craft on this section, all going as fast as we were, but with much more wash. We saw one chap in a forty footer go shooting up the bank at eight knots as we came through a swing bridge. He had come shooting round a corner, heeling over like a destroyer on the turn, seen us, banged the gear lever astern and steered into the bank. It took both crew considerable effort to push her back into the canal.

It was half past eight when we passed through Skipton; then doubled back to moor in Skipton Springs branch for beer and chips. We did the pubs in Skipton, ending up at a "singing" pub. I thought this was an unusual occurrence and was not surprised to see three Wiganers creating all the racket. That was the signal for a good booze-up. When my Widnes upbringing became known the conversation turned to rugby. Widnes and Wigan were keen rivals in rugby league. Nick had made appearances in rugby for Surrey in his youth; so many words were passed about the oval ball.

The next morning was a horrible morning as *Deva* swung into the Leeds-Liverpool Canal, with rain pouring down in a fashion reserved for Manchester. Swing bridge number 194 will have unhappy memories of that day as well. There were many swing bridges along this section of canal. Many were of newer steel type, which were not as easy or light to operate as the wooden ones, so one member of the crew walked far ahead preparing the bridges in advance.

As it happened I was trotting along the canal bank, just keeping ahead of *Deva*'s stately five knots, bursting my lungs on each swing bridge. Just before bridge 194 there is a sharp turn in the canal so *Deva* was out of sight and out of sound. I put my back into the bridge and heaved. No good. Try the other way round - like a rugby forward - still no good. Then I heard her - the Stuart was running the finest she had ever run in her life. The sound of bow wave was ominous too. She must be really motoring - obviously Nick had stopped to light a fag or to spend a penny and was catching up lost time. I heaved frantically. What a way for *Deva* to go, sunk in the heart of Yorkshire, a hundred and fifty miles from the nearest wave! On she came round the corner at five knots. Nick looked ahead, fag in lips, eyes half closed in the haze of last night's boozing. Then he saw what was going to happen. He went as white as I was red with pushing, throttled back and ran forward, and sat down with both legs stretched out on the bow as *Deva* coasted towards the bridge. A brave man, I thought, to stop four tons of prawner at four knots with two feet, risking rupture and two broken legs.

There was a sickening thud as *Deva*'s bullring, wrought iron of another age, dug into nuclear age nationalised steel. I opened my eyes, expecting to see Nick swimming to the bank. No, there she was, completely undamaged - they knew how to build prawners in those days. I fell flat on my backside. The bridge had opened - no wonder, for *Deva* must have rattled every bolt in it. The chaos was not over yet as *Deva* drifted astern. When Nick opened up to take her through, she would not steer because her propeller is a quarter installation. Thus until she starts moving she will not turn to port under power; her propeller just paddles her stern sideways.

On account of this peculiarity under power, *Deva* clipped the edge of the concrete base to the swing bridge at about three knots. It was pitchpine of half a century ago versus concrete. Luckily it was no worse than *Deva* scraping her paint and the concrete cracking off into the water. Gingerly I closed the bridge and joined Nick on *Deva* for a thanksgiving smoke and brew of tea.

It was not long before we came to Bingley, famous for its staircase lock. For the uninitiated a staircase lock is a series of ordinary locks joined together without any canal in between them. This is a magnificent piece of engineering. Five "steps" take you some fifty feet down. Although I suffer from vertigo, no topmasts for me!, I think anyone would agree that the sense of height is tremendous as one gazes east over Yorkshire from the top of Bingley five-rise.

We were helped through the staircase by several small boys and their enthusiastic fathers. Cameras clicked and by the time we had descended we felt quite the centre of attention. We had also acquired a couple of lads as crew from an interested father - we agreed he would pick them up in a few miles further down the cut in his car.

So the little lady of Lancashire trundled on to the next lock. Just before we arrived we saw another craft move into the lock - a floating gin palace if ever we saw one, with white topped caps to all the officers, glittering chrome, forty feet of fibreglass and perspex windows. However, *Deva* is not too fussy about with whom she shares a lock and I hailed them to keep the gates open. But it seemed that gin palaces are more than particular about mixing with real craft and as *Deva* steamed up to the lock the gates were slammed shut by officers. It took three of us to stop *Deva* from ramming the gates, straining two cables from the stern. No damage resulted, but I was fuming with rage. One of the lads ran up to the gin palace and told his equivalent "officer" on the gin palace exactly what he thought of them.

The race was on now. Lock after lock passed, pound after pound was navigated, and the little old nobby, whilst gaining on the pounds, was just short of locks as the gin palace barged into locks. They must have been in a hurry too, leaving sluices open at locks, risking flooding and drying out the uphill pound. Seven miles into this race it struck us that the two lads should have disembarked but apparently they were now near their homes, so we gave them a couple of bob for their help and bade them goodbye. Shortly after the temporary crew had gone an interested spectator asked me if *Deva* was built in fibreglass - a reflection on her topsides if ever there was one. Admittedly she was looking very handsome. All the brass work was glistening like a corporal's badge, shone every day, and the remaining wood topsides and cabin were brought up to a very rich gleam with constant polishing.

With all the hammering, the Stuart was getting rather thirsty so we moored at a small Yorkshire town to fill the petrol can. Just as I was returning with the fuel a Mini-

Cooper screeched to a halt and the father of the two lads came rushing over. Even a sports saloon hadn't been able to keep up with *Deva's* stately five knots. Apparently at every bridge he had come to he had just got out of the car to see *Deva* disappearing into the distance! He was relieved when we told him that we had dropped the lads off near their home.

The chase continued through Yorkshire, *Deva* slowly catching up the gin palace, until, about ten miles from Leeds, we overtook the monstrosity and having achieved this minor victory we moored at the next convenient pub. Throughout the voyage Nick and I had been arguing whether to drink first and eat afterwards or vice-versa. My northern upbringing suggested we should do the latter, but with true English diplomacy we arrived at a compromise. We would drink before and after the meal, and, to save loss of face on my part, the "jam-butties" (Liverpudlian Knotty Ash style) would stay routine issue in the morning.

The next morning we set off for Leeds. The only interesting part about this journey was the tow we gave to two canoeists. Within a mile one chap had capsized and the other had sheared into a tree. Happily there was no loss of life. We did have a polythene bag round the prop for the last five miles to Leeds which slowed us, but the water was too dirty to clear it. At the last lock on the Leeds-Liverpool Canal we waited for ten minutes for the gin palace, which had gained on *Deva's* crippled pace. Considering that there was no wind and their craft was twin screw with astern gear giving good manoeuvrability, I did not think it possible for a forty-foot craft to enter a fourteen-foot lock beam-ways. After more swearing, we managed to warp her in the right way.

After victualling in Leeds we set off down the Aire and Calder Navigation, the gin palace hot on our heels. The navigation was like an American freeway compared with the cart track atmosphere of the Leeds-Liverpool Canal. The locks were about three hundred feet long - long enough for *Deva* to keep going while the water made a level. There were traffic lights on a gantry over the lock. The waterway was tremendously busy with oil barges and coal carriers, but even so the lock keepers were very courteous. They let the water down very gently and strolled over for a chat. They were amazed that a craft of *Deva*'s size could have crossed the Pennines - compared with a two hundred ton lighter she does look puny.

At one of the huge locks the keeper came over and told us that he stopped work at half past five, and we would be the last boat through that day. This cheered us considerably as the gin palace was fifteen minutes astern. The remaining locks remained open all night. *Deva* ploughed on through the evening - we wanted to get clear of the Leeds industrial complex - and it was interesting to see the road bridges kept open for waterborne traffic. The waterways round there take more than the roads.

The next morning was not a good one. We met our first nasty lock keeper. He swore at us for using fenders - thought we were bourgeois - and dropped us like a ton of bricks. Shortly afterwards the Stuart decided to take a breather - fed up with the same old spark plug. By sweet coincidence a tanker came past at eight knots, pushing the whole canal in front of her and *Deva* hit the bottom with a bang and went on her beam ends as the convex surge revealed the canal bed.

The navigation was in many parts a canalised river and thus we had the help of about one knot of current; it had rained every day on the cut. At one point *Deva* overhauled a taxi running on a road by the canal!

One feature of the north-east waterways was the use of trains of canal craft - really lighters of from fifty to one hundred tons towed ten at a time. *Deva* was stuck behind a train of these "Tom Puddings", as they were known locally, in the New Junction Canal, a link to the Sheffield and South Yorkshire Navigation. It was impossible to overtake these strange vehicles, for they were swinging from one side of the bank to the other. We ate luncheon while they locked through. Soon it was time to turn to port for the Stainforth and Keadby Canal, which was to take us to the river Trent.

This canal is not quite so advanced as the other North Eastern Waterways - locks were operated by hand. One had to sound a siren for the keeper to emerge from his hen house or vegetable patch and operate his lock. This was all right for the motor barges but the only sound we could manage was by clouting the stew pan, which was often laundering underwear, with a spanner. The canal to Keadby is for the most part very boring. We nearly ran down a small coaster coming through a swing bridge - we thought it was too good to be true to see the bridge opening well in advance! Otherwise the only thing that happened was that I was soaked in a torrential downpour, which lasted four hours. A fair amount of water went through the mast hole, which was only covered by the w.c. seat. We arrived at Keadby Lock to find that the tide was wrong for locking out into the River Trent. So I went to bed for the afternoon while Nick went out for some cigarettes.

The next morning we took the flood up the tidal Trent. The current was very strong giving *Deva* an extra four knots. We were passed by a few motor "keels", which were doing at least ten knots. Before engines, the barges or "keels" on the Trent went under a square sail, which must have required some rare skills. The river also had very difficult bends to negotiate. Another craft passed us; she was the ultimate in luxury motor yachts - too classy for a gin palace!

After three hours had passed we came upon the biggest barge jam I had ever seen. There must have been fifty barges anchoring, going aground, turning about and hooting, and the luxury yacht looking very confused in the middle.

Well, *Deva* couldn't stop - no brakes. I did not want to drop one of my anchors in the Trent in those days - the river was so polluted and foul bottomed, water quality not then being an issue. Anyway we were doing at least six knots over ground so anchoring was out of the question. The inevitable happened. The Stuart wanted a bonus plug cleaning for dealing with barge jams, and promptly cut out. I gave the helm to Nick while I dived below to change the plug. Luckily the Stuart started fourth swing. As I emerged on deck I saw *Deva* pick up just as she was about to be swept on to a nasty looking tree trunk on a plinth of rocks. Nick did a beautiful helming job. It would have done credit to a taxi driver in London's Marble Arch. We must have "carved up" twenty barges in two zigzags across the river. After missing a stone embankment by three inches he handed the tiller to me in a cold sweat. The whole episode had been like a nightmare. Nothing was real, nothing logical.

We forked off the Trent up to a cut to Torksey, for the Fossdyke and Witham Navigation, but our scrapes were not over yet. We could not see the lock for a round-arched bridge, so we did not slow down at all. Some twenty yards from the bridge *Deva* was still steaming at her regular five knots, when, like a thunderball from hell, a British

Waterways hotel barge came surging out of the tunnel on the top of a seething muddy surge. I swung the tiller to starboard and old *Deva* heeled her gunwale under and spun to port, missing the barge by inches, thank the Lord for rockered keels. She was now heading for the mud bank. The helm was reversed and her podgy quarter swung right up the bank. With the force of gravity behind her, the old nobby dived into the water again and, gathering speed, shot through the tunnel on a port turn. *Deva* finally skidded on her fenders to a halt in the relative peace of Torksey Lock.

About five minutes after we had tied up, the luxury yacht tried to enter the lock. To begin with she managed to mangle her bulwark plates on her port bow. She went astern out of the lock, and stopped to go ahead again. With a roar of twin Rolls Royce diesels she made one more attempt. This time she only scraped the paint off the dent. Twelve feet of bows entered the lock and then no more came. She had grounded on the lock sill. The lock keeper went up to her captain and told him that it was high water now. Furthermore the water wouldn't be so high for another week! So the poor chap had to go astern, back to the ebbing Trent and a mud berth for another seven days!

Apparently *Deva* had only just scraped through - the indicating marks read only three feet. If the sill hadn't been worn slightly we would have scraped our keel.

It was pleasant to be back in the placid waters again. The canal had been dug by the Romans in the days of their occupation. Like their roads, the engineers had built it straight, so it was a case of *Deva* guiding herself along the canal. It must have seemed strange to towpath walkers to see a craft motoring unaided up the cut, guided by the equal pressures of liquid between the nobby and the banks. We occasionally looked where we were going but the general form was that one brewed tea whilst the other slept off the previous night's excesses.

The countryside appeared very fertile. Huge fields of grain extended behind the canal banks. I would have liked to have a better look at Lincolnshire's countryside, but the thought of getting to Lincoln in time for a good drinking session made us spur *Deva* on. I had told Nick that Lincoln was a good place - better than Keadby. (Nick thinks that the North is all the same from St. Albans upwards.)

We were not disappointed with Lincoln city. We moored in a huge basin where the Fossdyke Canal joins the River Witham. Architecturally Lincoln is so well known that it needs no describing. It is certainly a very interesting city, although poor new buildings have been erected. We spent some time walking the streets before diving into a pub. The pub was rather refined - unusual for Lincolnshire - and the beer was refrigerated and not cellar temperature, which curbed our capacity that night.

The next morning we set off for the last inland leg - Boston in eight days or bust. We had on the previous days made enquiries about time for the Liverpool to Boston run; not many people have done the exact passage, but the best times we had come across were in the region of a fortnight. *Deva* had been averaging well over four knots, including locking and swinging bridges, through the Leeds-Liverpool Canal and on the north-eastern waterways slightly higher, although tides had not been favourable at Torksey, where we had lost half a day. Hangovers also accounted for ten per cent extra time. Anyway *Deva* was making excellent time. Most waterways people I had spoken to reckoned three weeks an average allowable time for a power cruiser. However, it is the lines of a craft which count for speed rather than a hefty power unit.

Deva's mini-powered unit was making itself noticed. We passed through the Glory Hole in Lincoln, a narrow enclosure of tall, old buildings with the cut running through its axis, leaving it full of smoke. We couldn't see the other end. We emerged from this Lincoln feature to find another craft waiting to go through a guillotine lock. An official was working the lock, winching the blade ever so slowly. Having a following wind, no convenient towpath and no stern gear, all we could do was to throttle back and hope the guillotine would have been raised enough for us to pass under. We cleared confidently by half an inch.

It was not long before we had another clearance problem. Just down river from Lincoln there is a large swing bridge. When we came upon it there were several craft waiting to go through. Apparently the bridge keeper had a reputation for deliberately delaying waterborne traffic and some craft had been waiting for half an hour. Well, I have always been an advocate of low freeboard. There are too many motor galleons in commission - and some Bermudan rigged ones too. So, *Deva* stayed on course. I'm pretty sure that we saw the bridge keeper deserting his post at the sight of a bridge-breaking gaffer. Nick lay up forward to lower the bows half an inch so that the mast, laid on deck, would clear, and clear she did, leaving astern half-a-dozen peeved motor galleons.

There's not much more to be said about the River Witham. It was straight, wide and high banked. It is a good navigational river but it lacks the intimacy of a run-down canal like the Leeds-Liverpool.

We were relieved to see the end in sight - the Boston Stump, a huge church structure, a branchless tree towering over the town more famous for its namesake in America, which hosted the "Tea Party" and the start of American independence.

For the next two hours the stump grew larger as *Deva* steered herself along the canal while one crew slept and the other brewed tea, sheltering from the rain. Gradually the remoteness of the fens became busier, moored craft becoming more numerous, and eight days out of Liverpool the little Lancashire nobby steamed into Boston, appropriately within spitting distance of the pub. She had made very good time. We managed to slip in "last orders", which lasted a lot longer than they should have done, and went into town to do the victualling.

It was interesting to see a port where a large fishing fleet still flourishes. I must have seen some fifty smacks, but not one of them set a scrap of sail. The lines of a Boston smack do not look quite as elegant as a bawley or a prawner, the bows giving a sluggish entry but they certainly have a good run aft, with a good rake to the sternpost. But it was upsetting to see that none set sail. The nobbies fishing in Liverpool Bay set sail - reduced sail at that, equivalent to a double-reefed main and small staysail - but relied mainly on motors. However, I suppose that the Irish Sea can give a worse motion than the North Sea, for no craft without sail would give a stable enough fishing platform in *Deva*'s old waters.

As I turned away from the sail-less fleet I saw a craft rather strange for those waters. She had tugboat counter stern and yacht-like cut away forefoot, and was beamy and had low freeboard. Only Crossfield built them like that.

Unfortunately, when I went up to the chap working on her mast I found that he was converting her to a Bermudan rig. Prawners do sail well with Marconi rig; several of *Deva*'s sisters have had a neat Dragon rig dropped straight in and have sailed well; but in these days of super aerofoil sails and wing masts one might as well set an old fashioned rig to identify oneself. So many craft look the same nowadays.

This alien prawner had been motored single-handed from Fleetwood to Boston by the same route as *Deva*, but had taken nine months. The owner had stopped to earn money at Wigan and started a pleasure steamer service at Botany Bay by converting a barge. He had many an interesting yarn to tell.

That night Nick was signed off. Needless to say we crawled around every pub in Boston. We ended up in one pub where I won the jackpot on the bandit, which kept the pub open until 01.45 hours.

As daybreak came Nick hiccupped his way to the main road to London, to hitch a lift on a lorry.

"South until the butter melts - then west"
-
Passage to London

While I was waiting for Dad to bring the dinghy and sails from London I spent some time wandering around Boston, looking for a small crane to lift the mast. One would have thought that a bustling port like Boston would be able to oblige. However, to compensate for my disappointment, I purchased a new peak halliard - sufficiently over measuring to leave me with three fathoms slack.

The people at Boston were a very friendly crowd down by the riverside. One couple cooked me a meal and took me out for a drink. Or did I take them? Apparently there are two distinct "sets" of yachtsmen on the Witham. One is the "gin set" while the other is the "beer set". They are as different as steam and sail. Each set has to moor in a confined space, generally alongside, but woe betide any unfortunate visitor who doesn't know his place in society. I had not seen such obvious discrimination before. What the difference between one set of fenders and another is I do not know.

Soon the family arrived, dinghy and dog included. Jenny, the dog, was looking very old now - and so she was. But she still enjoyed being in the middle of the family scene of action. The next day *Deva* said goodbye to British Waterways as she motored through the lock into tidal water. We passed the man in the prawner; *Deva*'s glistening paintwork and bright work seemed to please him.

We moored alongside the dock wall astern of another fishing boat from the north-west. She was a Liverpool MFV which had come a colder way round. *Deva* dried out in the softest of muds some forty feet below the top of the wall. It seemed that it would be easy to slide the mast over the quay side and drop the stick in. However, try as we might with the help of onlookers, we couldn't get the correct angle to the mast. The dockers went home in the end while we sat disgruntled. In the evening the tide came in and with a casual attempt by just my father and myself, the mast dropped into perfect position. Within thirty-six hours *Deva* was at sea again, her faded gaff mainsail lightly filling in the north-easterly draught. The fishing fleet came past us without a stitch of sail set in fifty craft.

We made a mess of pilotage out of the Wash. I swore that my compass was not ninety degrees out of true as we rounded a red target buoy!

The light air developed into a flat calm as we were swept towards Wells by the young flood. Dad decided to go for a swim and even that did not bring any wind. Eventually we made Wells harbour. During our stay in Boston we had filled in a "66" form at the coastguards, so we were expected at Wells. The entrance channel is very tricky there, as well as dangerous in rough weather, and it was with some relief to the crew that *Deva* motor-sailed into the harbour, her gaff mainsail towering over the considerable crowd of onlookers.

We spent a very pleasant evening in Wells, supping our pints on quayside. *Deva* settled down to her drying berth to await the next tide. As she came to life in the early hours the sun shone beautifully. The gaff mainsail creaked up the mast, the faded red sail hanging limp from its yard. Whilst this hot weather was very pleasant, it also killed the wind. Even nowadays when *Deva* sets a topsail she still needs a force three to pass the five-knot mark when running. The coast in these parts is devoid of comfortable anchorages so we were in a fair hurry to reach the relative safety of the Thames Estuary. So it was main and motor that day as *Deva* chugged past the bleak East Coast at a stately four knots. The light air began to draw round to the north as the tide turned to ebb. And ebb it did. With the engine resting and *Deva* under goose-winged jib and mainsail, her speed through the water was still near the four knot mark but speed over ground was but a quarter of that. This seemed an ideal opportunity to try tacking down-wind. This had worked for me in racing dinghies so why not on a nobby? Apparently Royal Ocean Racing Club and Junior Offshore Group yachts use this tactic with success, but *Deva*'s speed on the run compared well with her reaching speed. In fact she lost ground tacking down-wind. Thus we risked grounding and headed for the shallows where *Deva* made good progress against the tide. And she made even better progress when the tide turned. We chose then to top up the engine gearbox with oil which had the disastrous consequence that *Deva* "steamed" in her own personal fog belt.

The clock struck 20.00 hours as *Deva* coasted through the pierheads of Yarmouth, with space age accuracy on her "estimated time of arrival" (ETA). Yarmouth was quite a pleasant anchorage. The strange craft serving the North Sea gas rigs were interesting to see.

The next day, again in light airs, *Deva* wafted over to anchor off Southwold harbour. According to the pilot book, one should only enter when the correct signals are shown. We waited. We ate. We waited again. Still no signals. Dad took the dinghy ashore to find out the form - apparently there was a huge sandbar just outside the pierheads, which stretched right across the entrance. Caution on our part had proved justified. A month previously a newcomer entered unknowingly, and ran aground on this bank, and, almost immediately, the tidal surge meeting the river water produced a wave of tidal wave proportions which made the yacht a total wreck, the crew nearly losing their lives. To enable our entry, a pilot, Trinity House, no less, would be required, complete with heavy pilotage fee too. However, the pilot would come out to check his lobster pots and we could follow him in.

With such news Dad returned to *Deva*. To dampen down the rolling I had set the staysail to starboard and the jib to port - an unorthodox practice, no doubt, but successful.

Presently the pilot appeared in his motor lugger – a local craft, but bearing a striking resemblance to her West Country counterparts. He circled round us, and, taking the hint, we weighed anchor and followed him in cautiously under headsails and engine tick-over. Nowadays, 2001, the entry into Southwold is very much easier following extensive work to the north pier. *Deva* could get in at most states of the tide, although the current still runs very strongly.

We stayed all the next day in the harbour, visiting Walberswick and the Harbour Inn and touching up paint. We also lent our charts to Boston to a yachtsman going north. Early next morning the old nobby crept out of the harbour and set her worn-out sails to a fresh north-easterly. The day was fairly uneventful, except for the dinghy parting its three-inch warp.

The entrance to the River Ore was pretty terrifying, but despite the fierce currents we could still see the shingle banks. It was a matter of minutes before we moored off the pier of Orford. Orford was a pleasant, if pricey, anchorage so I returned to London to check my mail and rugby club for a couple of days. Luckily the weather decided to break while we were away and had finished relieving itself by the time we returned.

It was a good run down the coast past Woodbridge Haven, Harwich and the Naze, and up the Wallet to Brightlingsea, although the entrance at the Colne bar was hectic with the wind over tide. The dinghy sought my company in the cockpit on more than one occasion. The run up the Colne was pleasant, though, in the brilliant sunshine and with the background of barges. It was the first time I had seen a Thames sailing barge under canvas and I was duly impressed with her pace and handling.

We blotted our copybooks at the entrance to Brightlingsea creek. We went round the wrong side of the middle ground buoy and ran aground. We ran aground so hard that *Deva*'s keel stuck in the sand like a knife. This did assure me of the strength of the keel bolts though. When the flood came we drifted up the creek and moored alongside a motorised bawley. She was a far cry from her days of sail. It appears that when they motorise a working smack on the East Coast they do the job properly. It would be impossible to set a shred of sail on most of the working bawleys these days. Surely a small mainsail and storm staysail would give a more kindly motion with the added bonus of emergency power in the event of engine failure? Brightlingsea needs no description for the east coast sailor.

In fact most of the craft on the North Sea seem to moor in the creek, it seems so crowded!

The shipping forecast next morning gave a force six wind from the north-east which might go up to seven, or down to four. Either way it was favourable for the run down by the Maplin Sands and with all those sandbanks around the channel would not be that rough. Even so I took two reefs in the main, becoming fully reefed.

It was a hard beat out to the Wallet Spitway buoy against the wind and young flood, but as soon as *Deva* weathered the spitway the wind was freer. Somehow we got lost in the mist and spindrift. I don't know which bank we crossed and re-crossed but it was some time before we found a buoy that looked like the right one. We were not used to this Thames Estuary Pilotage. We were used to a few Welsh mountains to take a bearing from! With *Deva* careering about at terrific speed, her wash playing havoc with waves and breaking in shallow water, it was a miracle that she was not wrecked.

However, we were on course now. Dad was puzzled again in his navigation – the buoys seemed to be fairly shooting by. In fact we were so puzzled at the calculated speeds that we timed *Deva* as the water came slack on the measured distance between two buoys. She was averaging over seven knots in still water! This would not be amazing if she were carrying full sail, but, reefed down and riding easily with the wind fine on the port quarter, she felt as steady as a Pullman Express guided by rails.

At this sort of speed it was not long before Southend pier was abeam. We had shaken out the reefs to fight the ebb and the wind was down to force four. But not for long. The spring ebb took its brakes off and the wind went round to the east and blew.

Deva was almost out of control. With all plain sail hoisted and vertical waves in excess of ten feet, breaking at that, she had gone mad.

There have been sceptics about prawners' low freeboard aft being dangerous in following seas, but now I know that they are wrong. Even though *Deva*'s quarter waves were towering over me, like the gaping jaws of a lion, not one green sea came aboard. Nevertheless life was pretty terrifying for her crew; the spray blown off the top was stinging the back of my neck. The little prawner seemed to be loving this weather. She kept hopping on the top of waves and staying there for a free ride. She would sit her squat little bottom on the soft crest of the wave, lift her prow high and plane with a speed that would be the envy of the Flying Dutchman. Then her mainsail would show signs of going limp and she would drop back. The dinghy, on two lines now, took this chance to catch up and cheekily draw level. *Deva* didn't do anything about this, but now I know that she meant what she said when she conveniently wrecked the dinghy off the Goodwins the following year.

We must have been travelling at a fair speed, for we overtook a fifty-foot ketch under sensible storm staysail as if she were standing still. Not one tug or tanker overtook us either. It was with some relief that we bore off to starboard to moor in Holehaven, a dirty little creek, which smells as nice as the River Mersey. Holehaven had some strange beauty at night, the brilliant flames of the nearby oil refinery glistening over the mud. The anchorage can be crowded, but the wash from passing ships does not disturb the peace of the creek. The Port of London Authority (PLA) had a jetty there, which they use once in a blue moon, but yachtsmen had to make do with mud to avoid trespass!

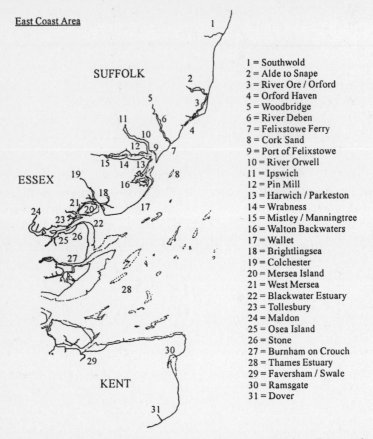

East Coast Area

SUFFOLK

ESSEX

KENT

1 = Southwold
2 = Alde to Snape
3 = River Ore / Orford
4 = Orford Haven
5 = Woodbridge
6 = River Deben
7 = Felixstowe Ferry
8 = Cork Sand
9 = Port of Felixstowe
10 = River Orwell
11 = Ipswich
12 = Pin Mill
13 = Harwich / Parkeston
14 = Wrabness
15 = Mistley / Manningtree
16 = Walton Backwaters
17 = Wallet
18 = Brightlingsea
19 = Colchester
20 = Mersea Island
21 = West Mersea
22 = Blackwater Estuary
23 = Tollesbury
24 = Maldon
25 = Osea Island
26 = Stone
27 = Burnham on Crouch
28 = Thames Estuary
29 = Faversham / Swale
30 = Ramsgate
31 = Dover

The last leg under sail was a calm day except for the wash of freighters. The flood tide was strong and *Deva* quickly covered the thirty dreary odd miles to Tower Bridge. When we reached the Prospect of Whitby pub we lowered sail, my head cushioning the gaff's descent, and moored at the entrance to Shadwell Dock. We had taken the precaution of seeing the relative powers in the PLA, explaining that we would like to dock to take the mast out for the Upper Thames. We even gave our time of arrival - Bank Holiday - and asked to be put in a dock where there was a small hand crane. The superintendent had recommended Shadwell and said he would have everything ready for our arrival. Regretfully, the wheels of bureaucracy had not turned enough and those on duty didn't know anything about our arrival. However, they opened the lock gates and road bridge and let us in, with one of them aboard. He was impressed with *Deva*'s acceleration and in general they all liked her.

Deva made her way to Shadwell basin and we looked around for a hand crane – not one in sight. The cargo cranes were all having a holiday too. In fact there was nothing to lift a mast out. No ships were in dock either, but there was a diving barge, which had a couple of pulley wheels, set in her prow. However, special permission would be required, even though it hadn't been used for years and was awaiting breaking up, and that would take some time to get. So we waited and thought. The officers went back to their hut. The policeman was looking the other way. It is not usually possible to get a prawner to tiptoe across a dock but *Deva* slid silently over to the diving barge with a whiff of two-stroke exhaust. A hemp warp was silently rove round the pulleys and stropped to the mast. The height of the pulley was about seven feet above water and with *Deva*'s low freeboard we just managed to lift the mast clear of the deck and lay it down silently along the top of the deck. *Deva* tiptoed back to her mooring. Within an hour she was ready for the lowest bridge. One of the officers came by and inquired how we had unstepped the mast. We muttered something about a helicopter and whistled.

The drinking was originally to have been at a famous old pub but with beer at three shillings and sixpence a pint (17.5 new pence) we went to the one next door. The famous pub had at that time some rather dubious clients from gangland. Occasionally local scores were settled and some friends of mine were witnesses to a murder there.

The final leg up to Richmond was uneventful except for the Stuart. Dirty petrol and choked filters ensured that we were not able to overtake a string of barges before the next bridge. Luckily the outboard engine on the dinghy started and pulled us clear of trouble. We were glad to reach Petersham Meadows and we soon were moored at the entrance to Ham Dock, a basin used by the Thames Young Mariners. Dad, a Director of Education, had "arranged" a winter berth there.

Thus ended a voyage of several hundred miles over two months, the longest *Deva* had ever done. Little had gone wrong and despite bitterness at having to pay £3 for a night in Shadwell basin there were no regrets.

I think I would have sold any other craft rather than risk stranding on the Pennines, but somehow *Deva* seems to like staying with us. Perhaps she too, like Dick Whittington, wanted to see the South where the streets are paved with gold. Or was it because there were no old gaffers races in the North-West?

Introduction to Tollesbury

1967

We had *Deva* lifted ashore at Petersham, and gave her a thorough going-over; she had not been slipped properly for a few years. Ron, the man who looked after the boats at Thames Young Mariners, was a shipwright and he put our minds at rest. There were a couple of cracked frames, but these were due to splitting shakes with natural timber movement rather than collision damage. The boat was still tremendously strong, and fit for a season or two yet.

All winter we looked at possible mooring locations. All were very expensive and with waiting lists, even on the East Coast. Purely by chance we heard that someone was giving up a tidal mooring at Tollesbury, in Woodrolfe creek. A man called Lennox Levitt would help us locate it. I had barely heard of places like Burnham, Maldon or West Mersea. No-one I asked in London seemed to have heard of Tollesbury. Even those who sailed the East Coast shook their heads and said that if it existed it was probably just a little tidal creek used by a few fishing boats, hardly a suitable place for a yacht. Eventually I managed to locate it on a chart, after I saw a reference in our 1960 Admiralty Pilot to Tollesbury Fleet off the entrance to Mersea Quarters. Careful study of an old chart indicated something more

than just a simple creek. The place appeared to have a
railway and a pier as well.

We turned up one bleak day and found this funny little
village. The Essex vernacular buildings were strange
enough to my eyes, with the weatherboarding and
pantiles. However, these were mixed with buildings of a
much more opulent nature, and it was clear that this place
had had unusual aspirations in its past. Over a pint in the
Hope Hotel, we learnt that Tollesbury had tried to become
a packet port, with a railway and pier. Unfortunately the
steamer traffic never materialised, the pier had little more
than fish landings from carriers and smacks, and the
railway line became known as the "Crab and Winkle". At
the Hope we were told Lennox Levitt's address and we
went round to see him at his cottage. This was quite an
experience. This fine old sea dog, wearing a Guernsey with
a J class yacht's name on it, appeared, smoking a cigar and
speaking in a drawl like I had only heard in Earl's Court
but much more ruralised. My sensitive northern ears
thought he was speaking Australian!

Lennox told us of the whereabouts of the mooring and of
its construction. Apparently it used an anchor and a
"cross" on the ground chain; I had never come across this
system before. The wooden cross was apparently buried in
the mud and would be there forever. We walked down to
the head of the creek and I was absolutely amazed. There
was all the infrastructure for a busy fishing port, although
most of it was now dilapidated and disused. Apart from
the boat yard, Frost & Drake, there were some delightful
sail-loft buildings on stilts. There were oyster packing
sheds and pits for the oysters. There were marine railways
disappearing into the mud. But the most amazing aspect
was the number of interesting boats laid up in the saltings.
There were barges, trawlers, smacks, racing cutters,
gentlemen's yachts and many other craft in final stages of

decay which today would have warranted *Classic Boat* magazine setting up a sub-office to cover all the restoration work which would have been in hand. Many of these vessels would have been of priceless value to the marine historian, but they lay neglected and unrecorded. A couple of the sounder yachts which were being used as houseboats have been saved, but the rest have since perished. However, the smack *Boadicea* (1808) was being totally rebuilt at the time, a sight I had not seen before, but which was to become increasingly common towards the end of the century. Was this restoration or replica building? Perhaps the latter in practice, but the spirit of the original boat never disappeared.

We did look at Portsmouth, and we also put our name on waiting lists at Southwold and Orford. But Dad's frugality got the better of him, and the nearly free mooring at Tollesbury seemed to appeal most. At least it would do as a temporary measure, and, as it turned out, *Deva* was based at Tollesbury for the next twelve years!

Our voyage down the Thames was relatively uneventful. We gave Shadwell and the PLA docks a miss this time. We found a high jetty from which we could step the mast, and we moored overnight at Holehaven. The westerly helped us up the Swin, and then it was a relatively calm plod under engine to moor in the Leavings, at the entrance to Tollesbury. The next day we found Lennox's mooring.

The mud at Tollesbury was something special. A friend of mine, Ken, and I had been out for a sail, but had returned rather late on the tide; we were too late for Woodrolfe creek, so we left *Deva* on anchor at the end of Old Hall, then took to the punt. Although the ebb had set in, there appeared to be still plenty of water for the skiff. Indeed, we made good progress until we grounded about 25 yards out. We tried shoving with the oars but nearly lost them.

We tried pushing from over the side, but sank up to our midriffs. We were actually quite worried now. It was getting dark. Eventually we stripped off and staggered/swam through the slurry with a warp. We attached this to the car, and eventually the skiff was pulled free. We stank.

In those days Tollesbury was very quiet and informal, and it was still very much a village and fishing community. People were always very friendly to me. I always used to chide the smacksmen for not setting sail any more, but then they used to tell me what real commercial fishing was about. Despite how much we romanticise about working sail, it was not even then an economic or practical proposition. The shrimp trawling nobbies of the North-West which still used a little sail did not need to beam trawl as fast or hard as a sole trawler with otterboards. Also a smack needs much more sail proportionally to be any use, whereas a slightly less stable yacht like a nobby can do very well with mere steadying canvas. And also the seas tend to be higher in the North-West. However, I remember "Southerly" Frost (I don't know why he was called "Southerly") explaining all the grants and scams with the White Fish Authority which helped him keep his motorised smack *Varuna* in fine fettle. Some thirty odd years later she was still a sound boat, being restored to sail, with a counter added.

Another working smack or, rather, bawley at Tollesbury which came to fame in later life was the *Helen and Violet*. She had shed all sign of sail, but when I saw her slipped, well wow! she was a real beauty underneath. With hollow entry, plenty of keel depth and lateral resistance in that shape, and hollow garboards and sharp turn to the bilge. The bluff-bowed broad-beamed square-sterned fishing platform above the waterline sat on a really sleek yacht under-carriage. She was eventually restored by three gents from Brightlingsea, including sailmaker Jimmy Lawrence and Cyril White, former shipwright at Crossfield before the war. Whatever misgivings we may have about the archaic boomless bawley rig, on that hull she was still the fastest East Coast fishing boat around.

There were relatively few Bermudan rigged yachts based at Tollesbury in those days. There were about ten or so converted smacks and gaff cruisers. I recall two smacks. One was *Phantom* which was moored in Woodrolfe creek. She was owned by a chap called Quill at that time. I seem to remember that her mast was in a tabernacle. She had a coach-roof and cockpit, like a yacht. Later she was restored to near original format at Shotley, when she came into the hands of a young millionaire. When his fortunes declined she was bought by Harry Bird of Ardleigh. He had sailed on her as a lad when she was a working smack at West Mersea. She sometimes moors up in Thorn Reach at Mistley, when not in Mersea Quarters. She has a strange turn of speed. Many a time I've seen her sneak over wind and tide through the shallows off Mersea Island, still outwitting to this day all the racey smacks with their giant rigs. Mind you, Harry's topsail arrangement is rather neat for light weather.

The other smack was the *Taffy*, owned by Walter Bibby. He cruised her extensively for several years before selling her in exchange for a beautiful classic ketch *Gudgeon*. *Taffy* did not survive until today's era when people will spend fortunes on smack rebuilds. And yet at that time she was sounder than *Phantom*. Such a pity.

A group of earnest young men had bought a big Lowestoft smack near our mooring. Unfortunately she fell apart before she could be slipped, and was hulked on the saltings. Another pity. But the saltings also gave sanctuary to a number of notable craft which survive to this day. About the time *Deva* came to Tollesbury, so did *Privateer*, a sturdy Boston smack yacht, built by Gostelow before the war, in 1930. To my foreign eyes she looked a bit like a cross between an Essex smack and a prawner. This is probably not surprising in view of the similarities between the Wash and Morecambe Bay. It was very nice to see such a vessel rigged for sailing, after sadly seeing scores of them at Boston without a rag of sail. She was skippered for over 30 years by the late Martin Eve, a fascinating man whose delightful eccentricity summed up what real old gaffers were about. He and his wife Pat really fitted in well in Tollesbury. *Privateer's* story can be read in *An Old Gaffer's Tale*. She is now being restored by Nick Relf in Kent, at Hollowshore.

From the other extremity of England we had the pleasure of *Greenshank*, a Falmouth Quay Punt with a "goose-arsed" stern. She was, and still is, owned by Don Hunt of Witham. She had a very substantial jetty up one of the creeks, which, despite her huge draft, she was able to use for two hours either side of high water. She had a big topsail rig with a lug mizzen, a very powerful boat, and she could go.

Another boat which could go was the *Fearnought*, owned by Mike Gibson. She was a bit like a larger Itchen Ferry, with a unique hatch which could slide over her cockpit when left on moorings. She had been converted to Bermudan rig. Confused at what size to make the main, the converter had plumped for making a Bermudan main the same size as the old gaff. She ended up with a boom that went well outside her transom and a mast which went to the heavens. A few years ago she was restored to gaff rig of more modest proportions.

Perhaps more appropriate to the waters was the gaff cutter *Rose of Pagelsham*, owned by Kit Hughes. She had a centreboard, a nice little cabin and a decent engine. Kit eventually replaced her with *Miranda*, a handsome smack yacht built at Smeeth's of Dedham. For well over 30 years Kit has kept a boat on a mooring at Tollesbury.

With my girlfriend now living in Birmingham and with commitments to rugby and college studies, I was not able to get to see *Deva* as often as I wanted to. My mum and dad would occasionally go down for the weekend, but the boat would go no further than the Leavings. Dad would spend the time sawing away trying to fit the proverbial quart into a pint pot to improve the accommodation. Thirty-seven years on we still have not cracked it! Mum would read several books in the cockpit. My girlfriend, Margaret, who was now my fiancée, used to sail with me a lot. We used to take one or two holidays a year. In those days it was frowned upon in some quarters for a young girl to spend a night aboard a boat, just with her boyfriend. So Margaret stayed at the Hope each night, and came sailing with me during the day. Why what could happen at night was not perceived as possible during the day I do not know. It was not until I got to know Tollesbury a bit better socially that I realised it wasn't quite as straight-laced a community as was first apparent. We needn't have worried; they would not have said anything!

Later, we often sailed as a family from Tollesbury with Margaret , now my wife, and my son Andy.

Dad's ambition for our first summer cruise in southern waters was to sail to the Channel Islands. Bearing in mind the size of the boat, and with only a puny Stuart to cope with the extreme tidal streams, this was probably a little ambitious in retrospect. However, we borrowed some charts, and duly set off. A fair wind and a pleasant day brought us to Ramsgate without any bother. We spent a pleasant day there, and talked to the fishermen about the local conditions and the best time to set off. We thought it would be a good idea to slip across to Calais for some duty frees, then carry on down Channel. So we set off in our tiny boat, still towing our big skiff, in calm winds and glorious sunshine. Towards the afternoon Cape Gris Nez showed up; we turned to port as we closed the shore and followed a ferry in. We picked up a mooring in the outer harbour and went ashore to seek out the authorities. As it turned out, they weren't at all interested in our passports, or our ship's papers, which we did not have. We returned to find our skiff being freely used to serve all the local craft. The French couldn't believe that we had come over in such a small boat, but the skiff was "très bon" and "merci beaucoup". I was impressed by how well my dad conversed with the locals, although he had but a dozen words of French. Where he did communicate was in expressions - facial expressions, the odd scratch here and there and a colloquialism or two. But I suppose it's the same in any language. Anyway it turned out that we must go into the inner harbour, because a gale was expected. Tie up on the left hand side and it won't cost you anything.

The gale blew and blew day after day. We sought refuge in the yacht club, where we were regarded with great suspicion. Then I realised that the barman was counting the little biscuits on the tables, which we had been pigging at because we were hungry and thought they were complimentary. They were not. The trouble was that at that time the English were restricted to £50 to take abroad. It was also the time of Wilson's devaluation - "The pound in your pocket remains the same" - Huh! The gale had raged for over a week, and now the harbour authorities wanted paying too.

It had raged on so long that one chap thought he would fill in the space between his bunk and his wife's, so that they could be together - desperate straits for married people too! Actually it was quite interesting to be marooned with other Brits and discuss and look over their boats. One boat I had to do a double-take on was a white Bermudan sloop. There seemed something very familiar about the shape of stem and bow rollers. I looked at her stern and then saw the familiarity. She was a big sister of *Deva*. Indeed she was Delmar Morgan's *Laura*. Delmar Morgan was famous in yachting circles for his pilot books, and a Bermudan rigged *Laura* features quite often in them. Delmar Morgan also wrote the book - *I Bought a Prawning Boat*. More on that later.

Day 10 arrived and we were stony-broke. The forecast was down to 5-7 WNW but with a big sea running. We had to go. Two reefs were put in the mainsail. We only had one strong jib. The sea outside was big but not breaking too badly - basically because the tide was heading east. A few hours later we came to a mark, which we thought marked the western end of the Goodwins. It did not and shortly after we headed off for Ramsgate the seas began to break horrendously. The skiff sank and dragged *Deva*'s stern down. The jib blew out and we were nearly on the Goodwin Bank. Our "dead reckoning" had been way out. This was a disaster.

To free *Deva* to fight the seas again, we cut the skiff adrift. Thankfully the Stuart started. This was no good for progress, but at least it would help us to get through the wind and the massive breaking seas. We managed to go about and start heading out into deeper water again. Fortunately we did not ground in the troughs. I then saw my dad dive into the cabin and come out again with the old Seagull outboard in hand. He was about to chuck it over the side to claim the insurance. How could he think about such things? We had nearly bloody well died five minutes before. I persuaded him that it would be tempting fate.

The tide turned to the west, making the big seas break, even in the deep water. We thought it would be safer to take them on the bow by beating to Dover. Many boats could not have made to windward just under reefed main alone in such conditions. But *Deva* could. With the main fairly well out, she headed about five to six points off the wind, and she made good speed in the troughs, so good in fact that we could head up through the frothy bit on top, then bear off and skate down the back of the wave to build up speed again. It was exciting stuff, but we did not know how much longer we could keep going. The old inefficient semi-rotary pump could not keep up with the ingress of water from spray and spindrift.

Fortunately Dover hove into sight and we followed a ferry in. We weren't in a position to follow any instructions - we were blinded through the spindrift. But the relative calm in the outer harbour gave us our bearings again. We scooted across to the entrance to the Wet Dock where somebody passed us a couple of beers. We were caked with salt, cold, and half starved through lack of food in France, and we were ready to pass out.

I remember going into the Hostel for Distressed Seamen, where we were given a meal. We spent a couple of days in Dover. We bought an Avon Inflatable to replace the skiff. Never again would we compromise our safety through towing a big rigid skiff. We limped round to Margate for the night, then sailed back to Tollesbury. It would be twenty years and more before another foreign cruise would be made in *Deva*.

Student Days - Felixstowe Docks

1967 - 1971

One of the features of my student education was that students were given major design projects to be carried out over several weeks. Often the detail design brief was determined by a feasibility study.

Quite naturally I tried to turn these studies to maritime advantage. One project, for instance, was for a sports building/clubhouse of some kind, so a lot of research was required at Tollesbury. A scheme for a magnificent clubhouse and sailing centre was designed for where the Fellowship Afloat centre is now. All the mooring arrangements and mud berths were sorted out properly, too. Fellow students soon cottoned on to my little scam. I might be able to fool the lecturers about the sincerity of my studies, but they knew darn well that I was sailing round the East Coast rivers while they were researching through dusty old books in the Royal Institute of British Architects Library and British Museum, or even more boring places. Worse still, my projects were being awarded good marks as good as or even sometimes better than theirs. Bullshit was certainly baffling brains!

As we progressed through the course, the projects became larger and involved group working. It was important for me to work with a team which could be influenced in the direction of sailing and drinking. Bryan and David were two such fellow students.

At that time there was a lot of political unrest in the major ports in Britain, such as London and Liverpool. The old methods of cargo handling were dying fast. The traditional method of dock working, with ships tied up for weeks while being unloaded by stevedores working in holds, was being replaced to a large extent by new cargo unitisation systems and more mechanical handling. Jobs were being lost at an alarming rate, sending the local economies of dockland areas into free-fall. Strikes abounded everywhere, and many shipping companies were relocating their operations to mainland European ports such as Rotterdam. Politicians, businessmen and trade unionists were at each other's throats. These were the headlines of the day. Thus it was quite feasible for a group of forward thinking students to consider a study of containerisation, its social and economic effects and the new type of port facilities required.

The lecturers swallowed the bait hook, line and sinker. Other students muttered "Bastards" as Bryan, David and I slid off to the Hampshire Hog pub to plan our first voyage of the project over an afternoon's drinking. Charts were studied for suitable port locations. The Government was promoting London Tilbury in a big way to appease the unions more than anything else. Although we had to give Tilbury a looking over, we did not rate the idea highly, and apart from anything else it wasn't much of a place to sail to. So we studied charts of the Thames Estuary and a map of the country. We believed that the trade with Europe was going to be more important than anything else. And the main way in and out of Europe was up the Maas to Rotterdam. For this reason the country's manufacturing base was likely to centre round the Midlands and East, with offshoots to Manchester and the North-West. Now draw a line between Birmingham and Rotterdam, and it goes nearer Tollesbury than Tilbury.

However, much as I would have liked Tollesbury to become a container port, and realise its nineteenth century dreams, it could not be so. Apart from the total lack of infrastructure on land, so much off-site dredging would be required for ships of any size to use the place without recourse to high tide. Furthermore there was a myriad of sandbanks to negotiate to get to Rotterdam. So we turned our thoughts northward. Harwich/Parkeston Quay was a possibility, but it would need Bathside Bay reclaiming. The Stour was also a little narrow for turning really large ships. Road access to the Midlands was poor, although the rail link was quite good. Ipswich had some potential, but it was up a narrow river, and, like Harwich, would require quite a bit of land reclamation. But what about Harwich Harbour itself, where the Rivers Stour and Orwell meet before going out to sea? The north side looked quite promising, where the channel scoured the beach. There was a small dock, owned by the delightfully named Felixtowe Dock and Railway Company, and next to that were some old seaplane hangers. Well worth a look, and it was on the way to the Butt & Oyster at Pin Mill on the Orwell.

The project team's first survey trip in *Deva* to check out Felixstowe for suitability for development as a container port got no further than Bench Head, as we ran out of wind. But we had a bit of fun scuttling round in the dinghy taking photographs. The next trip had more than enough wind. We wasted most of the ebb in calm winds and got no further than Bench Head, and then it came on to blow hard from the south-south-west. We tucked in a couple of reefs and plugged a serious tide up the Wallet. Darkness fell before we had doubled the Naze and turned north for Harwich harbour. I could not work out where the top mark on the breakwater had got to. I shouted "We should be seeing a beacon to port any time now", peering towards Dovercourt. "Is that it?" said some bright spark who pointed to an errant beacon, shooting by on the starboard side! My sphincter muscles flexed, but it was too late; we had already sailed over the breakwater. We tore up the river Orwell to Pin Mill, found a mooring and took to the Butt & Oyster. In those days it was still very much a country pub, and most of the people there were either involved with the sailing barges or agriculture. The police did not know where it was either, for the singing and drinking went on into the early hours.

The next day was a sunny one as we sailed down the Orwell to have a proper look at Felixstowe. They had already started doing containers in a small way, and had one of those huge container cranes working busily away. It looked a hive of activity, well worth further investigation. After we had finished our mini-cruise, we rang up Felixstowe Dock and Railway Company and made an appointment to visit the docks. I should say at this stage that we had already done quite a bit of research into handling equipment, van carriers and containers, and had gone to trade exhibitions. Although we were only students, we were quite well read in the subject, well enough to convince commercial operators like Felixstowe or Tilbury.

When we arrived at Felixstowe, we were very impressed with the hubbub of a port working hard. Everywhere else we had been to people just hung around idling. But at Felixstowe everything was done at the double, and it was clean and tidy. They had their own shunting loco, the Colonel Tomlin, which was immaculately polished and painted. It was clanking up and down, pushing and pulling container flats over a maze of shiny rails. Van carriers (massive vehicles on legs for moving containers about) tore round the site with containers clasped to their bosoms. The big prehensile container crane lifted massive containers straight from the waiting ship on to lorries or bogie flat wagons, while Ro Ro ferries disgorged hundreds of lorries on to the quayside. The original little harbour was also very busy with grain barges and other conventional cargo vessels. It all seemed very efficient and so it was. We had a long meeting with the management of the Felixstowe Dock and Railway Company. All the strikes elsewhere had brought them a huge increase in business, and they were determined to keep it. Although they only had a small facility, they worked it hard and fast, and could turn round ships in very few hours, faster than anyone else in the country. We asked about unions and the Dock Dispute. A lot of their men were not in unions. They were paid a lot better than dockers in the striking ports anyway; they were making good money and had no intention of stopping work. They had proper contracts for employment; there was not the casualisation of dock labour. In the traditional ports a stevedore never knew if he would have work. He would have to report to the docks, where foremen/leading gangers would make the choice of who was going to be working for them. Naturally the system was open to corruption, in lean times especially.

Another factor in Felixstowe's favour was the relatively uncongested roads in East Anglia. Lorries could spend two or three hours extra on their journey stuck in London traffic. The meeting stopped briefly to jeer a containership coming out of Harwich. Felixstowe had turned round two ships with more containers in the time that Harwich had taken to do one.

The more we researched the subject, the more convinced we became that we were right in our choice. Yet when we talked to top civil servants they tended to stick to the government line. Her Majesty's Government (HMG) was not keen on privately owned and run docks. Tilbury was the place, followed by Southampton. But from what we could see on the ground, why on earth should a freight-forwarder taking cargo from Manchester to Rotterdam or vice versa bother to go through Tilbury when he could cut several hours off the journey by going through Felixstowe? Even students knew that time was money. HMGs implied response was that if Felixstowe got too big for its boots it would be nationalised. It was only because it was such a piddling little place in the first place that it had escaped nationalisation. But politics apart, we thought we were right. Leading consultants Mckinsey & Co then produced a report which confirmed almost word for word what we had said. Time was money, and distance was money too, when considering high value manufactured goods in transit. And Europe was where it was all going to happen. Deep Sea ships from the Far East and the Atlantic would tend to go to Rotterdam or Europort, not Liverpool, London or Southampton. From there "Short Sea" container ships would serve the UK, and inland transport would service the rest of Europe and beyond.

Where we did differ from Mckinsey & Co, and indeed Felixstowe Dock and Railway Company at that time, is that if Felixstowe container traffic developed beyond a critical mass, deep sea shipping would return, with short sea container runs to Europe. Our plans were big. We designed a huge container quay, with lots of service buildings and transit sheds. There was a big port office building, a multi storey complex. The railway layout was improved so that more freight and containers could go by rail. It was completely beyond the ken of our lecturers, so they had to award the scheme good marks. Thirty years on it is interesting to see what has actually happened in the area. In terms of general size and scale of development we were spot on. Felixstowe was the right place for development, and had the governments of the day invested in East Anglia, rather than elsewhere, we would have had much better infrastructure in terms of motorways and rail to service it. Britain's busiest port only has a single track railway, albeit greatly improved, and only recently has it had a dual carriageway trunk road, the A14, to the Midlands, and that is already congested. Felixstowe had grown entirely in the period of central and local government planning, and yet the powers-that-be totally misread the situation. A bunch of students could have done better! We did expect a larger amount of conventional cargo and bulk cargo handling; this seems to have gone up the river to Ipswich. The smaller operations in the area seem to have kept busy - Mistley and Harwich Navy-yard Dock, for instance. The train ferry service and a lot of car transporter business has gone with the opening of the Channel tunnel. Parkeston, whilst it has done well in car and passenger ferry business, has never realised its full potential with Bathside Bay reclamation despite promises on privatisation. It has recently been acquired by Felixstowe's owners. It will be interesting to see what they do. New plans for a big container terminal are now being drawn up. There has been a huge dredging operation to enable the largest container ships in the world to use the port. In terms of management for commercial and leisure craft, the harbour authorities appear to be very competent.

In contrast to all this sensible study and research, I did of course take part in student rag weeks. One year we decided to build a raft to cross the Channel and collect money for the Spastics Society. We used scaffolding poles, reinforcing bars, scrap timber and oil drums. The design was a lattice space frame supported on two rows of oil drums. I also worked into the design twin rudders, a centre plate and sprit rig.

We had a two day procession through London and down to the South Coast, with a stop at Maidstone. People were very impressed at the ease with which I found my way around a strange town, till they noticed that I was following the trolley bus wires! We launched at Folkestone with a blaze of publicity, including TV. Unfortunately the wind was blowing a full Beaufort 6, and I said we could not go. But in the end we did set out to sea from the harbour for the benefit of the cameras, with a fishing boat in discreet escort. Amazingly the raft proved to be very seaworthy. The waves just washed harmlessly through the space frame. The catamaran hulls kept her level. The vessel steered well, pivoting on her drop keel. She was not very fast under sail to windward, but she tacked. The boat was towed back in as arranged, unrigged and abandoned in the Inner Harbour. The fishermen said it was OK, and indeed they used her as a landing pontoon for several weeks.

Ken Herbert, one of the prime instigators and constructors of the raft, was determined to make another crossing attempt. It was a matter of professional pride, so after finishing for the summer Ken went down to Folkestone, armed with my working drawings for rigging the boat. Unfortunately I was not able to go myself, but Ken made a successful second attempt at crossing, with help from a British Seagull Century and escort from his Uncle Dick's fishing boat. They tied her up to a quay in the dark at Boulogne and came back. No publicity, but what an achievement!

My final year of student life was a busy one, with a written thesis and a design thesis to do. The written thesis I did jointly with Bryan, which was an excellent scam. Computers were still driven by steam then, but people were talking about them doing more than a few sums and cracking the Enigma Code. We wrote a thesis on Computers in Architectural Practice. Not only did we get paid for writing it during holiday jobs with the Ministry of Public Building and Works, but it was also published as a book. Five pages a day of bullshit, which no one could understand, but dare not admit it. Unfortunately I did not milk the opportunity of sitting on prestigious government or academic working parties and get into "computers" at ground floor. Getting married and getting out of London were more on the agenda.

The last little adventure we had as students involved the delivery of the Itchen Ferry *Dilkusha*. David Webb, a fellow student, lived on a houseboat at Kew Bridge. It was quite a nice arrangement, mooring costs being minimal, electric supply unmetered and free. There were several other old craft round there as well, including the famous sailing barge *Ironsides* under restoration, which was particularly attractive to look at because of the Swedish lady working on her. I was too shy to chat her up, but our paths crossed many years later and we have become good friends; she was none other than Lena Reekie, of Swale Match and Medway and North Kent OGA fame. She is probably the most intrepid female sailor I have come across, and can be seen sailing her little Dauntless class gaff cutter, *Linnaea*, winter and summer, and looking particularly elegant whilst doing it!

David had bought the Itchen Ferry in pretty dilapidated condition somewhere further up the Thames, and brought her down to Kew under outboard. Dave was a very practical chap with his hands, and I was amazed at how much he was able to achieve with the boat afloat - serious structural work like replacing floors for instance. There was a boat breakers yard in Southampton where we bought many bits. With the government surplus stores about then it was possible to fit out a boat in rudimentary fashion very cheaply.

The exams had finished, and David wanted to get his boat up to the East Coast where he could sail her. However he was worried, quite naturally, about bringing an unknown boat without an engine down the Thames. Although a four horsepower engine hardly qualified *Deva* as a tug, I suggested that we took *Deva* up to Tower Bridge and towed *Dilkusha* to Holehaven at the mouth of the Thames, where we could rig her before sailing up to Tollesbury. Four of us then went up to Tollesbury - myself, Ken, Bryan and Dave. The plan was for Bryan and Dave to get off at Tower Bridge and fetch *Dilkusha* down from Kew under outboard, then for *Deva* to take her in tow.

We got to Tollesbury and found that the wind was blowing old boots from the south-west; no way could we beat down the Swin. So we decided to abandon the project and have a sail up to Pin Mill and Walton Backwaters. We had a boisterous sail up the coast, and a boozy time at the Butt and Oyster, then slunk into the Walton Backwaters and anchored in the Twizzle, somewhere near where the marina is now. We went ashore, walked across various gang planks and ended up with a skinful at the Walton and Frinton Yacht Club. Out of habit we listened to the shipping forecast - north-east4! - so we decided to sail at 04.00.

It was a beautiful sail down. We even rigged up a jib topsail to give ourselves even more speed. We carried tide past Holehaven, then had to plug the long ebb. The tide turned at dusk. I remember passing a replica galleon going the other way under tow; *Deva* was under topsail, gliding up the river. Which was the genuine article? We were told to get out of the way once by the PLA, but I did not expect them to understand the limitations of a sail driven vessel constrained by nature. We arrived at Tower Bridge, and tied alongside a PLA pontoon. Bryan and David caught a night bus to Kew. It took a couple of hours for the PLA to notice a little nobby illicitly moored to their property, and they told us to "Go away!" in time honoured fashion. I said I would have to wait for the tide and they gave me another hour's grace, by which time our consignment had arrived.

We started off by towing alongside, but the wash from commercial vessels was too great, so we towed line ahead. We rested the flood at Greenwich, got some well needed sleep, then resumed our journey. All went well until we reached Tilbury. The Stuart engine started spluttering and losing power. We were drifting towards a moored merchantman. Dave immediately cut the tow and tried to start his outboard. Meanwhile the tide swept *Deva* alongside the merchantman, whose cooling water was a two foot diameter spout which went straight down the hatch on top of the dying Stuart. This should have been the end.

I cannot think of a logical reason why, but the engine suddenly came back to full power again, almost as if refreshed by this thorough drenching. We dashed off to recover our tow, only to find *Dilkusha* pinned against a pier by the rushing ebb. We anchored with the intention of setting a line down to her, but a kindly tug came along and pulled her off. Thankfully we re-attached our tow, but decided that sail was more reliable than Stuart and did the remainder of the tow under sail and power. This did involve some tacking across the river, which was interesting at times, considering the heavy commercial traffic in those days.

As the Thames broadened and calmed David began to rig *Dilkusha*, and the boats had separated by the time they reached Holehaven. Thoughts about a couple of hours' kip and several more drinking at the Lobster Smack were interrupted by a hail from *Dilkusha*. They were sinking! I took *Deva* alongside, and lashed the boats together. Dave found that several seams had been opened up and ribs cracked with the banging against the pier. The damage was at the turn of the bilge, just under water. Well, there are times when low freeboard has its uses. With weights on the boom we careened or heeled *Dilkusha* right over. As *Deva* was so low in the water, we were able to put a canvas patch and tingles over the worst seams and staunch the flow. By daybreak *Dilkusha* was ready for sea again.

I thought I would have trouble keeping *Deva*'s speed down so that *Dilkusha* could stay with us. But as *Dilkusha* sped away from us I realised that this was no sluggard, despite her rough old sails. *Deva* had a reef in the main and was towing a rubber dinghy, but even so she had good sails and plenty of them on a slim hull. The race was on! Neck and neck we sped out of the Thames Estuary, only feet between us all the time. There were no rules. We even emptied our Elsan to put them off. The wind picked up, but the boats still stayed locked in combat, through the Wallet Spitway and right up to the Nass, where *Deva* nearly got away. Then *Dilkusha*'s longer bowsprit gave her the final edge by three feet. We moored, shattered, in the Tollesbury Leavings.

That was the last sail we all had together. Marriage and jobs put paid to this harmless fun of ours. David eventually went to America, then built his own boat to cross the Pacific. Bryan and Ken pursued architectural careers very seriously, and became very respectable and sober members of society. I moved a bit nearer *Deva*!

We were to meet again on rare occasions, but the era of student madness was over.

Old Gaffer Racing on the East Coast
1967 - 1972

Mention *Deva* on the east coast, and people think of racing. She does have a reputation, larger than she deserves. But she does have the heart to win, which is most important.

In the Mersey Rivers Class she was not that successful. Possibly it was because she was not quite the same as the others - a little beamier, a little heavier perhaps. She was the prototype, which was improved on. However she did win on occasions, mainly due to steering a different course to the others, which often caused outcries from competitors. The situation is the same today. The race may appear totally lost, but time upon time she will suddenly come up with some magic. A tide saving shoal here, a lee bow there, or a major disaster to a competitor somewhere else. No boat is immune to *Deva*, and others know it. Although she has no more victories than most boats, the ones she does have are most unusual.

Harry, her previous owner, used to race her with the cruisers at Tranmere with some success, but the first race I had with her was the East Coast Old Gaffers Race from Stone in 1967. Indeed this was the only race we did for many years. Anticipation of that first race made me very excited. I believed nobbies, especially *Deva*, to be invincible anyway. Then the cranky Essex smacks looked like lumbering cart horses with old tarpaulins for sails; in no way, I thought, were they competitive. Then there were all sorts of Itchen Ferries, Quay punts, Harrison Butlers, Hillyards and other fine, but sluggish, traditional vessels. This was going to be embarrassing.

The gun went, and suddenly all these stately old ladies gathered up their skirts and chased after the Wallet Spitway as if it were the new curate. *Fanny of Cowes*, late on parade at the start, not much bigger than *Deva*, shot by with spinnaker drawing and crew neck-oiling their beer in utter contempt of us. I realised then that I had so much to learn. However, I always believed in the boat, despite having to face up to her not being the most delightful being afloat.

Adherence to tradition was not as important in those days as improving performance. Some owners did look at pinching ideas from modern boats. *Fanny*, for instance, had a stretch luff mainsail. However there were limitations, and really it was a matter of improving the rig within the confines of fifty years old infrastructure. Two sails I bought from Taylor's of Maldon included a storm staysail and a topsail. The topsail was very important to *Deva*, for some reason, and became an obsession with me. I did not feel that I had had a sail unless the topsail was set. It was very effective off the race course, and we made some splendid passages with it. On the race course I always seemed to make a mess of setting it.

The other significant alteration I made to the rig was a third set of reef points from throat to second reef clew to create a trysail or balanced reef. The need to study rig more carefully for racing actually created a better, more seaworthy rig for cruising; a better range in both light and heavy winds. The latter was to prove particularly useful for the 1970 race.

1970 was a tragedy for the Old Gaffers Association (OGA). The East Coast Old Gaffers Race had become by far the largest race of its kind in the country, and one of the biggest events of any kind on the East Coast. The OGA, under John Scarlett, had really banged the drum, and the press and TV were there in force. Eighty entries had been received, the flags were flying at Stone and the great day dawned, blowing damn near a gale. Four of us were on board, Dad, Ken, Margaret and I. It was not going to be a pleasant race, so we put Margaret ashore by going in to the lee of St. Lawrence. We watched the mayhem as boats dragged their anchors into each other and the seas broke over the weather going tide. Only eighteen of the eighty made it to the start line. It was impossible to see or hear the signals, so the committee kindly sent out a boat to tell us all that the race had actually started!

Ideas of sailing double reef and topsail were quickly dispelled. We set the flying jib, staysail and double reefed main. By Bradwell, we decided to reduce this to the balanced reef. Several boats were already in trouble. By Wallet Spitway the local smacks had fled to Brightlingsea for shelter. By the beat back, we were in trouble too, trying to lower the flying jib. We hove to and formed a human chain from the mast, and my dad finally reached the jib with Ken holding on to his life jacket as the foredeck was mostly 3 feet under water. Down to balanced reef and staysail, the boat was relatively steady again, and slowly beat back to Stone. Only four other boats were in the race. *Fanny of Cowes*, reefed similarly to us, a 30ft prawner, a bawley rigged dhow which had sailed from Cape Town and a big double ended cockle boat, *Amity*, from Brancaster. No smacks could handle the conditions, no yachts either. There are conditions which will overwhelm *Deva*, but she proved again what a wonderful sea boat she was. She may look a dainty lady with her fine lines and big rig, but there is a real toughie under the petticoats! She seemed so tiny compared with the rest of the fleet, but everyone now looked at her with new respect. The aftermath of the race was pretty bad. Lots of damaged gear every where, Ken grilling our cigs to dry them out. The Deben Cherub *Sea Pig* was nearly sunk, so with the help of a passing motor boat I ran her ashore to dry out.

For several years one boat had shone above all others on the East Coast Race - *Fanny of Cowes*. An Itchen Ferry built in about 1860, she was really a 30ft boat with the back cut off, but with beautiful lines under water. Every piece of timber had been soaked in linseed oil at construction, and she had lasted more than a century in very rude health. Her rig had a huge foretriangle with massive bowsprit, counterbalanced with a very high peaked mainsail and long boom. She was sailed by very experienced racing crew, and indeed campaigned with the East Anglian Offshore Group, the only gaff rig amongst modern offshore racers. Compared with the rest of us, boat for boat, she was unbeatable.

However she had yet to come under the spell of *Deva*. The 1971 race, in contrast to the year before, was on a much more gentle day, the light westerly wind wafting 92 of us down river. *Fanny* as usual shot off into the distance, massive kite pulling her over the horizon. The wind continued to lighten. Clearly something was on the cards when the tide changed. Weather experts scoff at the concept of weather changes being related to tide changes, but I'm not sure.

At the turn we tacked away from the rest of the fleet, and the wind started to bend and bend in our favour. We tacked back and it bent the other way. *Hyacinth*, *Fanny*, *Golden Plover* and other fast boats covering each other lay relatively dead in the water, whilst *Deva* tacked in clear water from shift to lift, creeping un-noticed upon her prey. Suddenly she appeared at the head of the fleet, and the hotshots looked on in horror, forgot their fight with each other and chased after us. Faster boats, they soon overtook us, realising that it's not how fast you sail, or even how well you sail, it's where you sail that counts. And, being a very small boat, we had a very good handicap, which they would not beat on a quick run up the Blackwater. Through gritted teeth the coveted East Coast Old Gaffers Trophy for the first boat on corrected time over fifty years old (affectionally known as the "Lump of Lead") was handed to *Deva*, for her name to join the illustrious good and the great of gaff rig.

Patchy conditions prevented *Fanny* from winning the 72 Race, and she was sold on after that. She never raced again, although she was kept in local waters. Occasionally she is seen in Harwich Harbour, and I describe her past to my companions, how for years she dominated the gaff scene. She appears relatively sedate in her speed now, many boats being as fast or faster. But she was the greatest.

Deva never really got back into the gold again. She would close up on the fast boats of one year, only to find that the next year even faster boats had joined the fleet. Occasionally she would get into the first six or ten places, but the "Lump of Lead" remained elusive. However, the search for speed continued. Learning from modern boats the value of balance, I trimmed three feet off the mainsail, and put three feet on the bowsprit. The next mainsail had a "roach reef" in it, so that the main could be flattened for windward work. This was later replaced with a traditional loose-footed main which did just as good a job! A traditional small flat spinnaker was acquired. But as *Deva* went faster, so did every other boat.

At Tollesbury I joined the local sailing club, and started to take part in the cruiser racing. These were very much social races, often ending up in local watering holes such as

Brightlingsea or Bradwell. This turned out to be very good fun, although I did get some funny looks from the Bermudan boats. One or two other gaffers such as *Greenshank* and *Miranda* joined in, and we did not do too badly, despite our funny rigs and heavy boats. Whether or not it was because old gaffers were taking part, with genuine handicap racing for all types of boat, cruiser racing really took off on the Blackwater as a whole. We sometimes had Blackwater Joint Clubs Racing Committee (BJCRC) races, with each club putting in a team of four boats. One year Tollesbury's team consisted of three old gaffers and a catamaran. We started at Osea, not particularly well, but most competitors made the mistake of cutting in towards the Thirslet spit too soon. The shortest distance between two points is not always a straight line, especially with a strong ebb running. After all, Thirslet spit would not be there if there were not a back eddy. Anyway it was very satisfying to zoom up the outside of all these modern Bermudans.

Crew or friends who used to sail with me at this time were a mad bunch. There was Tony Cox, a Welshman from the Valleys, who, apart from everything else, used to nobble other boats when we partied on them before OGA races. His speciality was swinging out on the rigging round and round the mast. There was Plymouth Tony, a surveyor from the Ordnance Survey. He was an ex hotshot crew from proper racing boats, equally as mad. You never knew where he was, but he always seemed to know and turn up in the nick of time. Richard Coe, a good old Suffolk boy from Haughley, stood nearly 6ft 8in tall. He could reach virtually any part of the boat with his long arms without moving, which was particularly handy when reaching for a beer out of the cabin. Beer played a major part in the racing, because really it was party time as soon as we climbed aboard. Beers were graded according to Beaufort Scale. Ordinary light ale up to a force 3, Abbot ale force 4,

Strong Suffolk force 5/6, Audit Barley Wine 6/7. We used to get some strange looks from competitors at the start, and some other crews might have been demoralised at the sight of us taking things so easy. But my premise was that if the enjoyment were the first priority, we would never have a bad race. Crew would return for future events, good team spirit would prevail, and if that team spirit developed into pride as well the boat might sail better too.

This did not always work out, especially with married men. "Yes dear, do go out for a sail, you have had a rotten week at work, you'll come back refreshed and relaxed". Unfortunately, with the emphasis on refreshment, too often they returned in a worse state than they left - bloodshot eyes, slurred speech, aching and bruised limbs. They were lucky if they did not need a Monday "sickie" to get over it. Occasionally wifey came along to check that it was nothing more than a boys' day out. But that was the last time hubby would be allowed out. "You are not going out on that dreadful little boat with that awful Wainwright".

But we played hard, we drank hard and we sailed hard. *Deva* would come out with a bit of magic, and the race would be in the bag when you least expected it. One marvellous race we actually began with us starting half an hour late; *Deva* had just had a photo session for *Practical Boat Owner* for a series on gaff rig. When we eventually started there was a light south-easterly breeze and all the Bermudans were pointing straight for the mark. There was no way we could do that, so we worked the ebb tide instead. We tacked toward Bradwell, into the deep channel and let the current do the work. We might have been pointing the wrong way, but we were going the right way. As soon as we tacked, we could lay the windward mark full and bye. The tide put wind in our sails, but did nothing for the Bermudans out of the current against the Mersea shore. Slowly we came abeam, then went ahead.

The Bermudans were pointing well up towards our track, but still well to leeward. We slid round, the tide changed to flood, we did a few wriggles round the remaining cans about the Bench Head, then bore off for a very pleasant reach up river, while the others struggled against wind and tide. We flashed through the finish line, where the chaps on the committee boat were dozing peacefully. They woke with a start. One of them reached for the horn, but was then restrained by his pal. Oh, a big rat was smelt! We had missed out a mark! *Deva* rounded up, back through the line, and went to find the missing mark, a wretched thing further up the river. What a stupid course! We still finished second over the line properly, but it was so nearly a complete whitewash. However, the point was made for the glory gaff rig.

Deva never lost a race until the line was crossed. In one race, beating back from Brightlingsea, we were at the back of the fleet not doing well at all. We were approaching the Nass when a huge black cloud appeared with a line squall underneath. We had no time to strike the topsail before it struck, with blinding rain cutting visibility to a couple of yards. One witness later told me that "*Deva*'s going!" was his last shout as he saw her capsizing. When the squall had gone she was no longer there. He thought she was sunk, and wondered what the hell to do. Then he saw her, crossing the finishing line ahead.

Deva was not the only old gaffer to compete with the Bermudans. *Miranda* was just as competitive. In my last season at Tollesbury the two of us contested the Cruiser Points series neck and neck right through the season. One race was held just for us, in three parts of a gale. Nobody else wanted to race, but *Miranda* needed to get a first to stay in contention, and *Deva* needed a second to keep in the lead. We had a very gentlemanly sail round the course, and *Miranda* won by miles. But *Deva* took the pot! Those days of informal cruiser racing were great fun at Tollesbury. Even the Cruising Club chaps from the marina joined in, and we had some super joint races, with thirty or forty boats taking part. Racing against the gaff riggers had some influence on the others - some started using watersails!

I moved to Mistley near Manningtree and eventually berthed *Deva* there. Tollesbury had become much more popular with yachtsmen, and moorings were in great demand. It was even getting difficult to berth a dinghy on the hard. New regulations restricting the use of the hard by foreigners from Tolleshunt D'Arcy (about three miles away!) and beyond meant that I had to park the tender a long way from the water. It was thus a struggle to get out to the mooring at Tollesbury. It was much quicker to get to sea from Mistley, although we were nearly ten miles up a river. The cruiser scene flourished there too, although the club, which had hitherto been mainly dinghies, did not give the prominence it should have done to the larger cruiser activity in the silverware stakes. *Deva*, with her heavy displacement and long keel did not fare very well against modern lightweight jobs, but when we sailed out to sea she would get her own back.

However, changes swept through racing to spoil all this. First of all it was the E-boats, extra light high performance boats which were essentially very big dinghies with lids. Stripped of full cruising gear and sailed by zealous racing types wanting to make an impression, they killed ordinary cruiser racing on the Blackwater. Whatever handicap was applied, ordinary people were no longer in the same race, the fun had gone out of it all. Within two years there was nothing and most of the cruiser races were history. On the Stour the Micros achieved the same end. The little man in his Lysander no longer felt part of it, and went off cruising on his own. No amount of fiddling with handicaps would bring him back, other than for the odd regatta. The Micros race on their own.

I would like to have said that the gaff scene did not suffer similarly, but I would have been wrong. After *Fanny of Cowes* retired, there was little room at the top for cruisers or working boats unless they were smacks and effectively sailed their private races. Old racing boats, discarded because they were obsolete in top racing circles, and useless for cruising, were being dug up in corners of boatyards. With all the gaff rig races going on they became a viable proposition. *Golden Plover*, an open Clyde Racer, took over where *Fanny* left off. She was followed by *Sheena*, a French 7.5 metre, converted to gaff rig from Bermudan. The little *Jade* of Tollesbury, a Seaview Mermaid, was the one which really heralded the new era, and I helped her, God forgive me. Hamish Stuart had just fitted her out, and could not get to Stone for the old gaffers race, so I towed her there in *Deva*. Hamish had just re-rigged her with a new gaff main, which had a near vertical head. Without engine, without cabin, without cruising gear, only 25 feet long and with a good handicap to boot, she had a tremendous advantage even before her natural performance was considered. She shocked everyone by winning by a great margin. It was not just against old gaffers; it was against anything. She was even banned from some regattas, she was so fast. Gayle Heard, the Tollesbury sailmaker who, I think, had made her new mainsail, then took her under his wing, and she won the "Lump of Lead" as many times as *Fanny*. In her wake all sorts of classic racers appeared. Many had never sported gaff rig before, and seemed to go even faster.

So *Deva* was never going to win the "Lump of Lead" again, or at least so I thought. But 23 years later she was to prove that her magic had not worn out.

One area where *Deva* has never been able to win is on the Crouch. Unlike many East Coast rivers it is straight with high banks or at least it appears so. The wind tends to blow up or down, so it is running or beating type sailing. *Deva* is slow on a run, and, whilst she can go to windward, she needs space to get going. The Crouch Rally is also held at Whitsun, so *Deva* is normally at her foulest underneath. But the worst problem is the locals. Because it is such a restricted area and so heavily raced, they know every nuance of the course. There is no way a foreigner can show them the best way round the course. So, denied her boatspeed and normal guile in sailing a better course, *Deva* would never win. But that is not all. The locals, better known as the "Crouch Mafia", have a lot more tricks to ensure that *Deva* comes last. They will even sacrifice their own to achieve this. Apart from using almost invisible secondhand dan buoys as racing marks, they are quite prepared to detail a couple of their boats to round the mark the wrong way, or round the wrong mark, so that *Deva* will make the same mistake. Beating up the shore against a foul tide, they will despatch two boats to shadow *Deva*, to make sure that when she tacks to port at least one of them will be on starboard with right of way. And, if that does not work, they will bring a boat out of a totally different race to catch *Deva* on port tack. Just assume that even that doesn't work, and *Deva* is lying third or fourth. Every boat behind *Deva* would retire, so she would still be last. This has happened on numerous occasions, but is all good fun really. The Godfather of the Crouch Mafia, Raymond Austeno, wears dark glasses and speaks with a Sicilian accent at our annual dinner at the Royal Burnham Yacht Club.

Deva still occasionally ventures down the Wallet to the Blackwater for races. But the scene has changed. Apart from the East Coast Race, there are many other races run for traditional craft by local clubs. It has all become very competitive, and perhaps rather incestuous. The same people race the same boats round the same cans in the Blackwater Estuary, week in, week out. A lot of them only come off their moorings to race, and rarely venture past Bench Head. Sometimes it is because the boats are only really equipped for day racing, sometimes it is because they are worried about someone else winning a local race in their absence. This situation is quite common in keen racing, and is one of its downsides. The intense racing ensures that there is a fine fleet of smacks in good fettle, which was the original object of starting up gaffers races. But perhaps some of the old camaraderie has gone on the Blackwater; most of the people just turn up to race, rather than turn up to celebrate. This stops many boats from outside the area taking part. How much more of an impression could be made if these beautiful boats were to be seen over more of our coastline or in Holland! How much more satisfying it is to have been somewhere different! I probably get more satisfaction from making a passage to an event, than from the race or event itself. Even if we come last, we still win hands down in other more important ways.

Great Plans, Great Despair

1979 – 1983

Work was getting boring. Had it got be like this forever, a wage slave for another thirty years?

I rang up Tony to share a few thoughts. How about our own boat business? We could play old boats for a living. He felt much the same way as I did, and within a few weeks we had our own letterhead and limited company, Coxswain Boats Ltd. While we were thinking about premises, we decided to start trading by getting in paint and chandlery, and flogging it to our mates. Tony lived in Bury and worked in Ipswich. I lived in Mistley and worked in Needham Market. We used to meet up in a lay-by on the A1100 near Bramford and I would load boxes of paint and boat bits into Tony's car for resale at Bury St Edmunds. On the Stour I did not do so well. I would get an order for some paint, then find it cancelled, because the purchaser was getting it from his "usual supplier". Then the usual supplier would come and get it from me. The local mafia prevented me from getting a foothold.

We had a look at one or two sites, including ones at Maldon and West Mersea, which had several moorings. It was a pity in some ways that we did not proceed. I could have had the pleasure of being one of those officials who wind up yachtsmen for a bit of fun. I remember once seeing a high ranking officer of the OGA run aground in Woodrolfe Creek in his beautiful canoe yawl. He did not recognise me when I shouted "Oi, you can't stop there!". "Can't you see I am _____ing aground," he replied from amongst an absolute cat's cradle of tangled halliards and sheets. "That's as maybe," I said, "but you are obstructing the fairway, and there are byelaws about this." He went absolutely ballistic and told me to put the fairway where it would never fit me. He still doesn't know it was I to this day, and this is the sort of fun you can have as a moorings master.

However, Eddie Williams, who was then in charge of cruiser racing at the Stour Sailing Club, heard about us and became interested. He'd come across a site at Walton on the Naze which might be of interest. Would we like to have a look? I wish we never had. It was a forty acre derelict site, with a twenty-five acre boating lake at the back of Walton, opposite the yacht club. Years of fruitless planning and feasibility work were about to start.

I prepared some preliminary plans for discussion. We could get a five hundred berth marina and a boating lake, and a traditional boat centre. Many an evening meeting was held at Portview, my house. We had a company jug which we used to take down to the Wagon & Horses off licence next door but one and fill with beer. It was not just marinas. Eddie kept coming up with little sidelines. We bought an old cruiser called *Merlynn*, refitted her and put her up for charter. This was not a very profitable business. By the time Eddie's expenses for maintenance and repair had been taken out together with the cost of advertising we lost considerably. The final straw was when we found she had been used for some very suspicious business to do with the ferries. We sold our shares to Eddie at a pittance, and he converted *Merlynn* to gaff, put a diesel in her and after a few years sold her to someone in the West Country.

Another sideline was dinghy kits - the Coxswain *Saluki*, which Eddie had designed. The *Saluki* was a simple little ply dinghy that was quite easy to put together. She could also be sailed with a sprit rig. There was quite a lot of interest in her, but again the cost of advertising and paying Eddie's costs made it a poor paying proposition. There was nothing left for Coxswain Boats admin costs when a sale was made. And we could not put the price up, because there was some competition.

A sideline which did have potential was epoxy resin. We had a line into a US manufacturer (Chem Tech) and a Canadian manufacturer (Industrial Formulators). America was streets ahead of the UK in epoxies for marine use. They were tolerant of damp and cold temperatures. They were less toxic as well as being a lot easier to use. The colonials actually had their trips to England paid for by their governments, so were very pleased to see us. We signed contracts to be European agents.

However, whilst the business looked good on the surface, there were a lot of set-up costs. For instance, we had to import in big drums and then bottle the stuff. There was all the rigmarole of imports and customs. I could never believe how much it cost to transport the "goo" over here, and how long it took. There was definitely a lot more money in freight forwarding, as the stuff came in at Felixstowe, went past our door to London then came back at vast expense. Another trouble was that it was often solid by the time it got here. Frozen on some freight train stuck in the Rockies, it took some thawing out. And we had to decant it by hand. We had various types - Lifebond, Lifecoat and Lifefil from Chem Tech. We rationalised the range when we started with the Canadians, with Coxwain's Cold-Cure epoxies. We even developed our own anti-fouling Copper Cure, which used epoxy and copper dust. *Deva* had a coat of that. It was very good. But again we ran into the problem of marketing. We had a better product and a cheaper product than was available, but we could not convince the boating public to go our way. So we rumbled on with a bit of mail order, getting nowhere. If only we had had the backing, we would have made it big time. We could have had all the osmosis centres for plastic boats.

The Yacht Harbour project, however, took up a tremendous amount of my time. Drawings showing all the major aspects of the project, including details of locks, weirs and dredging profiles, were prepared. We joined the National Yacht Harbour Association (NYHA), we consulted some leading Dutch engineers on my design and we went the rounds of various merchant banks to raise finance. Unfortunately, no-one would advance a penny without planning consent. Eventually, after much consultation with the local planning authority, an application was submitted. And then the balloon went up. The District Council, who had just become the planning authority on such matters, approved the project. It would bring much needed economic stimulation to the area, clear an eyesore and enable some of the traffic congestion to be eased. We intended to build part of the relief road to give access to the project - imagine the big sign "Coxswain Boats - Get in Lane!". Unfortunately the County Council, who had just lost their planning power, protested to the Department of the Environment, then run by Sir Michael Hesletine, who "called it in" and asked for a public inquiry. The financial stakes had risen several hundred fold. With the media interest and the public commitments we had given, we could not cut our losses and retire gracefully.

Meanwhile we had to assume that we were going ahead with the project. My long-term dream was to have a traditional craft base where we would regenerate the skills and recreate the scenes of our maritime heritage a small Mystic Seaport, or Enkhuizen, perhaps. It had been done before. And, of course, there would be *Deva*'s private marina. The local environment, the Backwaters in particular, was our concern. It was important that we had a vessel to pilot boats in and also make sure that the occupants did not land or disturb wild life in certain areas. We discussed this with the Local Authority, and they said they would create the necessary byelaws.

Deva was due for some major work, and I thought that she could be modified to be this pilot/warden's cutter. It was a lovely thought, to have the job of the warden/pilot. "Hard day on the boat, dear" my wife would be saying. I would spend a lot of the time drifting off Pye End, or, if it were a nice day and there were too many boats at Stone Point, telling them to move along, unless they were gaff rigged. Plans were prepared to repair, raise and strengthen *Deva*'s topsides. Also she would have a much larger engine, with hydraulic drive to twin folding props. She already had ex 1¼ inch planking and was a very strong boat for her size. However, she still needed to be beefed up for continuous lock work, coming alongside and towing. Also the original structure needed protecting. In the end the plan was to extend the frames and the stem post. A topstrake in 1¼ inch keruing laminated and spiked to the existing plank top and the frame extensions was to be provided, together with planted rubbing strakes 3" x 2" lower and 4" x 2" upper. In structural terms *Deva* would have a laminated I-beam following her gunwale, which would not only preserve her from all the biffing and bashing, but would also stop her going out of shape.

My next problem was finance. I was in a bad way with the costs of preparing the planning application, and the subsequent public inquiry documentation. My budget was £500, which would not even pay for a lift-out and storage.

Cyril White (now of Brightlingsea) sailing his Rivers class in the North West in the 1930s. This is how *Deva* would have looked before conversion to a cruiser.

The start of the Solent Old Gaffers Race off Cowes, 1998.

Good start at 1997 East Coast Old Gaffers Race at West Mersea:
Deva leads old Tollesbury rival *Miranda*.

Hounded by the mighty Essex smack *Sunbeam*, Pete the Knife takes *Deva*
on the way to win the 2001 Harwich - Southwold Passage Race.

So the work would have to be done afloat alongside the quay at Manningtree. I could run to keruing for the topsides work and a couple of sheets of ply for the decks, but the rest would have to be salvaged timber. I did have a good source of epoxy and gripfast nails, though! *Deva* became her own workshop, self-regenerating. A saw, a big hammer and a handplane were my only tools.

Exposure revealed a couple of major problems. The nobby's counter is formed by two long oak archboards, which curve to meet in a big dovetail joint at the stern. There was some rot at the point where they meet the pitchpine planking on the quarters, and the dovetail itself had disintegrated. Harry had let in a brass T piece, but this really was only cosmetic, and hid the real problem. I cut the oak back to where it was sound, which left a six inch gap. It was November, a gale was blowing from the north, and *Deva*'s counter was low enough without a six inch hole in it. It was a case of having to make a fashion piece to slot in before the tide came in. I worked feverishly into the night. The tide was rising all the time, waves slapping against the boat. I just managed to get the piece in before the first icy wave broke over the stern. Some water came in because part of the deck was missing, but not enough to sink the boat.

The other frightening area of corruption was the stem. I found that a split in the top of the stem had allowed water to get in and cause rot about two feet down. It had to come out. As I took it out the hood ends began to spring out. "Oh God, the boat is literally falling apart," I thought. God was on my side, however. I made a new stem out of laminated oak bookshelves from Stowmarket library, with a massive scarph so that it would join the remains of the old stem post. I had neither the means nor the access to take detailed measurements - it had to be by eye. I staggered across the mud with the new stem across my shoulder, and it just slotted in, almost as well as if a proper shipwright had done it. I used a couple of bolts and a bit of glue, and I could draw the planking back in, and *Deva* looked whole again. I needed to whack in a secondary apron on the inside to make the structure seaworthy, but my heart rate eased at the visual security of it all.

The counter-top was prefabricated in my garage from several curved pieces of salvaged iroko, spiked and glued together. This was lifted on to the stern and fixed. The half ribs began to poke up between the beam shelf and the top strake. These were bolted to the existing ribs, which had started to rot at the top. After the ribs were ready, the strip planking was fixed with glue and gripfast nails. There were a lot of nails, and the strips had to be bent round gradually to avoid splitting, which meant that I could work on the side away from the quay. After three strips I would have to swing the ship. "Bang, Bang, Bang-te-Bang" rang round the waterfront. I even had the vicar's wife come round to complain that I should be spending more time with my wife and children on a Sunday morning. But a job like this never finishes, once you falter. While the planking was being done, the rubbing strakes went on - two layers of keruing to give a total timber thickness of over three inches. This was backed up by the three inch oak frames, which in turn were backed up by the beam shelf which I doubled. For the size of boat, this was very strong construction. It was important that it was, to hold the shape of the boat. With the planking complete, some of the new deck beams were put in, with the mast partners as well. When these were fitted, the old deck beams were taken out. Nothing moved, thank goodness, and the old beams were fitted in their new positions. The old cabin sides and hatchway were recycled, and they still leak today. The new *Deva* took shape.

Major Works on *Deva*

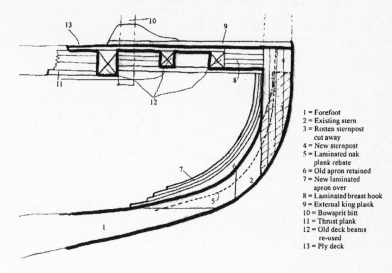

1 = Forefoot
2 = Existing stern
3 = Rotten sternpost cut away
4 = New sternpost
5 = Laminated oak plank rebate
6 = Old apron retained
7 = New laminated apron over
8 = Laminated breast hook
9 = External king plank
10 = Bowsprit bitt
11 = Thrust plank
12 = Old deck beams re-used
13 = Ply deck

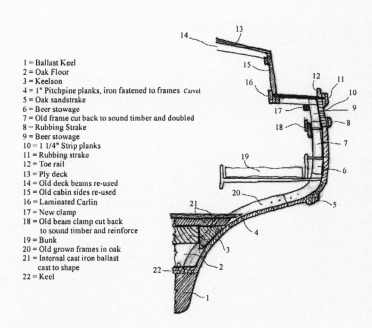

1 = Ballast Keel
2 = Oak Floor
3 = Keelson
4 = 1" Pitchpine planks, iron fastened to frames Carvel
5 = Oak sandstrake
6 = Beer stowage
7 = Old frame cut back to sound timber and doubled
8 = Rubbing Strake
9 = Beer stowage
10 = 1 1/4" Strip planks
11 = Rubbing strake
12 = Toe rail
13 = Ply deck
14 = Old deck beams re-used
15 = Old cabin sides re-used
16 = Laminated Carlin
17 = New clamp
18 = Old beam clamp cut back to sound timber and reinforce
19 = Bunk
20 = Old grown frames in oak
21 = Internal cast iron ballast cast to shape
22 = Keel

We often wonder how the old boys could build wooden boats at a commercial rate. Four men could build a 32ft prawner in six weeks. That is probably a tenth of the time it would take professionally today, or a twentieth of the time an amateur would take. These guys built at a more productive rate than today's Glass Re-inforced Polyester (GRP). The advantage they had was steady workload, standard designs, very standardized construction details, readily available local materials. The finished product would not win a prize at the Wooden Boatshow, but it was very fit for the purpose intended. Commercially it needed to last ten years; anything over that was a bonus. In my case repetition would bring large increases in productivity. The first half frame took me all weekend to fashion and fit. The last took ninety minutes.

The biggest hold-up was spectators. "Got a big job on there" was a comment which slowly drove me mad to the point at which I would say "No, it's nothing - give me a minute and I will come and start on your boat". Some were of course very helpful. John Hugget sorted out bronze rod and nuts for fastenings, as well as running up new chain rollers for me. Others would say "Oi, you can't do that" as a gripfast was hammered in where a screw should have been. Sometimes I had backhanded compliments. People would look at work I had completed and say "Look at that workmanship, you couldn't get anybody to do that these days." I would probably do quite well in the antique business; my woodwork comes with added distress as a bonus.

I often wonder whether these yacht quality restorations of smacks are quite the right thing. There is nothing of the old workmanship left on most of them. I do not suppose that the modern generation smackie knows what a real working smack looked like forty or fifty years ago. Most of them were cobbled together by old skinflints, held together with bloody great nails and stuffed with string. If somebody arrived with one at a smack rally he would be probably be told to go away!

Prawners, being half yacht and half smack, are a bit different. The planking was of a reasonable standard, and the frames were not too bad. But the fastenings, the joints, such as they were, were very crude. In some ways I would like to have *Deva* finished to "joinery" standard as a matter of pride. But then the maintenance would have to be equally high, and I couldn't do rough things like trawling.

During this period we had the public inquiry. The council said it would take a week. It took three. Essex threw in their top barristers from the Stansted Airport inquiry. One tried to roast me as an enemy of the state. Not only was I paying his exorbitant fee through my rates, I was also paying for two solicitors to watch him dissecting me. The conservationists were very sweet, but they did take so very long to make their points, and I was paying solicitors hundreds of pounds per hour while they did so. It was an incredible experience, and I learnt a lot professionally. Unfortunately the inquiry had a lot of coverage in the press, especially when we exposed one of the objector's lack of safety concern regarding pollution and explosives - the whole of Dovercourt and Walton might go up in a bang! I was also in the public eye in my day job, presenting projects at council meetings. In one issue of the East Anglian Daily Times there was the Chief Architect of Mid Suffolk District Council, Mr. Jon Wainwright, on the other side of the page there was company director of Coxswain Boats, Mr. Jon Wainwright. Legally I was not doing anything wrong, as Coxswain Boats was in essence just a very expensive hobby, but some might have interpreted it differently.

As the days dragged on the issues appeared to simplify. The threat to bird life and the site of special scientific interest was essentially the critical time of nesting by the Little Terns. How could we stop more yachts landing at Stone Point in the nesting season? Along with the District Council, we said that we would provide a warden patrol service, and back it up with byelaws. The other outstanding issue was heavy metals in anti-fouling. It was suspected that TBT in yacht anti-fouling was affecting shellfish. Our argument was that it was like lead in petrol - if it was found to be bad for the environment, TBT would be banned, and copper alternatives would be used, as in the past. On all the other issues the opposition were conceding defeat. The fishermen swung behind us, as did most of the local community. Some wanted us to do more. Why not cut a channel straight out to sea, and make the Naze itself an Island? There would be lift bridge for road traffic. Keep the riff-raff out and Naze properties would rocket. Frinton could have its level crossing to keep itself select, Walton would have its bridge.

At the end of the inquiry I felt sick, and even sicker when the really big bills came in. Tony could stand it no longer, paid his share and resigned. I had to take on his role as company secretary. Then it was a matter of waiting.

Work continued on *Deva*, the epoxy resin business trundled on, barely covering its costs. On *Deva* the budget had all but run out. The rates counter of the former Gipping Rural District Council formed the stern, Stowmarket library shelves provided the oak, and I had a small supply of iroko benching as well. Good things can be found in contractors' skips. But things were still getting desperate on *Deva*. I managed to re-use many of the deck beams forward, and create others by laminating off cuts. Old Wilf Peeke came along with two deck beams suitable for the cabin, which had been washed ashore at Wrabness. However, I was reduced to scrapping the interior of *Deva* to re-use the salvage to continue the structural work.

The result of the inquiry came through. We had lost. The Minister did not think that a warden's patrol boat with byelaw back up would be provided. He could not guarantee that TBT would be banned from anti-fouling. Heartbroken and financially broken, it was ruin for me. In hindsight we were right and the Minister was wrong. There is a warden's boat on the Backwaters, and TBT has been banned from yacht paint. But there was nothing I could do about it; the decision could not be reversed. I could make a new application, but the nature conservation movement had become so powerful and influential that there was no way in which the application would succeed.

We had one more go in the big league. A big wharf and associated land at Brightlingsea were for sale by tender. I assembled a local Manningtree syndicate. Experience with Walton enabled a fairly detailed assessment to be made of the potential of the site. The existing commercial use did not give a very good return. There would be potential for leisure and housing, but the planning gain elements such as an access road round the back of Brightlingsea would put a high initial charge on the project. We put in a tender, which turned out to be the highest, but it was still nowhere near what the owners would accept. I had the impression that the whole exercise had been a means of establishing a low asset value for accountancy purposes.

Work was eventually finished on *Deva* to the point where she was ready to rig for sailing. With the help of Eddie and John, we rigged up a tripod to step the mast. There was nothing in the interior apart from floorboards, as everything else had been recycled in the hull work. Although she had been afloat, the topside planking had shrunk to the extent that it was possible to hold a conversation through the seams. The Stuart, which had been under a mound of wood shavings for nearly 18 months was seized up, but I managed to free it with a hammer and drift. It would need a bit more attention before it would work.

The main was made ready for hoisting. I warped *Deva* to the outside of the quay and set sail. I had no idea of how she would steer after all the alterations, but she seemed better balanced than before, steering just under mainsail. There was a lot of hooting and cheering from the Stour Sailing Club. *Deva* was alive again, reincarnated. It had taken about a hundred man days over a year and a half to do the work. Changing the profile of a classic, or conversion, is always a controversial action. Had I been in my present state of having two boats, I would have had the luxury of being able to restore her to her original format, as a half-decked dayboat. *Deva* had already been heavily converted when we bought her. This conversion enabled her to do far more in terms of cruising, and be a much more useful boat. Had this not been done, or had the alternative of full motorization to commercial fishing boat not been done, she would have been scrapped through obsolescence. Keeping a dayboat of that size went out of fashion before the war. My conversion, for a use which never happened, has kept her strong and seaworthy, and she is not a bad cruiser for her size. When I have gone, someone wanting to restore her to her 1912 condition would find that most of the original hull remains. Several of the deckbeams are original, as is the mast. There is quite a lot of day racing on the Blackwater for classics, so it might be feasible. However, even without the cabin and cruising gear, *Deva* would not be a good "hotshot" racer. She is too shallow and very much too heavy. She is just a shrimper after all.

Deva
Standard Rig or
"All Plain Sail"

1 = Jewitt
2 = Tow forsail
3 = Mainsail
    (loose tooted)
4 = Topsail

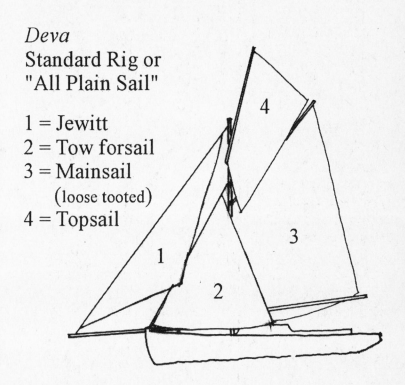

The experience of the inquiry not only left me ruined financially, but also my career as an architect was effectively finished. I no longer had the stomach for any more such ventures. The building industry went into recession, and by the time it re-emerged it was too late to save me.

So all that remains now as evidence of my dreams and a lost career is a couple of oversized rubbing strakes on *Deva*, and the warden's boat on the Walton Backwaters. Also, people who curse about the ineffectiveness of today's anti-fouling may know that the Walton Mere Inquiry had a significant role in the demise of TBT! However, *Deva* saved my mind. The little boat continued to give me delight and help me forget my troubles.

Heartbreak High

1986

Although I have always enjoyed a few beers, I had until that terrible day kept reasonably fit. After I finished playing rugby I still used to keep fit by running. Then one day, running up the long hill up New Road in Mistley, I had a pain in my chest. It was a bit like one I had experienced at the Club Dinner Dance which I had put down to gassy beer in excess. But this one stopped me. I could not run. I had to wait a little for the pain to ease. These pains kept coming back, so I went to my doctor for the bad news. It was angina, I was furred up at forty, and finished.

It had a dramatic effect on my life. Work prospects were zeroed, and I would have to take it easy for the rest of my life, which could finish at fifty if I was this bad at forty! The concept of mortality really hit me emotionally, which is apparently quite common in heart cases. Self-esteem hit rock bottom.

It was a very depressing Christmas, and the snow began to fall. I felt so low that I even did a "Titus Oates", walking out into the blizzard, hoping that the cold would kill me. Nothing seemed to happen so I came back. Down on the river there were reports of icing. John Huggett gave me a lift down to the Walls, on the bank of the Stour. There lay

167

Deva, riding the ice as in the Barents Sea. I was helpless to help her. I just watched the ice piling up against her. Heads were shaken as everyone watched a fine ship in her death throes. One day, after a huge gale from the west, I went down and she was no longer visible, just the ruthless ice. I rang up the Harwich Haven Authority and notified them of a possible wreck.

Everything was over now, not even the pleasure of looking at *Deva* in my last days. It was my blackest despair.

I didn't die immediately and so walked down to the river again. It did not matter if I could not get back up the hill again. But I did, without dying, albeit slowly. Day after day I went down to look, then one day a miracle happened. The wind had blown very hard from the north-east. *Deva* was back, moored about a hundred yards from where her mooring had been! She still had her mooring anchors with her. She must have come in on the ice pack in the gale and re-anchored herself. Rob Lewis helped me to get out to her a few days later. She seemed relatively unharmed despite her ordeal, and we took her back to the Manningtree quay. There was still a lot of ice about, so we had to sail through it, rather than use the engine. Arrangements were made to have her lifted out at Debbage's Yard in Ipswich. In February my neighbour David Warner and I sailed her down the Stour and up the Orwell to Ipswich.

Whilst I have never recovered my full self-esteem after the heart business, getting *Deva* back made me think more positively. I was ill, but not so incapable that I had died sailing in bitter conditions in getting *Deva* back to safety, so I could probably sail in better conditions without too much worry. I would have to make the boat less effort to sail, because I could not always rely on people to help me. So I started to study the rig and other boat equipment.

The gaff mainsail was only a small one, and, with my weight, not too much hassle to hoist. In any case it was a once-only operation. The mainsheet needed relatively little attention once the boat was on a course. But the headsails were possibly a problem, having port and starboard sheets to loosen off/harden in at every tack. I had been studying the rigs on traditional American boats, and many of these supported club-footed jibs. These were self-tacking jibs which had a short boom on part of the foot of the sail. They were sheeted down to a track on the foredeck, and went over at the same time as the mainsail. I placed an order with Gayle Heard for a new jib, for *Deva*'s "Cardiac" Sloop rig.

Deva 1987
Cardiac Sloop Rig

1 = Self tacking
   jib with
   club-foot

1

I considered an anchor windlass, but *Deva* was a bit small for that. Simpson Lawrence, however, produced an anchor winch a bit like a heavy-duty sheet winch. I consulted my physician, but he advised that the horizontal action would be bad for someone in my condition.

The Stuart was then studied. That little beast had probably contributed to the hardening of my arteries in the first place! The swinging of the starting handle was considered bad news for a "cardiac cripple", so an electric start was considered essential. The 4hp engine was underpowered enough without having to manage a dynamo and so another engine was required. Given the shape of the boat, the simplest alternative was to install an 8hp Stuart on the same line as the 4hp - the profile was the same. It just needed a larger shaft and extended engine beds. Coincidentally I heard through a sailing club member, Jenny Fiddler, that her father was replacing his 8hp Stuart with a diesel, so there was one for sale at Walton.

Debbage's were not keen to do the installation, but they did agree to fit the new shaft and lift the engine in, if I did everything else. So the deal was done and *Deva* was lifted out. Her hull was in brilliant condition, much to everyone's amazement. Not a scar, not a scratch could be attributed to the ice. The home-made copper/resin anti-fouling had acted like copper sheathing and was nicely polished by the ice, all ready for the next season.

Everything went to plan, and *Deva* was launched in the spring. The new Stuart gave her a tremendous burst of speed, and was capable of pulling her off astern if we went aground, as we found to our advantage when we grounded dramatically off Pin Mill on the way round to Manningtree. The "cardiac" sloop rig was a bit more of a problem; the track on the foredeck kept jamming, and the club foot on the jib was exactly that, braining anyone who went on the foredeck. We had a disastrous Crouch Rally at Whitsun, and failed to make any impression on the local mafia, but the boat proved a very able ferry to get people ashore at North Fambridge. Occasionally the arrangement did work, but *Deva* did not feel right with the foreign rig. With the club removed, the jib did find use later on in life.

Meanwhile Papworth Hospital had given me a thorough going-over. They thought they had detected a slight restriction in one of the arteries, but they put me on a rolling road/treadmill and tried to kill me before announcing that I had an excellent exercise heart rate. In fact as good as that of a professional footballer they had half killed earlier. So there was no immediate danger. I'd given up the pipe and cut down the drinking and so there should be no problem. But time was to prove them wrong. Living the life of a saint - well, in cardiac terms anyway - made no difference to the decline. Although regular exercise and swimming helped me along the flat, if there was a steep hill I was now having difficulty. All too often in Manningtree on South Street I would grind to a halt on the incline by the Red Lion, resisting the temptation to go in for a rest.

Obviously time was not on my side, and it made me realise that there were only so many tides that *Deva* and I were going to catch. That is the problem of having a real concept of mortality. I see so many people who embark bravely on big rebuilds of smacks and other large vessels, reckoning to take five years and often taking ten or more. I could not conceive that possibility. Even if I survived the effort of rebuilding a boat, how fit would I be to sail for much longer afterwards? Some of the re-builders who are fit when they start probably are not so when they finish; the brokers' advertisements feature vessels from such situations. But they do not see it that way. They laugh about being knocked down by a bus, but do not believe that it will happen to them.

So my situation meant that work on *Deva* is not to a cabinet maker's standard. It is fit for purpose, not built for posterity. The decks are painted rather than laid teak. Some jobs are neglected. The odd deck leak is ignored, at least until it starts raining. A temporary arrangement will be around for a long time - "if it ain't broke why fix it?" I do, however, do my best to make sure that everything that should be strong is doubly so. That boat has to take some hard weather, and she will survive. She has proved it. Yet I see so many situations where some exquisite joinery or finish is applied to a yacht when she cries out to me for a thicker mast, a proper rubbing strake or a decent keelson to give her some backbone.

My situation means also that I cannot be traditional in all my fittings if I want to do my type of sailing. Old working boats were built for real men who were far tougher and stronger than we are today. Whilst many of us sailing our smacks in the summer put on sea boots and smocks and pretend we are hardened smackies, looking with disdain at "yachties", most of us have no idea what it was really like to work a sailing vessel winter and summer, foul and fair weather. Very few of the modern day "smack yachtsmen", that's what we really are, have experienced using fishing gear at sea in the depths of winter. The real old timers had to be so hard and strong when working the fishing gear that to them working the heavy sailing gear was no effort at all. The other issue is that many of the smaller smacks, which are the majority of the survivors, worked very limited grounds, spending most of their working lives within sight of their home port. They were essentially day sailers.

The majority of *Deva*'s sailing is in coastal passages, which is probably one grade up from her original job description. She also makes offshore passages - short sea to Holland or Belgium rather than ocean going, but nevertheless considerably more than she was built for - so she has some equipment which was not aboard at the turn of last century. VHF radio, satellite navigation, echo sounder, sea toilet, cooker, cabin heater, winches lead back to the cockpit, mainsheet jammer block, electric bilge pump and some other things are not original equipment. This enables her to make passages in relative safety within the ability of her crew. Her inherent strength enables her to bash through weather which defeats many bigger boats, although there is a heavy price to be paid in comfort.

This is not pure heritage, but it enables a boat of some heritage interest which would otherwise be redundant to have a very useful role a hundred years after she was built. The alternative of restoration to original format would have produced a lovely little boat for fishing, racing and day sailing, and were the interest about, I might have done it. I can understand therefore the mentality of those on the Blackwater and elsewhere who rebuild local smacks and sail them without engines or modern equipment. However, the smack culture is very strong, and virtually any bunch of driftwood which might have fallen off a smack is turned into a magnificent recreation of a local oyster dredger. Such boats are not the tarry old things which were knocked together by cobblers of low order. They have the best shipwrighting to yacht standards and are rigged with a standard of sail which would have been mind blowing a hundred years ago, but the business executives and professionals who own them carry on the proud traditions of working sail, and indeed there are oyster dredging competitions, so the working practice carries on as well as the sailing. However, few of them venture beyond the mouth of the Blackwater, preferring to participate in the various local regattas rather than do any cruising, as some are limited by adherence to the original format.

The issue becomes one of preserving the paramount traditions of sailing and fishing in what are effectively better-than-original replicas. In *Deva* a lot of the old sailing tradition has been prostituted with gizmos, the engine and living accommodation, but the hull is mostly original, a tribute to the builders. It is an issue I do feel guilty about at times, but otherwise I am glad of what I have been able to achieve.

With an electric supply aboard, *Deva* quickly acquired the basics of lighting for navigation and cabin, plus an echo sounder and a Tiller Pilot. My young son Andrew did much of the work, which has survived for several years. For the navigation lights, we routed out a slot in the mast into which we put a conduit for lighting and aerial cables. This was then covered with a sliver of timber, which very effectively disguised what had been done. However, the Stuart began to give problems. The installation had not been properly aligned. The boring for the enlargement of the prop shaft was slightly askew, so at Maritime Ipswich. '87 I had the very embarrassing situation of the prop shaft disappearing when going astern. Water started pouring in, and I thought we might founder, but fortunately the shaft had not quite left the tube. Andrew bravely went over the side and pushed it in again and we refastened it. I was not aware that there had been an alignment problem, because the transmission was so smooth, and it was not for some time that I realised how the problem had arisen.

I fitted a folding prop as the sailing performance was significantly affected. The previous installation had a folder, and she had been rated by the OGA for that. For some reason the engine did not like this at times. Sometimes it went very slowly, because one cylinder would cut out.

About this time we returned to old gaffers racing. I had completed my stint as secretary. I would only carry on with the paperwork and organisation, if others did the race officer part. And that's the way it has been since.

Deva's "cardiac" rig was abandoned, and the cutter rig reinstated for the old gaffers race, but I did occasionally revert to the club-footer and retained a detachable forestay bottlescrew so that this could be done. The headsail configuration was changed again; we had a small red working jib, and a tow-foresail. Gayle Heard made some comment about one last fling. If it blew up a bit we could change down to the Huggett, an excellent working staysail cut with a hollow luff so that it would stand on a slack forestay. This was made by John Huggett, who had just got hold of a sailmaker's sewing machine. We sailed to the race in company with John Huggett's *Madeline*. She was a 30ft smack yacht, and may possibly have been a "tripper boat" in her youth. She zoomed ahead of us down the Stour in the early hours, with the light wind astern. But once we were out of the harbour into a bit of a sea and a headwind positions changed very rapidly. There was a big difference in not just speed, but ability to carry canvas. For all her weight and drag, *Deva* was a good windward boat like all nobbies should be. John subsequently cut two panels off *Madeline*'s main. He also shortened the mast.

When we arrived at Stone we realised how much had changed since *Deva* had last raced. The boats were all that bit smarter, especially the smacks, and there were several hotshot racers like *Sheena*, *Asti*, *Chittabob* and *Jade*. There seemed to be fewer of the small 20-24ft cruisers. It was bad beating down the Wallet to get to Stone, but at least it toughened us up for the race. There was a good entry of 104 boats, and the event was sponsored by Ind Coope. Interestingly another Rivers Class boat, the *Severn*, was entered. In *Deva* Richard Coe and I set reef and topsail and tow foresail, which was quite effective on the run out. *Severn* did not have an engine and sported a taller rig than *Deva*. Also she was not carrying the extra half ton of keruing topside rebuild. It would thus be interesting to see how my alterations had affected performance compared with the original format. *Severn* was a little faster down wind, her bigger rig and lighter weight making that only to be expected. But on the wind *Deva* just walked away from her. *Severn* was two reefs down and being blown all over the place. *Deva*, with working jib, tow foresail, single reefed main and topsail, put her shoulder down and went.

Logic would say that if the original hulls were of the same shape *Deva* with her additional top-hamper would be less stable. *Deva* was said to be the prototype of the Rivers Class, but checking her dimensions and one or two specification items against the official rules for the Rivers Class showed that she has some small but significant differences. She is wider in the beam, for instance. The mast is pitchpine, not spruce. She was built with trawling posts or nogs fore and aft, and there are many other details of difference. These days the purists get terribly worked up about whether a vessel is a workboat or a yacht - they tend to spit when they say "yacht"; it was the other way round forty years ago! However, I would think the reality was that boatyards like Crossfield's just built "boats". If you wanted to use a nobby as a yacht, a pilot cutter, a tripper boat or for fishing, broadly speaking you got the same product. Anything different from standard cost money. The Royal Mersey Yacht Club would have approached Crossfield's knowing what the local nobbies looked like, and asked for a half decker which Liverpool gentlemen could sail. Crossfield was building shrimpers of 22-23 feet for the Dee, as were a number of other local builders. The RMYC might well have seen these vessels as well, and it would be logical for Crossfield to point to one and say "How about a class of these?", pointing to *Deva* herself perhaps - for *Deva* is Latin for River Dee. They may have agreed in principle and said "Yes we'll take her, but on the next ones could we have..." This would tie in with the old Welsh sailmaker's recollections in 1966 as well. Certainly you cannot compare the construction of Rivers Class boats with any other half decked racing yacht of the period. They are really little fishing boats.

Back to the East Coast Race: amongst our own kind we were not too bad. We were ahead of the Deben 4 tonners like *Janty*, we were good against sister *Severn*, and when it came to the beat back we really picked up, zipping across the shallows on the "direct" route. *Francesca* followed exactly in our wake and grounded. The topsail heeling us over must have saved us.

We had quite a good sail and did well against similar sized boats especially on the beat back. That is apart from the Itchen Ferry *Blue Jacket*, which seemed to like the conditions even better than *Deva*. We ended up twelfth overall, but did not pick up any of the twenty-five pots on offer. The marvellous thing about Old Gaffers Races is that even if you think you have done badly there is a good chance that your boat is the only one to qualify for a certain pot. The prizegiving was held in a marquee with one or two mud banks sticking up above the floodwater, and our presenter from the sponsors in wellingtons. The Suffolk Bilge Rats tried manfully to entertain us before abandoning us for the higher ground in the Stone Sailing Club.

But if I thought that the East Coast Race had been badly hit by the weather, it was nothing compared with what was in store for the much vaunted OGA Silver Jubilee Rally, Ramsgate, which was our next port of call. Our plan was to make for Bradwell at the mouth of the Blackwater, and make a dash across the Thames Estuary. The wind was nearly a gale, so we blew down the Blackwater on staysail, and put the engine on at Bradwell Spit. Unfortunately it decided to run on one cylinder only, which was not enough to beat ebb and gale. An emergency hoist of sail was arranged and we had the most terrifying sail in beating through the moorings. One certain collision was averted as at the last minute the moored craft jerked up its mooring buoy just in time for our bowsprit to strike the buoy and not the boat.

We eventually sailed into the marina and berthed safely, and made for the Green Man pub. The next day was still blowing old boots, so I walked into Bradwell to get some high tension cable, to rewire the engine. Whilst we were in the marina we went on board *Blue Jacket*, which was weather-bound like us. She was an amazing boat. She had the feel of a 32ft boat with 8ft cut off the stern. Perhaps they started at the bow and found that the shed was too short - I don't know. But she was a powerful little boat, so beamy that she could have her engine in the middle of the cabin with room to walk round her - ideal for maintenance, ideal for saloon table top. Her beam and powerful sections made her a superb sail carrier, and she had a massive rig. In her earlier days she had been owned by Uffa Fox, the famous yachtsman and designer. I believe that he converted her to Bermudan rig, a folly soon put right by subsequent owners of better taste. In later years we were to have many a tussle with *Blue Jacket* on the Swale Match. We managed to improve *Deva*'s performance so that we could hold or even beat her to windward, but down wind the huge rig, and the spinnaker she could carry with it, put her way over the horizon every time. There are some boats which get it exactly right, and she was one of them. They are magic by behaviour, rather than by stealth as with *Deva*. Another boat similarly just as irritatingly perfect is *My Quest*, a 24ft traditional gaff cutter built on the East Coast. Fair wind or foul, up wind or down wind, she is so good that she doesn't need an engine. Sister ships have been built, but for some reason they are only very good, not perfect.

Anyway, we set off across the Thames Estuary with a reef in, and managed to find slants in the very brisk wind at the right time to take us through the various gats and gutways across the banks. The sea was very brown and angry, and seemed quite furious with us as we sailed into Ramsgate. We looked round, and wondered where all the others were. There had been 113 entries and I expected to see a veritable forest of gaff, rather than a few pathetic specimens scattered around the harbour. Then the stories began to come in about boats setting out and being swamped and having to turn back. Then the disdain about *Deva*, "Well of course *you* must have come across in a window in the weather." Perhaps we did or didn't, but perhaps it was more to do with course we had steered. Most people from the Blackwater seem to think that it is mandatory to beat up the Swin in a weather-going tide if they are going to Ramsgate. That's fine in a north wind, but hopeless in a west-south-west 6 and a bit. *Deva* had dodged across the fingers of banks which make up the Thames Estuary, steering a course south by east most of the way, so we had the wind on the beam. They had a slog to windward, and wondered why they got even wetter than *Deva*. However, the boats which were there were interesting to look at. I went on board David Cade's converted bawley *Storm*. She was at one time owned by Maurice Griffiths, the famous yacht designer and journalist, as well as former editor of *Yachting Monthly*.

The racing from Ramsgate was ruined by the weather and the restrictions of the port. Friday was abandoned altogether, but we had a go on Sunday. Because everyone was in the locked basin, we couldn't leave before two hours before high water, so it was going to be tight beating the tide into Pegwell Bay anyway. Then we were held up by a report that the harbour patrol boat was in difficulties with a broken rudder. We had to wait while the lifeboat went out to tow it back in. On the way in the tow managed to straddle a navigation buoy. The reserve lifeboat had to be sent to tow in the first lifeboat and the harbour patrol boat. When all that had been done all the ferries that had been held up had to get out. When the professionals had finished making such a hash of it in their state of the art boats the geriatric old gaffers were sent out in totally unsuitable conditions. All the south-going current had gone.

The dozen or so boats on the line included the Blackwater sloop *Adele*, ferro gaffer *Sea Eagle*, replica Itchen Ferry *Alice*, another traditional South Coast boat *T Jay*, prawner yacht *Bonita*, Pilot Cutter *Noorderzon*, Cornish Shrimper *Aussie II*, *Blue Jacket*, Bawley *Fly of Halstow* and a couple of other pilot cutter types. I had Richard Coe and Brenda Jago aboard as crew. With the forecast as it was I had put two reefs in the main under the topsail, which was a big mistake. The wind was not that bad, but the current was worse. I could not work out where the line was, what the new start time was, where the course was; it was crazy. Eventually I noticed that boats were vaguely all pointing south. The seas were the wrong length for *Deva*, and without the drive from the sails we were not going anywhere, in fact progress was negative. If I had known how the water was by the Ramsgate Harbour sea defences, I might have done a lot better cutting inshore. I had totally blown the race.

In desperation we handed the topsail, shook the reefs out, and set the tow foresail. The boat now moved through the seas better, but I had made a big mistake in the design of the cockpit. I had made the cockpit almost the beam of the boat, which was fine as far as steering goes. I thought I had protected it from water coming down the side decks with a coaming or breakwater, and it had seemed to work for a few years, and in some heavy winds too. But these were different seas, and going into them at speed was putting too much water down the side decks, water which was cascading into the cockpit. In the front corner of the cockpit I had a little cupboard with a flap, which contained the echo sounder. That was now full of water.

We sailed on and on, trying to get over the tide. We even went to the Goodwins to see if there was a back eddy we could work, but there was not. After three hours we decided to retire. Funnily enough, everyone else bar the two fastest boats, which managed to get round the windward mark, seemed to retire at the same time - we had obviously been watched. We started the engine, and then found that it kept stopping, due to fuel starvation. All the bouncing around had shaken up the dirt in the bottom of the tank and clogged the filters. I had to keep undoing the feed pipe and blowing through it, not a pleasant task in those conditions. In the end we had to sail back against wind and tide, which was something we had failed to do when racing. Bloody boat, like a stubborn mule, refuses to move when asked, yet bolts when turned for home! You can't tell me that boats don't have minds of their own.

The whole event had been a fiasco, not helped by the weather or the antics of the lifeboat. The tidal conditions and the restrictions on the lock to the inner harbour had made it almost impossible to sail the course that had been set. The mighty *Noorderzon* and *T Jay* just scraped round to collect deserved prizes, the rest of us received the remaining pots because they could not be used again. It was a good party in the club afterwards anyway.

My plan had been to sail to France afterwards, but Richard did not seem very enthusiastic. The constant soakings and rotten weather had taken their toll. I happened to overhear him asking about train times. I had to cut the holiday short. We crossed the Thames Estuary in a flat calm, the engine failing about ten times. Afraid of running out of fuel, we put in at Shotley Marina. They no longer served petrol, so we had a long hike to a garage. We returned to Mistley in thick fog. Hardly the most successful of voyages, but we had excitement and I learned a lot.

It was interesting that in all this I did not give my "dicky ticker" a second thought. In fact I did not suffer an angina attack despite the stress and physical effort. Yet on land heart pain was quite common. Perhaps the alcohol and the sailing environment relaxed me.

That race was the first time for some years that the OGA had run to filming an event. Ron and Di Davies shot the video film for us, and I had to do a commentary. This was quite difficult as I was speaking over a musical background, and the opportunities for editing were very limited - basically it was one take for ninety minutes of film. Not being a professional, and having a bit of a stutter, I did not find it the easiest thing to do properly, but I was the only one who knew most of the boats. The Jagos supplied me with a libation to ease the stutter, and it became a slur in reality. It was not until I sobered up that I realised how awful I sounded. We made several films with Ron and Di over the years, both for this event and the Classic Boat Festivals. In the end we used to do them as outside broadcasts, which meant we could make mistakes and get away with it.

It was quite interesting to see *Deva* sailing off Ramgate. She looked very impressive, sailing with a nice motion. Just a pity about the land in the background going the wrong way!

Classic Boating and Dutch Days

1991 - 2001

The growth and recognition of Shotley Classic Boat Festival also bought us into contact with other organisations. One that seemed to crop up regularly was the Dutch Classic Yacht Regatta (DCYR) at Hellevoetsluis. Everyone was talking about it and I had not been there - well *Deva* was too small, wasn't she? A number of Dutch classic yachts came over for our festival. Why did a British contingent not visit theirs? I worked out that we could get over there if we went straight after the East Coast Old Gaffers Race in July. The Dutch could leave their boats at Shotley and sail over with us. Thus the North Sea Classic Passage Race was conceived.

The race was envisaged as more of a timed cruise in company. We were worried about staging a full offshore race for old boats, because of liability issues. So that people were not encouraged to take chances, we did say that engines could be used with a time penalty. We did not want boats to be out there too long, we did not want boats becalmed in a shipping lane. In other words people would sail their boats as if they were cruising, keeping best passage speed. That seemed fine from an OGA standpoint, but would *Deva* be able to play?

Bryan Hammet and Rob Williamson, both seasoned offshore cruising men on the OGA committee, started to worry me. "You're not thinking of taking *Deva* over are

183

you?". I looked at *Deva* laid up ashore. Normally she grows a bit as the painting season looms. However, she had now shrunk to the size of a winkle brig.

I don't mind admitting it, but I am not one of those brave or foolhardy types who think nothing of sailing across oceans on rafts or row boats. I am just the ordinary chap at the sailing club bar, pretending to be an old sea dog to impress others so that my pot never runs dry. There are millions of us; we have even infiltrated the RYA, RORC and the Stour Sailing Club. Old Gaffer versions are worse. We try to pretend that our boats are the finest sea boats, even if they can't sail to windward. And the smackie versions of Old Gaffers are worse still. They not only pretend that their boats are the finest sea boats, but they work rather than just play at it, and through the winter too - wooden ships and iron men. You really feel that you are not worthy to buy them a drink. The weather-beaten face of a thousand winter gales, the frost bitten fingers that have gutted a million fish, the sea boots, the rolled cigarette and all the rest of the gubbins set them apart from the plastic navy.

The reality is that an old half decked boat held together with rusty hundred-year-old nails and kept from sinking by bits of string stuffed between the planks is not as seaworthy as a modern glass reinforced plastic vessel with self draining cockpit. A properly constructed modern boat should survive anything as long as you can hang on. I know that we get a few disasters in the Fastnet or the Sydney-Hobart race from time to time, but that is down to corner cutting on design and construction and human error in a crisis. *Deva* could probably recover from one major knockdown or broach before she filled up with water, but not two or three in succession. She could probably take four or five swampings from following seas before she went to the bottom. But a pitchpole? No, apart from the beer being shaken up, the ballast would probably be thrown about, the deck would rip off and that would be that. There are some old wooden boats which are capable of handling the worst. A Falmouth Quay Punt goes everywhere in the South Atlantic, but not only is she twice the size of *Deva* she has also been modified and strengthened by someone who knows what he is doing.

So yes, I was scared!

Then I started thinking. We often thrash down to Burnham from Mistley in bad conditions without any serious trouble. Holland is only three times further, and the natives are certainly as friendly as the Crouch Mafia, so if we can have a fair forecast for the next thirty-six hours or so, which should be possible in these days of computers and satellites, the odds are better than even for making it. I began to think "How do I find my way?". Stellendam entrance buoys are only fifty metres apart, a pretty small target after more than a hundred miles with crosstides and an inaccurate compass. My navigation was a bit like Columbus's - aim a bit to the right or left of where you are going, then you know which way to turn when you find land. But you can't do that sailing for Holland, as it is so low you would hit it before you knew which way to turn. I did try a sextant once. I have one from a German U Boat. It is probably a duff sextant as the vessel was captured aground on a sandbank. However, not only would it be very difficult to take a sight with a sextant on such a cramped boat, but also it was impossible to do the mathematics and chart work to the required standard below.

It was actually easier for the old-timers. There were more buoys about, more slow moving vessels to ask or follow. With ships being sailed by computers and robots, there is no-one to ask now. However, I did notice a gadget at the boatshow, called Dinghy Decca. It gave a position and one waypoint. I know that it is cheating. I know that my smacksman would have just spat over the side and known exactly where he was. But it opened up a new world for me. It was such a small, discreet piece of apparatus that I could still go through the process of looking through the sextant at midday, in the morning and at night and in fog too, look very studiously through incomprehensible tables, mutter a few calculations to myself, and point to the chart, spit in the water in front of the smacksman, and say "We are there!".

The other issue with open sea crossings is safety equipment - equipment to keep you on the boat, and equipment for when the boat sinks underneath you. Modern yachts tend to have guard rails running round them. When my son was young I did put guard rails and a pulpit on *Deva*. But I took them off when I did the new deck job. They were high enough to be of use for a toddler or small child but I am not convinced of their usefulness for adults. Because they are so low, they would be unlikely to stop anyone going over the side, and more likely to trip him over. They also give a false sense of security. On a small boat you must hold on all the time, however excellent your sea legs are. With guard rails it is easy to become careless.

On balance guard rails seem to cause more problems than they solve. Clambering across a raft of modern boats is particularly painful! In some ways rails are very dangerous when coming alongside in a marina. I have seen several nasty accidents in which people climbed over guard rails and slipped down topsides, sometimes getting trapped between boat and pontoon. With *Deva* we have level access and just have to lean over from the cockpit to tie on.

One piece of safety equipment we do have is a safety harness for each member of crew. On *Deva* I did have a line of webbing down each side deck as a jackstay to clip on to, but this was later abandoned, as there are so many potential attachment points. But even with safety harnesses there are problems with small boats, especially at night. I have seen some spectacular cat's-cradles when crew got their harnesses crossed. This tends to happen when the rigging requires urgent attention, and the ship can thus be put into danger by a safety measure.

Another piece of equipment deemed essential by the pundits is a liferaft. In theory it sounds an excellent idea. On big ships and large yachts liferafts have occasionally proved their worth, but I am not sure that this would be so in a little boat where disasters happen so fast. Presumably the likely scenario would be a sinking following a sudden swamping in gale force winds. If we chucked the thing into the water and tied it on so that we could get in, we probably would not have time to do so before *Deva* sunk, taking the raft with her. If we had sprung a leak which we could not hold, possibly we could launch in anticipation, but we could do that with the ordinary rubber dinghy. If *Deva* were run down by a ship, at what stage would we reach for the raft - just before we were hit, or after we were smashed to pieces? Possibly with a liferaft to hand there is a tendency to abandon ship too early. Even a waterlogged yacht is far safer than a liferaft. I am surprised that more attention is not given to having buoyancy in the boat - for instance, air bags that would inflate inside the cabin, as in a car.

However, if there were a disaster and all *Deva*'s crew perished, no doubt I would be castigated in memoriam for not having the boat properly equipped. So I have often carried a liferaft on *Deva*.

As far as *Deva* herself was concerned, she had metamorphosised now more or less into her final form. The cockpit had been revamped; a new elliptical coaming had been crafted and the side decks widened. The trawl nogs had been reinstated and new bowsprit bitts fitted. After a couple of years of experimenting with a short curved bowsprit we reverted to a conventional straight one of prawnerish proportions.

My college friend Bryan and his son Nick had offered to crew for the Old Gaffers Race on the Blackwater and the North Sea Race, which was straight afterwards. We met at Mistley Quay and loaded all the stores, kit and liferaft, and set off early on Friday morning. As Bryan did not have complete confidence in the boat or its equipment, he supplied the liferaft and a chart. We had the normal gentle run down the Stour and reach out through Harwich Harbour and across Pennyhole Bay to the Naze. Then it was the usual force five south-westerly on the nose all the way down the Wallet, wind over tide, tacking between the shore and the Gunfleet bank.

On the way there I thought I would check the location of the temporary North East Buxey mark for the race. Unfortunately I could not locate the mark in the mist, but I did locate a very hard sandbank which I think was the Buxey Sand. The echo sounder drowned at Ramsgate had not been replaced. We managed to get off without too much trouble, but the bumping was very worrying. There are dangers a-plenty in local waters without having to cross the North Sea.

The race itself was a magnificent sight. We didn't get anywhere until we were fouled horribly by *Bonita* and forced to tack at the Knoll. It was the best thing *Bonita* could have done, sending us into slacker tide and steadier wind, and we gained places by the score. Most of the "professionals" who are meant to know the waters with all their smack races and Mersea Weeks seemed to choose to try to head along the rhumb line to the North East Buxey, and found themselves swept north by the ebb. They closed the Buxey Bank, then risked running aground. One potential race winner did that and had to retire. When the tide turned to flood, we again went into the shallows and picked up many more places on the way to the Wallet Spitway. Once we turned with a fair tide for home, all the other boats caught up or overtook us. It was only a matter of relative boatspeed; there was no deviousness we could think of. However, we had done very well on handicap. We were fifth overall and had the Hunt Trophy to take home.

The next day it was back up the Wallet in the Tendring Coast Passage Race. The sight of the smack yacht *Merlin's* kites being set made us dig out the "Bastard" from the forepeak. With the wind on the beam we flew along, overtaking Vertue *Maid of Tesa*, the ocean racer *Nutcracker* and even the brilliant little *Blue Hawk*, which was setting a huge jackyard topsail. That topsail seemed to claw a wind out of the sky when the wind dropped, and she sailed over the horizon as if by magic. We closed the coast at Holland Haven to dip out of the now foul tide, which should have been to our advantage, but instead a wind offshore sent the whole fleet past us.

Deva Light Weather Reaching

1 = "Bastard"

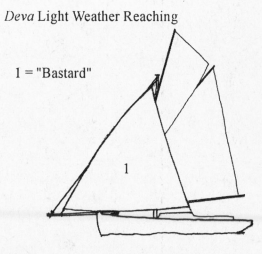

When the wind eventually reached us our path was blocked by a big modern yacht which took great exception to being overtaken by a maritime fossil. As we arrived at Medusa we ran into the Haven Series Race rounding the mark in the opposite direction, which was interesting! The wind came just ahead of the beam again and *Deva* took off, even passing some of the Haven types. They could not carry their chutes, but we could carry the "Bastard". We closed *Merlin* again, and I hoped that she would let us pass to windward at a decent distance. But the thought of causing chaos with our kite was too much for Clare Thomas, now Mrs Catchpole, and she began to push us up to windward, where we could not carry the "Bastard". To change down to working rig meant us going slower than *Merlin*, for she was actually a bigger and faster boat. And Clare was not going to let me through her lee either. And I thought she was such a nice girl! She is really. The only option was to drop back and sail well down on *Merlin*'s lee side, and drop the "Bastard" for the last stretch so that we could point up into Harwich Harbour. We got through Clare's lee. I took a nice photo of her and *Merlin* which made the front cover of the OGA Journal. As it turned out, although we were well to the north of the rhumb line, we picked up such a lovely lee bow on the tide at Outer Ridge that we were swept into Harwich without having to "de-bastard". The two bursts on the close reach with the "Bastard" put us into second place. *Blue Hawk* was already in.

On shore there was something of an "admin" panic between the OGA and the Dutch Vereniging Klassieke Scherpe Jachten (VKSJ), which required some hasty cobbling together of instructions, handicaps and declaration forms. We then loaded even more provisions and made some last minute adjustments before posting our Customs notice and locking out of Shotley Marina. We fired up the Decca, set the topsail and set off for the start line off South Shelf. The start was a beautiful sight, 18 classics including a

Thames barge, *Thistle*. It was lovely weather, the only trouble being that the wind was in the south-east. The fleet sailed on starboard tack towards the Shipwash and the really open sea.

As we lost sight of land, I tried ringing up my office on my mobile phone. Mobile phones were just starting to come in then. They were huge and very expensive, but it was considered a good thing if management was always available. I rang not so much for work reasons, but to speak to Rosie, who was my gorgeous PA, just to hear her voice for the last time for several days. But I was told that she was still not back from the pub, being with my deputy. When the cat's away!

Sailing out at sea gave me a different feeling. Somehow - possibly because the water is clear - I seemed to be more aware of being suspended in a depth of water. *Deva* felt even smaller. The evening fell and the wind went light. We were foul underneath and heavy inside and we started to fall back. We kept crossing tacks with the barge, and put in an order for three egg rolls, sunny side up, to *Thistle*'s caterers. Then the wind went east and almost by magic the boat picked up speed again. She seemed to be telling us something, and I had some tactical thoughts. The longer term forecast was for the wind to go south-west, and perhaps this was the start of the change. Now if we could use the east wind to get us south we would be sitting very pretty for when the wind changed. We would get the fair breeze first, and set the "Bastard" again, and sweep up the Belgian coast to glorious international victory.

With new spirit we sailed on, slicing through the lee of *Raoudor*, a Dutch Folkboat. She tacked to the north, while we sailed on for one of our finest beats to windward, all sails drawing on the port tack with the best phosphorescent wake I had seen for many a year. All the time we kept plotting our position, and watched our course creep across the chart. By the time we reached the shipping lanes halfway across the south-westerly had not materialised, and we had thus made one almighty tactical blunder.

Mist fell as we crossed into the no-man's-land sea between the shipping lanes. With Decca plots we did a series of short tacks to the north-east, until the mist lifted sufficiently for us to cross in safety. It was a worrying time. Mid-morning I put a call to *Avola*, Brian Hammet's sturdy Francis Jones cutter. He was about twelve miles ahead, now motoring in a flat calm. We still had a light headwind, making about two knots. The tide was due to come in our favour and we still hoped for the south-westerly.

There was a rather sad occurrence. A pigeon circled our boat and tried desperately to land, but without success. Eventually it settled on the water, patiently awaiting its inevitable death as its feathers soaked up the brine. I wished that I could be as brave as that little bird over my "dicky ticker".

The tide swept us past our destination up to the approaches to Europort. We had to start the engine, but the Stuart had other ideas. Not only did it fail to start, but it took down all our electrics as well - no lights, no Decca, not a clue! I dismantled the engine and found that the dynamo bracket had broken. I managed to secure the beast with a wedge between it and the structure of the boat. The engine ran smoothly and there was not the vibration of a diesel to loosen the temporary wedging, which actually lasted the engine for the rest of its time on *Deva*. With some other broken bits I managed to crank start the Stuart and we went towards a buoy to establish where we were. Absolute shame fell on us as we shone our torch and found we were at the Hinder, not the Haven, buoy, and some three miles on the wrong side. An hour later we crossed the bar into the entrance channel to Stellendam, some thirty-six hours out of Harwich. The promised south-westerly came in with a vengence, but it was no good saying better late than never!

We tied alongside the ocean racer *Nutcracker*. Nick and Bryan celebrated *Deva*'s historic arrival with a rush visit to the toilets. Despite its fail safe design, they had reservations about *Deva*'s en-suite bucket. Nick Zeinau's *Jasmine*, a 30ft cutter was in port, together with the John Leather cutter *Pleione*. The Folkboat *Zoetje* turned up. She had started a day early and had taken three days to cross, confounded by calm and headwinds.

Nick and Bryan left the boat at Stellendam, leaving me to take *Deva* up the Harringvliet to Hellevoetsluis on my own. *Deva* entered the lock, which was a lot gentler than that at Shotley, but had inset bollards to lasso, to make things challenging. It was very satisfying to enter the wide, safe inland sea. I opened a can of Dutch beer and ate some Dutch cheese to celebrate. However, the sanctity was soon shattered by a squall. The Dutch masters had not lied in their paintings. I was amazed at how quickly the seas went on the boil, and how the buoyancy of the boat suffered in the less dense fresh water. I quickly shortened sail to deep reef main and staysail, and, arriving off the entrance to Hellevoetsluis, hove to, to make ready for berthing. It was strange not to suffer tidal currents and stay on station. A small group cheered *Deva*'s arrival, and we berthed in the historic port.

It had not been a particularly memorable crossing for *Deva*, and weatherwise it had been calm. But she had made it safely without giving us any serious worries. I was still frightened about sailing back though. Once those big locks shut behind, the open North Sea seemed a frightening place by comparison with the well-organised inland waters I was now sailing in.

In those days one had to have clearance at an official entry port when going to Holland. The event organisers had arranged for the Dutch officials to check us out at Hellevoetsluis, but we were confined to the harbour, confined, as it turned out, for three days. Imagine my envy when the barge *Thistle* turned up with a crew which had clearly been in party mood for several days. They had entered via Flushing, and had a lovely cruise through Zeeland, calling at several watering holes on the way. I made a mental note to change to that for the future. Taking a fleet of antique nonconformist gaffers into a very busy port was a bit risky. I had noticed in the sailing directions that there was an entry port at Roompot on the East Schelde where there looked to be several potential watering holes we could call at, so the next time we did change our finish to Roompot, much to the puzzlement of the Dutch. The break of a relaxed cruise between the passage race and the Hellevoetsluis regatta proved so popular that we continued the practice after entry formalities between Britain and Europe were lifted. The Dutch worked out the method in our madness, and the boats coming down from the Zuider Zee have made the trip into a mini cruise too, calling at Gouda and meeting us at Willemstadt.

Waiting was very boring, and some Dutch wag suggested that I went out for a sail - "If stopped just claim to be from Friesland and say you can't speak Dutch." I have since learned that indeed many Frieslandlers do not speak Dutch, and that their native tongue is actually quite close to

English. I often wonder if many years ago there was a common language spoken by seafarers in the Southern North Sea. In the days of isolation and lack of communication links on land there was no need for common folk to speak a national language. That was for the aristocrats, who spoke French anyway. Seafarers from what is now the Dutch coast would probably have spoken as much to people from England as to landlubbers from the hinterland.

My son, Andrew, now in his teens and wife Margaret arrived at Hellevoetsluis, having taken the ferry to the Hook and worked their way south via a complex system of trains, tubes and buses. Many years ago Hellevoetsluis did have a rail link, and it was important enough to justify its own harbour. The railway was actually known as a Stoom Tram or steam tram. These used to be all over Zeeland, puffing their ways along the top of dykes and through streets. Apart from a preserved line at Hoorn, they have all gone now that the building of motorways and bridges has linked the islands, but their memory carries on in place names. Virtually every little Dutch port has a "Tramhaven". It is a great pity that the Stoom Tram did not survive to the present era, when many countries are considering light rail systems, their modern equivalent, to combat pollution and road conjestion. Even the normally well-organised Dutch did not anticipate the problems universal car ownership would bring.

We did not have a very good time in the racing at the DCYR. It was good fun, but the boat did not go well in the conditions; I think we came 89th. After Hellevoetsluis we cruised back via Willemstadt, the Volkerak, Zierekzee and Veersemeere to Middleberg to await the passage crew, Bryan and Nick. I had a day to spare, so walked along to Flushing, and gulped at the huge expanse of wavy water. Some tiny yachts were setting out - tiny until I realised that they were three times as big as *Deva*.

I left Fushing and the West Schelde via the little fisherman's channel across the Raan bank. This seemed the most direct route and the Stuart was compliant. The wind was westerly, so we were close hauled under sail all the way over on the port tack, and the boat sailed like a dream - five or six knots over the ground, never less than four. Why couldn't she have done that on the way over? I had a scare when I came on watch in the night and saw no one in the cockpit. I thought Bryan had fallen overboard - the tiller was lashed, the boat sailing full and bye on the port tack like a dream through the night air. I started to panic, then heard snoring in a dark corner of the cockpit.

The rest of the journey was a piece of cake and thus ended our first passage trip.

The Curse of the Stuart
is Lifted

1992

The next winter saw the end of the Stuart era on *Deva*. With my heart condition continuing to deteriorate I needed a more reliable engine. Swinging the Stuart in stressful conditions was not recommended. Problems with the Stuart were the petrol consumption and the lack of space to store fuel. So I went the whole hog for a diesel, my worried mother giving me a substantial subsidy. The engine chosen was the Yanmar 1GM10 9hp, and French Marine of Brightlingsea fitted it, using the old bearers and existing sterntube. The propeller on *Deva* is offset on the port side, and this was suitable for left hand propellers. The Yanmar had a right hand propeller, but to re-align the engine from twenty degrees offset to port to twenty degrees offset to starboard would have meant a lot of upheaval. New engine beds and shaft log would have had to be fitted, and there was a lack of both time and money. This economy was to prove a problem later.

I actually managed to sell the Stuart without any trouble, and, strangely enough, I was quite sorry to see it go. It was a bit like a divorce. You want the woman out, but you remember all the fun you had together in the past, as well as the scrapes you survived together. And you do make comparisons with the replacement. The nine new Japanese horses weren't actually as good as the eight very old

British horses on a good day, with a comparable fixed three-blade screw. But the new engine was lighter, simple to start and much easier on fuel.

During that winter I met Bob Farrow and Mandy Steer at the local sailing club dinner dance. Mandy says that it was the most expensive dinner she has ever been to, as she became infected with gaff. At that time they sailed a Silhouette, and *Deva* was almost capacious by comparison. They started to crew for me and the rot set in. It wasn't just the drink. They then bought a smack, the *Polly*. She was the last smack to work under sail out of Maldon in the 1950s. And they rebuilt her at St Oysth. A smack rebuild is the true definition of a hole in the mud into which you stuff twenty-pound notes very tightly. They do not sail with me anymore, since they found out that there are one or two gaffers which you can not only stand up in, but which have all "mod cons" as well. I lost them when Ray Walker of the super pilot cutter *Noorderzon* lowered a bar of soap down the companionway after a very wet crossing of the North Sea a couple of years later.

There was not Hellevoetsluis that year, 1992, but Bob Farrow and I planned to have a week of sailing in Holland directly after the Swale Match. The passage from Hollowshore in Kent to Roompot on the Osterschelde is about 130 miles. The weather forecast was south-westerly 7 decreasing to 4, with rain overnight.

Having spent a peaceful night at anchor in the Swale, we motored back up Faversham Creek to Hollowshore, tying alongside *Sallie*, the smack, so that Andrew and Mandy could get ashore with their gear. Just before high water at 10.30 we made our departure, but a lapse of concentration on my part while sorting out which sail to set caused us to go out of the channel into the mud. This could have been embarrassing, but fortunately a "drop of diesel" pulled us out of our groove in the mud.

The log entry, in the ubiquitous surveyor's pad which can just about survive the damp environment on the *Deva* which is more than can be said for the expensive proper logs shows merely "Swale-East". With a strong wind warning of south-westerly 7 our plan was to sail in the lee of the Kent coast to the North Foreland, then put into Ramsgate if the promised moderation did not come about.

The south-westerly 7 started to materialise as we left the Swale, so we changed down to balanced reef, which makes the gaff main into a trysail. *Sauntress*, on her way back up north, passed us, a fine sight in the choppy seas. Our journey became smoother once we rounded the Whitstable Street Buoy and closed the Kent shore. The sun even started shining. By the way, in this account assume that it was raining unless otherwise stated. Bob put it down to my shorts. A reef was shaken out and the flying jib set. I have never quite understood why they put a sandbank off Margate. There is no natural reason. However, we picked up the narrow entrance channel into the Gore, and soon we were sailing in the Margate Roads with the fishing boats. At the North Foreland there was a horrible sight. The north-east swell from the previous day was surging against the fresh new south-westerly waves coming round from the Channel. It was the clash of the Titans. Ramsgate looked a long way off, as it always seems to when there is a headwind from the Foreland. With my heart in my mouth, on the strength of an easing forecast, we sailed on into the North Sea.

Deva Heavy weather rig:
Force 7 upwards

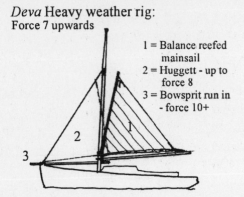

1 = Balance reefed mainsail
2 = Huggett - up to force 8
3 = Bowsprit run in - force 10+

The beam seas were frightening, considering the open cockpit, and the waves were going in opposite directions. Every so often they would meet in conflict and stand right up to each other, trying to outface each other, to see which was the taller. Then the combined whole would break and come crashing down on us. Strangely enough we only shipped one of these unnatural seas, and even that was totally absorbed by me, very little going into the bilges.

Looking at the chart, I see that it says "Strong Ripple" by the Drillstone buoy - masterly British understatement! Certainly the weather began to improve. The remaining reef came out, and with "tinnie" in hand it was really very pleasant. If Bob had not gone below for a sleep I might have set the topsail!

We crossed the shipping lanes in daylight without any problem, and our plan was to skirt north of the lanes leading into Zeebrugge. The wind went as dusk approached, but we were not in any hurry because we wanted to arrive at the Roompot entrance in daylight. In the dusk I could see ahead an inky blackness and hear the sound of breaking water. Suddenly we were in it; the boat pitched violently; twenty minutes later all was quiet again. We had crossed the West Hinder bank.

Then the lights of Belgium vanished from view, and this time a total blackness descended, encompassing both water and sky. It rained as I have never seen rain before. From where I was standing in the cockpit I could not even see the hatchway light. I was standing in water, the deck was under water, indeed *Deva* had disappeared, technically foundered, no longer afloat. Bob had been buried at sea. Was I to call the lifeboat, or would that be thought of as just typical British obsession with the weather?

Fortunately the rain did ease off and allow the pumps to clear her, and the most depressingly grey daybreak saw us thundering along up the Westpit in front of a stiffening westerly wind. Soon it was Steendiep and "land-ho", as we headed for that grey strip on the horizon that was the Netherlands. There seemed to be quite a few freighters working off Domburg, possibly with sand or aggregate, as we approached the Roompot Channel. The seas astern were growing and breaking, making me worry about shallows and causing us to take in a couple of reefs. It was a good job that Bob did not look behind him, it was a good job that he steered a true course.

However, by Manningtree standards there was plenty of water, and it became quite a pleasant sail alongside a fine sandy beach. In more seasonal weather I could imagine the big Dutch girls bathing topless, but not today thankyou! We passed two boats coming out, beating to windward; they would really have a beating before they were much further out to sea. We rounded the end of the Hompels bank, then sailed between the pierheads of Roompotsluis harbour, and headed into wind, lowering sail before coming alongside, twenty-three hours out of Hollowshore.

Bob had brought along his Walker's micro-log, which tells you all sorts of information, a bit like a digital watch with a fish spinner. According to this, our maximum speed through the water was 7.5 knots, although the average was quite a lot less because of the calms of the previous evening.

As we stepped ashore and looked back over the North Sea it looked horrible; the wind was up to gale force and it was sheeting with rain. We had thought that all the big Dutch yachts tied up to the pontoon were waiting to lock in. No, they were having second thoughts about going out, and they could not work out how such a strange little old boat had crossed from such a funny place as Hollowshore.

It took all day for the Customs man to arrive, but we used the time to catch up on a great deal of lost sleep. Once we had cleared, we had the problem of leaving our berth. The gale force winds pinned the boat down on her fenders; expensive plastic yachts were in immediate danger of being "bowspritted". Bob worked out an ingenious system of extrication by using the seaward after-trawl nog, and taking a line round the elliptical counter, then forward on the pontoon. We cast off the warps, going astern against Bob's line, and *Deva*'s bow miraculously pulled away into the wind. This really impressed the locals, and it was not until I did a "semi-Keeble" that British prestige was put back at the bottom of the league again. Mike Peyton's book of cartoons shows Arthur Keeble in his ketch *Gem* getting wedged diagonally across a lock in Holland. Unfortunately his neighbourhood cartoonist was on hand to record for posterity that on entering the lock our bowsprit and counter chose different sides of the chamber.

Once inside the Oosterschelde we motored across the sluicing currents to the new marina at Roompot. The modern holiday village left much to be desired architecturally, but the facilities at the marina were absolutely superb, all paid for in the very reasonable mooring fee. The voyage was celebrated with several beers at the holiday camp bar.

We took *Deva* to Zierekzee and Goes before returning via the Veersemeer. The rain continued, and a solitary prawner beat her way against a gale under spitfire jib, Hugget and double reef main. More trouble was to await us.

We motored round to the lock for the Walcharen Kanaal at Veere, and were directed to the ship lock in company with two ferry boats on a special outing. Joining us in the lock was *Spirit of Boadica*, the Ocean Youth Club training ketch from the East Coast. OGA member and former owner of sister *Severn*, Roger Parrimor, and the new owner of *Severn* were aboard, fascinated by the coincidence of seeing little *Deva*.

At Middleburg we went ashore for a quick tour and a bite to eat, tying up to the shoppers' stage. Then it was off again down the Kanaal, through the several bridges. The *Ram-Ship* at Middleburg was looking very spruce, clearly much work had been done in the twelve months since I had seen her.

Whilst motoring down the canal I put in the balance reef. The wind was too strong for the scheduled voyage to Blankenburg, but we popped over to Breskens, as it was meant to be a good setting-off point for the voyage to England. I later wished we had not. We motored in astern of a gin palace, which suddenly went hard astern and swung across the lock. I put the Yanmar astern, and the bowsprit swung to port, catching a timber pile. The resultant force ripped the bowsprit bitts out of the deck, leaving a gaping hole. The lock gates were opened and we were emptied out into one of the ugliest estuarial scenes I have witnessed - Force 7 wind over a four knot tide, monster shipping going up the river, and ferries going across while pilot cutters zoomed back and forth, just to make sure that every wave possible broke over our foredeck.

I did not wish to risk setting headsails amongst the broken heap of firewood that had been the foredeck, so we went under main and motor. I followed the ferry over, and wondered what the yacht harbour was further up the river. Apparently that was the proper place, so we had to plug the vicious tide for a mile or so. It reminded me of the Mersey of my youth. Once in the relative shelter of Breskens, we set about repairing the damage. Using some brass brackets which I had earlier used to hold down an errant deckbeam, a floorboard out of the stern locker and lots of waterproof grease, we managed to re-structure the bitts. Considering that this operation was carried out in torrential rain, and that the repair lasted to the end of the season, we did well. It was a good job that we had aboard basic tools such as a saw, a drill, a hammer and screws, and were on a wooden boat where cannibalisation was possible.

Having been shifted from an outside pontoon to an inner berth, and sandwiched by three other boats alongside, we had to sit out Friday because of strong north-west winds approaching gale force. We felt sorry for a number of Brits who had been gale-bound there for several days.

The most interesting part of Breskens was the large active fishing fleet, who were in to spruce themselves up for a local festival. It reminded me of how Fleetwood used to be when I was a boy. We do not seem to have very many places like that any more on so much of the UK coast, yet in mainland Europe they are quite common.

Weather forecasts were listened to avidly, but it appeared that most of the English were waiting for *Deva* to make a move, judging by the questions. Probably it was because of my salt-stained smock. When I said we were sailing the next day my questioners would look rather concerned and shudder, then go off and talk to their companions. I would see groups talking about the weather, one would see me and turn back to his cronies and say "Well he's going." "What? in that!" One or two people came round to look at the boat, the smallest, most cramped and aged in the marina. Low freeboard and the open cockpit really worried them. The insensitive man that we had spoken to in Goes had turned up as well. I was more concerned that Bob might start to believe them and jump ship!

At 05.00 on 15 August we tried to get some life out of the outer layers of "sardines", and it was not until 06.30 that we were leaving Breskens with one reef in the main, Huggett and working jib. It was still lumpy in the Westerschelde, but the north-west wind was fading all the time as we tacked out to sea. By the time we headed west along the coast, the wind had gone west too. Sailing along the coast, I tried to distinguish the Dutch/Belgian border. There seemed to be a narrow inlet between two sets of buildings. Perhaps in the olden days there was a proper channel dividing the provinces as indicated on the old maps. One day I will go ashore and have a look.

Off Zeebrugge the wind almost died and I set the topsail before heading out to sea. The waves were still confused, the north-west wind's mark on the sea was far from gone, and now there was occasionally a south-west wave. On a little boat, especially one with overhanging ends and a long heavy bowsprit, pitching can be a problem. Certainly our speed through the water was only about two knots. I could have opened up the diesel, but the motion would have been intolerable.

Overground the tide was still taking us to windward, and by 15.00 we were as far west as the West Hinder bank. As the favourable tide petered out the wind strengthened, and the speed crept up to 4.5 knots, *Deva* now sailing herself with helm lashed, full and bye. We crossed the shipping lane at a good pace, and were well clear before dusk fell.

Unfortunately, the Met. Office had had a change of mind, and instead of the Force 4 maximum at lunchtime we were now being offered a full Beaufort 6. We hove to, handed the topsail and reefed the mainsail at 20.00hrs in the rising wind. Back on course, we noted that reducing sail actually increased speed by nearly a knot, and, still sailing on lashed helm, we sped off into the night.

With the wind came more rain. The seas started to boil at the crests, and by the time we crossed the Galloper it was diabolical. Down below I clutched my chart and my ruler while pandemonium broke out. Everything started leaping out of lockers and shelves as *Deva* rolled to the seas. They talk about not relying on Decca, but the nearest I could get to navigation was to make a stab for the little magic box and plot its numbers on the waterproof chart.

At midnight the Sunk Light Vessel hove into sight as we crashed along. Felixstowe, Clacton and Walton sometimes flickered into vision, only to be wiped out by great black seas. The Decca started to cut out, possibly because of the motion, possibly because of the waves dwarfing the aerial. Fortunately, because we were taking regular plots, we could work out by dead reckoning where our approximate position was, then re-set the miracle box. The tide was now setting to the north, and we were concerned that we would be swept past Medusa on to the Cork. However, we eventually saw the little green fellow, Medusa, and by 03.00 European time we were heading north for Harwich. At about 04.00 we were into the harbour, but not until after a very worrying time caused by hallucination over the lights. I kept seeing the breakwater across our bows, I kept thinking the breaking seas astern were because of shallows.

Another hour on and we had picked up a spare mooring at Wrabness, then crashed out in our sodden gear, 23 hours out of Breskens. The log had recorded a maximum of 8.2

knots, and an average of 4.8 knots. Allowing for the fact that we had barely exceeded 2 knots in the calm part of the day, the last section of the passage must have been covered at some speed for an eighteen-foot-length waterline boat!

The next morning we took the young flood up to Mistley Quay, where we unloaded our gear. The rain stopped, our holiday having finished! The voyage had been quite an achievement for *Deva*. She had shown herself capable of still making good passages in moderate to rough conditions, despite her size and age.

A Rebuild for the Skipper!

1993

My heart was giving me a lot more trouble by then. I had always had a problem convincing specialists of the deterioration, because I looked too healthy. To maintain any sort of lifestyle I did a lot of gentle exercise, basically walking and swimming, so I did not appear very feeble. I had excellent blood pressure, cholesterol levels and lifestyle. There was a heart disease check at work. I had one of the best results - "Excellent - shouldn't think you will ever have heart trouble, keep it up!". Think again Sunshine, I thought. We love to blame sin and pleasure for our ailments, but sometimes one cannot help being ill. Eventually Papworth gave me an angiogram; dye is squirted up the arteries and the results are seen on a screen. They were not very good results - two blocked arteries. If all my exercise had not enabled my heart to develop capillaries to get round the blockages I would have been dead long ago. I was surviving on tickover. The surgeon said I must have an operation in two months, but as usual there was a long delay. My doctor raised hell with the authorities.

Eventually, just before Christmas, word came through for a January operation, and I was booked into Papworth. Compared with most of the other patients, who could hardly stand, I was pretty fit. I kept going out for brisk walks. But I had a terrible operation - "came to" on the slab, and had a serious out-of-body experience. I was able to go out into other rooms. I went to a nurse's leaving party, but, being out of my body, I couldn't have a drink. I couldn't even chat up the nurses either, as my voice box was still in intensive care. Being a ghost is a right Devil. I did have one advantage though - I was being wheeled along the corridor and the porter did not know which ward I was to go in; I zoomed out of my body to the end of the corridor, read the list and reported back; the chap was dumbfounded. And yes, there really was a nurse's leaving party, so make of it what you will. They did have a lot of trouble in starting my heart up again after the operation. It kept flashing from tickover to full revolutions and cutting out (damp in the electrics again - the heart is really just a Stuart), so they fitted a pacemaker. Possibly I was not always with this world, but halfway to another. My recovery was very poor. The eighty-five year olds were skipping around like lambs in no time, but I had infections, a collapsed lung and raging constipation, and was getting very, very, bored. I had one very nice visitor, Jane Rule from the smack *Ellen*, who showed me all her snaps from a big rally in Brittany. I had to get out, and eventually departed with a huge sack of pills.

Apart from one scare, I was soon on my feet, but I was not allowed to drive for several weeks. I had planned for this of course, and had some timber for a new gaff and boom in the garage. I occasionally got caught out by staff from the office, as they found me hand-planing the spars when I should have been a good little invalid in a bath-chair. Soon I was up to walking over to Brantham to work on *Deva*. She was to have the luxury of a sea toilet to replace the Elsan. It was one of the Lavac range, which uses a vacuum to operate, and is very simple and efficient. I had to keep Mandy somehow. People soon forgot where I had been. Somebody at the sailing club read about my operation in *Yachting Monthly* and said to me "When did you have the operation? I don't remember you not being in the bar". Well, I think I only missed one weekend, so it is not surprising.

After a few weeks I went back to the office. Oh dear! With me out of the way, chances had been taken by the power hungry to get rid of me. A major restructuring was in hand, with all the usual sorts of underhand deals which go with that type of operation. People I had supported for years and counted amongst my friends had sold me down the river for the promise of thirty pieces of silver. People whom I respected for their commitment and integrity had dumped responsibilities and grabbed early pensions and lump sums. I was told "You can't possibly carry on in your condition. You must take early retirement." I did not particularly like my job at times, but I did it reasonably well in difficult conditions when many others had already given up. There were a lot of building sites with my name on, and a lot of new projects coming in. I really resented having my job taken away from me, but there were no other options. No provision had been made for me; my job had been split into several pieces and given to other people in exchange for extra money or status while I had been away sick. I could have tried to hit my employers for all sorts of wrongdoings under employment law, but they would have got rid of me at any price, as I was still a threat to the new order. I managed to negotiate a deal for part-time consultancy work, and an enhanced pension. Although they had got rid of me, there was no one else who could do the strategic work or set up the projects. I was then sent to a specialist doctor, who said that I had the eyes of a young man, a pity about the rest of me. There was no question of me ever being fit for full-time work again. Strangely enough, I stayed in full-time employment, considered fit, until December 31st. It was deemed that I was then suddenly unfit for work on January 1st.

A Rebuild for the Skipper! 1993

In the middle of all this there was another North Sea Passage Race, preceded by an East Coast Race and a Tendring Passage Race. Bob and Mandy crewed for me again. The forecast was a bit strange, and was changed repeatedly. *Avola* went early to miss some strong north-westerlys. However, we then had a less worrying forecast, about force 4-5, so we started the race from Harwich as scheduled. The wind was fitful at first, and we had problems even rounding South Cork. But further out to sea we had a gentle breeze which wafted us along nicely. Very kindly the Met Office then revised the forecast to force six plus from the north-west. The wind hit us in the middle of the night and we hove to in order to reduce sail. *Deva* at this time had two jibs on the bowsprit. The outer one was a "long roper" which was fairly slim but went from the top of the mast to the end of the bowsprit, where it was shackled to a Wykeham Martin furling gear. The other working jib was on the traveller. The thinking behind this arrangement was that it gave very good flexibility in headsail operations, without slowing the boat down. For light winds we ran out the bowsprit spinnaker, "Bastard", then furled the outer jib. In heavy weather we could furl the outer jib (called the Jewitt, after the sailmaker), which was much easier than changing a jib on a plunging bowsprit. However, to get the topsail down we had to go on the starboard tack and heave to, and then put a reef in the mainsail. With a stiff breeze and flat sea, *Deva* really took off. However, the sea began to build in the night.

Deva "Reef and Topsail": Force 5 - 6

1 = Flying jib
2 = Huggett
3 = Tow foresail
4 = Reefed mainsail
5 = Topsail

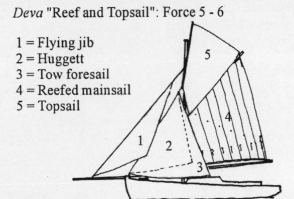

Dawn broke fitfully, with a very uncomfortable sea astern, and all through the morning the waves built up. At 09.00 we saw a small pinnacle of sail astern, quite often going out of sight in the troughs of the waves. This we deduced to be *Yachting World* Five Tonner *Elfreda*. The strong winds now gave her boatspeed over *Deva*. For the rest of the morning the two boats strained for the Dutch coast, still not visible. The seas were slightly on the quarter, and now thankfully longer as well as higher, giving the little boat a chance to lift. The main problem was to avoid making them break, and, if they did, to put the helm up so that they would break underneath. With the working red jib and tow foresail we were over-canvassed and driving too hard, but on the other hand we were in a race! At times I could not bear to look forward to see how close the long bowsprit was getting to diving straight into the next wave, where, with the jib attached, it could stall the boat and make her pitchpole. Suddenly the concept of the all-inboard rig appealed!

But the boat kept going as we clung on, and I even managed to grab an hour of sleep below. I awoke as *Elfreda* drew close, and saw how well her deep hull managed the seas. But even she was having a rough ride; the outboard motor attached to her pushpit was in danger of jump-starting in the following seas. We exchanged photographs, neither of which came out, and at 11.00hrs she drew level as we passed the MSB buoy which marked the passage across the Steenbank. People scorn Decca (as it was then, but which is now GPS) but in conditions like that to be able to work out on a small boat almost exactly the boat position and check tidal sets and leeway accordingly is a tremendous contribution to safety, and completely justifies the departure from tradition! To find that one buoy in poor visibility in the middle of the North Sea right on the nose was incredible.

It was not until we had picked up the Roompot Channel buoys that we could see land. The previous year we had come in on a south-westerly, and the waters had become smoother as we closed the shallows, but not this year! A horrible squall came over, so strong that it flattened the wave crests to start with, the stinging rain it carried nearly flattened the crew too. It was so strong that we had to lower the main, hooking in another reef, but, worse still, the outer jib Jewitt decided to unroll, the Wykeham Martin gear not being strong enough to resist the unfurling action of the wind. Very bravely Bob lowered the jib halliard, and because this particular jib was shackled to the bowsprit end he had to furl it alongside the bowsprit and just hold on whilst the bucking bronco of a boat plunged her way to the finishing line.

The seas off the sluices were horrible. The waves came straight across the Hompels bank at high water and crashed into the Oosterschelde barrier, whereupon they rebounded and joined forces with their cousins which had spent a hundred miles building up across the North Sea. I had never seen such angry seas before. Trouble was not over, for the sluices were open, sucking in the little gaffer towards her destruction. Amongst this mayhem were chains and steel buoys at close intervals, all ready to catch the unwary, and we made a rapid tack only just in time, the engine being called upon to drive the boat offshore.

We sailed into the little harbour, rounding up to lower sails before motoring into the lock alongside *Elfreda*. The peace was utter.

Elfreda's Stuart was playing up. The cooling system was blocked, so we gave her a tow into Roompot Marina, where many of the classic fleet were berthed. After handing our declaration race list to *Avola*, I had to check that all the boats that had started were accounted for, and let my wife know back in England in case of any queries from anxious relatives. Only *Nutcracker* was missing, and it was believed that she had gone straight for Stellendam. Amazingly, we were less than two hours behind the first boat. When the time at South Cork was taken into account, we had actually "crossed" more quickly than the 8 metre! Working the tidal sets, streams and windshifts had paid off handsomely, the reverse of 1991, when we went to the Channel Approaches looking for a promised south-westerly.

Mike McCarthy of *Elfreda* claims that I luffed him. One of his favourite stories in the bar is that he was sailing in this vast waste of tumbling North Sea, not a soul, ship or land in sight, straining to keep the ship on course. Then across the horizon came this little gaffer and started a luffing match with him. I was actually broaching Mike. Would I do an ungentlemany thing like that? I remember getting a real earful from Bob after we surfaced in Roompot Harbour. "Why is it that whenever I come out on this bloody boat I get scared shitless and nearly lose my life?"

It was a fairly hairy Hellevoetsluis regatta too. We had come from Willemstadt where we had berthed alongside my medical support unit, *Bydand*. She had come via Flushing. My doctor, in a party mood, gave me some expert medical advice At Hellevoetsluis we had the usual receptions and parties, and some strong winds to race in. The setting of reef, topsail and three headsails on the reach caught people's attention, and we actually made the cover picture of

Waterkampion, the Dutch equivalent of *Yachts and Yachting*. There was quite a lot of confusion over the signals and courses, and most of us sailed the wrong course at the right time or vice-versa or both. To avoid 185 protests against the committee, and in the family spirit of the regatta, it was decided that the results would stand. In our race we went from "Did not finish" to third in one leap. Everyone seemed to be happy about it when a group of worried Dutchmen from the race committee approached me and said my doctor did not appear very well, and could I come and look at him. He was in advanced state of seizure. His was the only boat to have sailed the right course on the right signals, and should therefore have been the only boat placed! He was not happy, so we increased his rum prescription. I do not think that we did particularly well at the regatta, but our taking short cuts across shallows had been noticed, and rules would be changed. However, we did win the Passage Race, which was a great improvement.

The weather was too bad to return straight after the regatta, so I sent Bob and Mandy back on the ferry, while I planned with the rest of the British fleet to work our way through the inland waterways to Flushing. The trip from there would be easier if the wind carried on blowing from the west or south-west. A group of us decided to head for Ooltgensplaat, one of the little villages off the Volkerak. Sailing single-handed out of the raft-up in Hellevoetsluis was problematical in the high winds, the difficulty being to set some sail in confined waters before entering the open "sea" without the bowsprit making a beeline for some immaculate topsides. Indeed such was my concern that I ran in the bowsprit, deciding that with the wind as strong as it was storm staysail and balance reefed main were perfectly adequate for cruising!

In quite a pleasant run up the Harringvliet the only difficulty was the need for the occasional gybe to avoid some of the banks and shoals. My real concern came on entering the big lock at Volkeraksluizen, with the wind howling down it. The quarter-mounted prop installation means that steerage is not possible until the boat is moving forward, and whilst the boat is picking up way she can have her bows blown off - embarrassing in a confined lock. Similarly, the boat can "jam" on her fenders when alongside to starboard, which on this occasion made it difficult to come alongside the inset bollards common to Dutch lock chambers. Fortunately *Pretty Kitty* was able to take a bow line from me, enabling us to haul alongside.

It was a short dash under power through the chop to the entrance canal to Ooltgensplaat, which led through a secret gap in the old sea wall, then through fields into a small basin in the centre of the village. Originally the place was a smaller version of Willemstat, and had extensive fortifications nearby. I took a quick look at these fortifications. They had been converted into a holiday camp.

Several other classics rafted up alongside, including *Pretty Kitty*, *Cachalot*, *Elfreda* and *Korybant*. The weather continued to be an awful mixture of rain and gales, and we were held at Ooltgensplaat for two days. In the local hostelry we played Dutch billiards, a strange game in which scores are made only in the manner of the English game's "cannon". The local hostelry also provided us with a super meal, but unfortunately many of us were running short of currency, the result of being forced to frequent too many bars when, had the weather been better, we would have been sailing. Because of this, on the second night we decided to have a dinner party on *Cachalot*, where each boat contributed a course, *Deva* providing the soup.

Although it was still blowing on Wednesday, the rain had stopped, so we decided to head for Zieriksee. The wind being right on the nose, I decided to motor down the Volkerak to the interchange lock at Krammersluizen. The small boat locks were only being used one way; our direction made use of the ship lock, which was the largest I have ever been in, about half a kilometre long. Several hundred yachts were jilling around, waiting for the entry signals to proceed, and in the wind it was difficult to keep station. I waited till most of them had gone in before entering myself, with the idea of rafting alongside a boat, rather than trying to grab two sets of those silly inset bollards in the lock.

On entering the salt water I did start by sailing under reduced canvas. The wind was not actually a proper gale, so progress was slow. Rather than go through the hassle of clearing out a reef and running out the bowsprit in such confined and crowded waters, I reverted to the iron topsail for the rest of the way to Zerikzee.

Despite being very crowded, Zerikzee was as beautiful as ever and well worth the stop. I met up with the rest of our classic flotilla, and we decided to go into the town for a meal. I had had a marvellous meal at a very reasonable price in Zerikzee some two years previously, and after a half-hour search located the restaurant. Obviously my patronage had enabled the establishment to go well up market, over the 50 dfl per head mark at least, so we went back to the market square for a beer and to reconsider our plans. We still had a Dutch couple with us, and it was quite amusing to watch the expressions of the waiters when, having practised their excellent English on us, they suddenly came upon one of our philistine group who could speak fluent Dutch. The Dutch came in very useful when ordering the take-away Chinese, although I have a feeling that they still use numbers a bit like the Brits.

The next day saw a reasonably fair wind to take us up the Oosterschelde to Katse Veer, towards the lock into the Veersemeer. All through the week I had been fiddling with the Wykeham Martin furling gear to try to make it set properly. The bowsprit had been run in and out several times, and the lead of the furling line was out, causing it to jump off the spool. I found a lee off Slikken van Kats, and hove to in order to unravel the beast. Unfortunately, the time taken to do this caused me to become separated from my flotilla, and miss the lock at Katse Veer.

The road bridge makes this always a slow lock, and the added complication of a freighter and an ambulance made the process so long that it stopped raining! After I locked out into the Veerse Meer I motored into the shallows to run out the bowsprit and set the sails. In the process *Deva* ran aground very gently, so I put the engine astern to bring the boat off. On coming off, I put the engine ahead and noticed that the thrust had gone, and now had vibration from the shaft. Clearly a case of weed, I thought, so I anchored the boat and went over the side. The grief at finding a blade of the propeller missing was only surpassed by the retribution I sought from the heavens concerning the way fate had sought to ruin my boat and my holiday. Of course *Deva* had sails, but we had the narrow Walcheven Kanaal to tack through single-handed. This would not have been popular. Then my time for crossing the North Sea was restricted. If the wind blew in the right direction all would be well, but we could be headed or becalmed, and perhaps lose a couple of days. We were all employees at that time, and I could only have Bob and Mandy for a set time, so a working engine was essential.

Needless to say, the wind was dead on the nose now that we had no engine, and I was faced with the difficulty of finding a landing I could go alongside under sail. The Delta Marina by Kortgene was nearby, but the dangers of putting a bowsprit amongst a thousand posh Dutch yachts on crowded pontoon moorings were considerable, so I had to sail on. Actually, unknown to me, *Avola* was berthed in the marina, and Brian Hammett was leaping up and down trying to attract my attention.

I remembered that at Veere there was staging outside the town, which would give safe berthing in a lee, so the long beat continued, involving many short tacks along the beautiful Meer. I did manage to raise *Pretty Kitty* on the VHF and report my situation. She was at Middleburg. Eventually I arrived at Veere, reduced sail and ran in the bowsprit. Fortunately there were people on the staging to take my lines, and we berthed without a mishap. Ashore I went to see if the harbourmaster could advise me of where repairs could be carried out. The slipway at Veere had now closed, but there was a boat repairer in the town who might help next day. Until then there was nothing I could do.

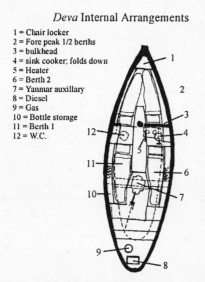

Deva Internal Arrangements

1 = Chair locker
2 = Fore peak 1/2 berths
3 = bulkhead
4 = sink cooker; folds down
5 = Heater
6 = Berth 2
7 = Yanmar auxillary
8 = Diesel
9 = Gas
10 = Bottle storage
11 = Berth 1
12 = W.C.

I wandered round the beautiful town, trying to find the restaurant where a year previously Bob and I had had a superb meal. I did find it, but felt so depressed that I could not go inside, and went back to the boat to open a tin. The cabin of *Deva* really was an ideal environment for complete self-pity and depression of the soul - cramped, dank and dark, everything sodden from the incessant rain, underwear and socks strung up on a line in a futile attempt to dry them over the cooker. For a week, the only way I had been able to dry damp clothes had been to sleep on them. I had a new Musto Offshore jacket, which I used to put over me to try and deflect the drips, but even this was no match for the interior micro climate of *Deva*, where rainstorms continued to rage irrespective of the weather outside. Musto's actually replaced the jacket for me as a consequence, but really the Ocean wear clothing is needed below decks on *Deva*.

Just then I was woken from my gloom by a rap on the deck from Mike and Steve of the *Elfreda*. Having heard of my plight, they had jumped into a taxi at Middleburg and come over to cheer me up. We went to the Yacht Club at Veere, and put back a phenomenal amount of beer with Dutch gin chasers, and whilst I hardly felt any happier my brain no longer registered mental pain. Good chaps, Mike and Steve.

The next morning I was awakened by the sound of the daily downpour which penetrated the hangover, despite its magnitude. I then realised that *Deva*, by herself, had saved Holland from a total disaster of flooding, far greater than that prevented by the little boy with his finger in the dam. Virtually all the rain that had fallen in Holland had been absorbed by my bedding and *Deva*'s bilges. Looking out from the hatch, however, made me blink twice. Tying up astern was a boat from Manningtree, the Maurice Griffiths cruiser *Thunderer*. The odds of meeting in foreign waters one of the few Manningtree boats to venture abroad must have been very slim indeed.

I explained my predicament, and very kindly they offered to stand by while I tried to find a suitable boatyard to deal with the problem. The Veere man could not help, but he rang a yard in Arnemuiden, about three miles away; they could slip the boat, and were Yanmar agents. Mike Moss on *Thunderer* offered to tow *Deva* up to Arnemuiden as the wind was dead calm in the downpour, an offer I readily accepted. At Arnemuiden they lifted the boat out straight away, and removed the remains of the propeller.

The boatyard searched high and low for a replacement screw, but without success. It would take two or three days to obtain a replacement. I did have a spare propeller, but it was in England. My holiday was running out, and there was nothing for it but to abandon the boat, send the yard the spare, and return to *Deva* by public transport as soon as I could find the time and raise a crew. *Thunderer* would be pleased to provide the homeward passage, so I transferred the liferaft and a few essentials, like the prizes and Mandy's warbrobe, and we were off down the Veerse Meer, myself feeling very wretched and miserable at having abandoned the love of my life on a foreign shore.

It was not until a fortnight later that we were able to return to Holland. Bob and Mandy, whom I had already "booked" for the Swale Match, very kindly agreed to help bring *Deva* back. The gales, apart from a very brief window, were back in full swing, but the long term forecast looked good as we took the taxi to Parkeston Quay. The Crown Prosecution Service's "Weight of Evidence" barrow, belonging to Mandy, (a trolley slightly bigger that a shopping trolley used for carrying files to court in), had been pressed into service for the liferaft, and this was invaluable as we made our way to Arnemuiden via Stena Line, three Dutch trains, which connected perfectly, and a taxi.

The yard had not lifted *Deva* back in, as they were worried about the amount of bilgewater she had inside her. However, the propellor was fitted and the sun was shining, and we soon had everything aired. The yard bill was only £60, including storage and lift-out, about a third of the English equivalent. There are a lot worse places in which to have a boat marooned than the Netherlands. The passage back to Mistley was uneventful, although tiring. When we were sailing up the Stour a Bermudan boat challenged us to a duel. Mandy's knuckles whitened on the tiller. Then she said "For God's sake put the engine on, I'm too tired to race."

That winter was when I was "put out to grass" and began my consultancy years. In the autumn I had started to get some aches in my chest. My cholesterol level was going up, and I was getting very concerned. The doctors and specialists said it couldn't possibly be my heart again less than a year after the bypass operation.

There Are Only So Many Tides

1994 – 1996

Beam Trawl

The political upheaval at work was only matched by that in the Old Gaffers Association. I was drafted on to a working party to find a new way of running the central administration of the OGA. Traditionally the secretary would have to do all the work during the year, only to be berated at the Annual General Meeting (AGM). We had a meeting in Richmond to set up a Finance and General Purposes Sub Committee (or "Politburo" as I love to tease them) to run the organisation between AGM's. I had a lot of pain getting there. On the way back I collapsed six times on the tube and the railway. Nobody offered to help. They just thought that I was drunk. My wife had to shield me from the wind so that I could inch my way along the platform. Soon I was in Addenbrookes Hospital, having to be pushed around in a wheel chair; I was too weak to walk anymore. It gave me an interesting outlook on what it is like to be disabled. I hated being helped. I wanted to do things for myself. People talk as if you have no feelings or mental functioning - the "Does he take sugar?" syndrome.

They sent me to Papworth for an angiogram, after which they realised that I actually was an emergency case and operated straight away. Normally they put people on waiting lists, but I suppose that because I was in a really bad way and they had only recently operated on me, they felt duty bound to act. Anyway, my wife, Margaret, refused to take me away. Unlike in the first operation I did not even know they had started until I came to in Intensive

Care, and came out in better condition than when I went in. It was nice being able to walk again. However, the doctors told me that the operation had been a bit of a repair job; one of the arteries had been so badly furred up that they had to cut it longitudinally and ream it out. They only gave me three years. But if it had been only three months I still would have been grateful. At Papworth you see people who have horrific operations, such as heart and lung transplants. In those days they only had a moderate chance of long term success and a high chance of mortality, but the patients were on top of the world just to have been given a chance of a tiny bit of "normal life" again.

I made a quick recovery and in a few days I was sent home. It was so nice to be able to join the outside world again, even if it was only to walk a few yards to the Wagon and Horses for a very weak shandy. They were launching the boats at Mistley Quay, however, and my dreams were forever seaward. Eddie took me out for a sail in the *Merlyn*, an Itchen Ferry. I was too weak to even haul on sheets, but it was so nice to be afloat again. Only a few weeks earlier this had appeared impossible. I worked hard to get myself fit again by walking and cycling. I even managed to run on the level, something I had not been able to do for years. *Deva*, however, languished in her shed, and it was not until four weeks after the operation that I was able to start work on her fitting-out. Bob and Mandy anti-fouled her bottom and she was soon being craned at Manningtree Quay. The engine started first time, we motored to Shotley Marina, finished rigging her, and started the Passage Race to Burnham the next morning. It was a nice trip down, setting twin spinnakers, and *Deva* won. The Crouch Mafia even allowed us to come third in the Old Gaffers Race there. The shock of seeing *Deva* again was probably too much for them.

Indeed, *Deva* seemed to lead a charmed existence on the racecourse for much of that year. We had two very good races at the Shotley Classics, one of which was the Pursuit Race round Pennyhole Bay from Walton to a finish in Harwich. We started from Island Point at the entrance to Hamford Water. The first mark down wind was Pye End. The second mark was Stone Banks, which looked like a simple close fetch, which the other boats all headed for like sheep. Somebody asked if we had left something at the barbeque at Stone Point as we rounded up and tacked into the Backwaters again. We beat round High Hill and slipped through the little fisherman's channel by Stone Point and reached for Stone Banks across the shallows. We noted that we had picked up the smack *Ostrea Rose*, with the two craftiest old devils on the East Coast aboard, Mike Emmett and Graham Brewster - not racing men, mind, but crafty. They had the same idea. Meanwhile the proper racers had got caught in the rip-roaring north-going ebb. It was going to take them hours to round Stone Banks. We sallied gently past Stone Banks, taking the tide down to Cork Ledge, by which time the ebb had slackened and a the seabreeze strengthened to give us a good reach. By the time the rest had rounded Stone Banks the tide had turned so they had to plug it down to Cork Ledge. The gap with the rest of the fleet was enormous, in fact embarrassing, as *Ostrea Rose* and *Deva* sailed neck and neck to the finish in Harwich Harbour. It was almost "After You" at the finish as *Ostrea Rose* crossed just ahead. Of course, we had taken a couple of chances. We had risked grounding in slightly uncharted waters. Another ten minutes later we would have hit the spring ebb coming out of the Backwaters and a very tricky cross tide round High Hill. The resulting delay could have affected our exit through the fisherman's channel, where there is a bit of a bar to hit. Had the rest of the fleet had a five degree windshift, they would have got there first anyway. When you don't have the fastest of boats you have to try something different!

If that was luck, it was nothing compared with the East Coast Old Gaffers Race that year. Boats like the *Deva* are well out of the running compared with the local racers. No cabins, no cruising gear, no engines, no victuals, no beer do they have to carry round the course. And they know the waters. We did not have a particularly brilliant start that year, and the fickle winds took the lightweights over the horizon in minutes. It was a long drag out to the Knoll, even with the "Bastard" pulling. Fortunately for us there was bunching at the front, where the hotshots battled it out with each other instead of looking for the best windshift or clear air. Some of the front runners took wind round the Spitway buoy, but the tide was still ebbing north and they went with it. We sensed that the wind would go from west to east as low water approached, laid a course across the tide, and steered to the east of the rhumb line, keeping the "Bastard" drawing on a reach. Many boats were just becalmed in the oily swell as we sailed in a half circle round them on the edge of the wind. We luffed the "Bastard" at the Spitway buoy and the wind swung round even more and filled the sail on the other tack, straight on course for the next mark at Jaywick. By chance this was picked up on the OGA film. We had such momentum that we overtook several boats we should not have overtaken. Then it was an easy run back. Of course, when the others got the sea breeze many of the bigger ones overtook us, but not at sufficient speed to beat us on handicap. *Deva* won the famous East Coast Old Gaffers Trophy (affectionally known as the "Lump of Lead") for the first time in twenty-three years. There were many similarities to the 1971 situation and a very large dollop of luck. Or was it the strange unpredictability that *Deva* possesses? She can seize defeat out of the jaws of victory and vice-versa; a race is never won or lost until she crosses the line. She seems to sense what to do in the most obscure circumstances on certain occasions. It makes her a very interesting boat to sail.

Her winning streak included the Stour Sailing Club Regatta. For some reason every windshift and every tack seemed to suit her. Bob and Mandy were absolutely perfect on the sail handling. *Deva* was amazingly ahead of all the Bermudan boats at the windward mark, and you would not expect her to give much away on the broad reach back to the finish. Even the Pin Mill Regatta in the heart of Orwell Mafia territory fell to the *Deva*. Actually she was only second, but *Snippet*, which was half a mile in the lead, missed out a mark and was protested out by someone in another class.

In the summer, at Shotley, I had exchanged an Old Gaffers Membership for a beam trawl. Melvin Fox, one of the lockmasters, had a Cromer crabber, *Paternoster*. She had enough power for an otter trawl, so the twelve-foot beam trawl was going spare. Whilst I had read about trawling under sail, I had never actually done it. We had a trawling competition at the classic boat festival for the local smacks. It made me wonder how *Deva* would trawl. She is very much smaller than a smack, but on a size for size basis she is heavier. I had actually had a chat with the owner of *Esk*, one of *Deva*'s sisters. She ended her working days in the early 80s as a motorised shrimper on the Dee with a 28hp Diesel and a twenty-two foot beam trawl, about the same length as the boat.

The trouble with putting *Deva* back to fishing was that her cabin and deck layout were not conducive to trawling in the traditional way. In the original deck layout the prawner had a long narrow cockpit and wide side decks. The decks were effectively work benches where the fisherman dealt with his catch whilst standing in the cockpit. He did not work at deck level as on a smack with bulwarks. The prawner only had a toe-rail round the gunwale, and the constant washing of the decks by the sea had the advantage of clearing all the rubbish, such as crabs and weed, that comes up in the trawl. On *Deva* the side decks are only a foot wide, and a cabin takes up half the length of the original cockpit. However, the trawling nogs ("tonking posts" in Essex) were in the right place, and we had a fish tackle rigged off the mast. I would have to work the net off the foredeck.

It was then a matter of putting theory into practice. The net and beam were stowed along the side deck, and I went to the fishing grounds. If fishing locally I would go just down river, off Wrabness, or sometimes Holbrook Bay. On morning and evening tides I would go out to sea. Once at the fishing grounds, the cod end buoy and line would be streamed astern and to windward, followed by the net, with the boat hove to. The beam would be partially lowered in the water, then "squared" to the boat. This was quite difficult to do single-handed. The forward trawl head slip had to be eased first, but not too quickly, otherwise the beam could go vertical or even capsize. Eventually I worked out a system that could be operated from the cockpit. Once the beam was "squared", both slips on the trawl heads were slipped, the trawl was "shot". The warp would snake out, and the ship be put on course. A preventer would be set round the warp back to the after nog, and the vessel steered with this rather than the rudder. Elements of the operation were dangerous, particularly as the big warp snaked out. This was coiled on the foredeck, and shortage of deck space often made it tempting to step into the middle of the coil. It is amazing how quickly a clove hitch can form around one's ankles and send one overboard.

Having got the gear overboard and on the sea bed, I had to adjust the power of the rig. Compared with the classic prawner rig, *Deva*'s mainsail is about twenty per cent shorter on the foot. I had cut three feet off the boom to ease either weather helm or a tendency to gripe to windward.

But when trawling, especially in lighter winds, the boat balances differently, and possibly a bigger main is better. In terms of vectors the boat is held about two or three points abaft the beam, so she will tend to slide to leeward. With a big main this effect is counteracted. With *Deva*'s smaller main I would have to ease the preventer on the trawl warp, pulling slightly more sideways than ahead. I often wonder why so many ex-sailing fishing vessels are so heavy on the helm. Surely the builders must have had a reason. Is it because they would drag a trawl better?

However, although *Deva*'s rig is slightly small for the type, the better cut and sailcloth of the modern day probably develops more power than the baggy old natural fibre cloth. Certainly she rarely lacked the power in her rig in anything from force two upwards, and the inertia of her heavy hull would keep a very steady pull on the trawl warp. The ability to set a jib on the Wykeham Martin was very useful when I was short handed. Messing about with sheets and sails on the already cluttered foredeck would have made for a real mess.

There were some quite challenging manoeuvres to be made when trawling the Stour. One of the big problems was that the prevailing wind was westerly, straight down the river. Owing to various obstructions it was often necessary to gybe and get the gear towing from the other side. This could be problematical and dangerous because the boat was not being steered by her rudder. It is too complicated to describe in detail, but it involved depowering the rig and lots of temporary hitches. A boomless and brailing main like a bawley's would have made it easier than lowering the whole sail or risking a slammer of a gybe. Sometimes the gybe would be put in out of sequence, and the trawl would be on the lee side, quite a difficult situation, as the boat could not be manoeuvred.

Ideally we trawled with the tide, about a knot or two faster than the current. But on a river the best fishing is generally on the flood, and the prevailing westerly on the Stour often made this practice impossible to follow. If there were a reasonable amount of beef in the wind, pulling the trawl should be no problem. However, the reaction to the current would be different, causing more gybes. The other issue was that there was a tendency for the beam to lift off the ground, as the weight on the warp would have to be higher to overcome the current. However, with the three or four hours I had on the tide, *Deva* could get out from Mistley, trawl down Copperas Bay against the tide, and come up the channel with the tide, but against the wind. Beating to windward with a trawl down is a bit of an acquired taste even out at sea where there is sea room. On a river with ships going up and down it is the foolhardy side of acquired, so we would round up to windward, lower the headsails and start the engine. Major changes of course with the gear down can be problematical, a common trouble being the capsizing of the beam as the tow comes cross current. More than once I found that I had been trawling with the beam upside down - great for getting up mussels!

With the trawl down and the boat under sail there would be little to indicate that *Deva* was fishing, other than her speed. A bucket or basket in the rigging would not mean anything. The speed - well, she was just an old gaffer; they are expected to be slow. There would then be the problem of trying to tell the skippers of Beneteaus and Westerley's to keep clear of the gear, pointing to the cod end buoy. Even that had its problems. Occasionally someone would try to pick it up, thinking it was a mooring. Other dangers were from the longshore mafias at Shotley Gate and Harwich. Most of them were not registered either, but they did not want any foreigners from up the river messing about in their patch. One might ask whether my little experiment was legal, with all the restrictions on fishing today. The net size was really only suitable for herring, which is not a fish one trawls for. Sole, skate and other "flatties" are the real target of the trawler. However a very pleasant man came up to me in Shotley Marina, where I used to winter when they did special deals for small angling boats. He shook my hand and asked me about the boat. I thought he was a member of the OGA, but it turned out that he was the fishery officer! He actually did not mind my activity. Probably he minded it a lot less than some of the expensive yachts which used to have to share a lock with *Deva* and her smelly trawl.

My worst experience was out at sea. There are parts of the Harwich approaches and Pennyhole Bay where the ground is fine for trawling, and some where it is not. Generally where there are lobster pots the ground is rough. Unfortunately a superb trawling breeze and a hard flood tide took me out of my area, about two miles off the Naze. The warp started stretching a bit, and I thought I had a bumper catch. I let go the preventer and expected *Deva* to swing round. Unfortunately, because the wind was cross tide, she would not swing properly. There was a bit of a sea running - it was blowing force four - and the boat was tethered like a captured beast, with the sails full. I managed eventually to get the sails down, but I had to cut part of the net before the gear could be lifted. The boat had netted a fine catch of cement stone, which was a commercial catch a few hundred years ago, before modern Portland Cement.

Getting the gear back on board was another interesting exercise. To take the power off the boat the main would be scandalised and the headsails lowered. The preventer would be eased off, the net would go out to windward. I would haul in the warp as quickly as I could until the bridle appeared. At this point the fish tackle would be hooked on and the beam raised to deck level to stop fish escaping. I would then rush to tie the beam fore and aft, before bringing the net in. Eventually the cod end would arrive, and the contents would be disgorged over the foredeck. Crabs, shrimps, shells, weed and a few fish would scatter everywhere. Just occasionally the boat would choose this time to go about or gybe. Once the gear was off the bottom the boat would behave differently and really needed the chap on the foredeck to operate the helm. With the cod end open, the net would be streamed in the water again to clean it, or it would be tied up, although I never learned to do a proper cod end knot, and the trawl shot again.

It was an interesting experiment to work a trawl under sail. It proved to me that the Morecambe Bay prawner must have been an excellent workboat. Her efficiency as a sailing boat and her manoeuvrability would have enabled her to fish the channels that criss-crossed the sands of the bay more effectively than other types of working boat. Her options on trawling up tide or down tide, up wind or down wind would have been considerable. Her buoyant ends and hull shape would help her lift to the seas, despite the restraint of the fishing gear. I am not sure about the boat's use as a commercial exercise today. Arthur Keeble saw me trawling one day and said "That's what you mean by being self-employed!". The fish caught was excellent in quality. Unlike in a modern power trawler, the fish is not squashed into a ball and bumped over the ground at high speed. It is very much alive when landed, and tastes the better for it. Unfortunately the catches were too small to be of interest financially. Obviously my knowledge, my skills and my reluctance to go out at the right time of the day affected the size of catch, but even when I have seen professionals have a go at fishing under sail they seem to have the same lack of luck. My view is that fish stocks in the days of sailing fishermen were a great deal more prolific than today's. In fact the sailing fishermen may have even enhanced them by just culling the excess. Statistics of landings at places like Lowestoft tend to back this up. The first powered fishing vessels would have had a field day on the fishing grounds, day in day out. They were not held back by lack of wind or direction of wind or tide, and of course it was a lot easier without all those sails around to get in the way. But, alas, it was the law of diminishing returns. The decline in fish stocks matched the decline in the number of those employed in the trade.

However, this in no way diminishes my respect for today's professional fishermen. Fishing remains a very hard and dangerous occupation, despite all the modern gear, and there are not many fish to catch now. It must have been a horrid life in the old smacks; no wonder sail was dispensed with when motors came in. Those who romanticise about the old smacks do not really know the half of it. Very few of them have even played at working their beautifully restored boats. They do a very fine job in investing in maritime heritage. They have ensured that some of the skills of managing the craft under sail have been retained, and we have the delight of watching their boats sail in regattas, probably more delightfully than when they were real working vessels. But, that apart, they are only yachtsmen like the rest of us. In recent years there have been oyster dredging competitions in the Mersea area, which a few of the East Coast smacks have taken part in. They race to the grounds, do a bit of dredging, race back, pick up the smacks boat and take the catch ashore for a social and party at the old packing shed. A welcome change from racing round the same marks in the estuary.

Deva Fishing

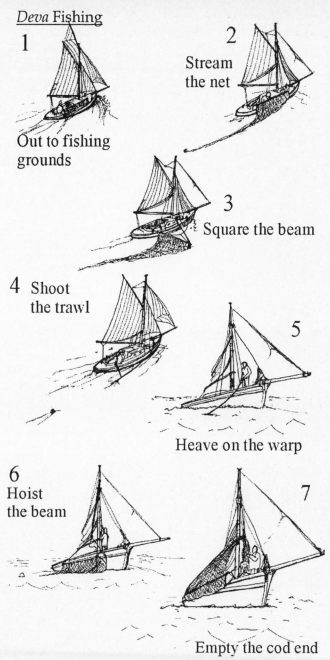

1

Out to fishing
grounds

2

Stream
the net

3

Square the beam

4 Shoot
the trawl

5

Heave on the warp

6
Hoist
the beam

7

Empty the cod end

Deva was to stay in commission for a number of years without the respite of laying up. Since the accident with the ice I have always been nervous about leaving her on the mooring throughout the winter. Often it is impossible to reach the vessel by dinghy in a crisis. The tides make it difficult to sail in the daylight. Now I keep the boat in a marina berthing for the winter period, and that helps for maintenance.

There are only so many tides or sailing opportunities allotted to all of us. My condition makes this more obvious to me than to most. I see people spend half a lifetime restoring a boat meticulously, then be too old to get many years of sailing out of her. I see other people working their hearts out for a big pension so that they can have their dream ship. But indeed their heart can be worked out by the time retirement comes. Sailing all the year does provide many more "tides", which is critical to those whose future is restricted. In other seasons the rivers are clear of moored boats, and the scenery can be wonderful and peaceful in a light which summer cannot provide. Good clothing and heating go without saying. In *Deva* I fitted a gas calorific stove which is cheaper to run than the cooker grill with which I would thaw my fingers. There are limitations on how long in a day it is reasonable to sail and because of that the nights at mooring or anchor are perhaps too long, so longer cruising is limited. But it is still so worthwhile. The winter passes by, and suddenly it is spring, with lots of newly painted boats about. It is a bit like going to an all-night party and coming home in the daylight.

The following year 1995 we were off to Holland again, this time with a newfangled GPS which Bob had bought in America. Times have certainly changed since *Deva* was a tree! Satellites now orbit the earth guiding her about the seas. We have VHF radio and cellular phones to contact people by voice, text message or email. A Victorian or

Edwardian sailor could have come on board *Deva* ten years ago and not have seen anything he could not understand. Even a Viking sailor could have worked out a lot of it, apart from the Stuart! In a few short years the problems which beset mariners for several millennia have been solved. The pace of change has been incredible.

However, some things do not change. The best way to cross a sea with varying cross tides is to head a straight course and sail a wavy one. The GPS does not appreciate the change of tide, and will keep telling the helm to point into the current, so we did not win the race across to the Roompot. The right way is still the old way - work out the duration of the crossing, work out how many tides, work out a course to steer. The GPS is only useful in its ability to give a bearing or position.

That was the year in which Bob and Mandy were seduced by the bar of soap being lowered down the hatch by Ray and John Walker of *Noorderzon*. The oodles of space for Mandy's extensive wardrobe, the crates of Grolsch stacked up by her bunk, the central heating, the showers and the rest were all too much temptation for her. *Deva*'s "boudoir" or forepeak could not compete, even with its unique micro climate. We sailed to Goes, the nearest railhead, where they left me. It wasn't really that bad of them. They had given me some very good years. Their beautiful smack *Polly* was restored now. She was the last smack to work out of Maldon without an engine. If they wanted to sail in the manner of the nineteenth century, they had a far more suitable boat. And if they wanted to go "yachting", *Noorderzon* was the best boat to be on, for offshore work particularly. Built out of steel on the lines of a pilot cutter in a Dutch shipyard, she was massively strong with a huge engine and a huge rig. If I had a lot of money and were not obsessed with *Deva*, I would have had her!

My son Andrew joined me at Willemstadt, and we actually had a very hot Hellevoetsluis. The first race was in light airs, the second was in a good "Reef and Tops'l" breeze, and the third was back to light airs. For some reason we won the gaffers series prize – it must have been the VKSJ handicap - and the third prize in the North Sea Race. Andrew went home, and Margaret came over for a cruise, which included a tour of the Biesbosh. This is a wild area of Holland with woodland and uncharted waterway, where the Dutch Resistance used to hide in the war. We again came back via Middleberg, where Bob and Brian Tower joined me for the trip home. This time we returned via Blankenberg in Belgium. Our passage to Blankenberg was a terrific sail, averaging 6.6 knots, despite a significant amount of foul tide. Our passage from Blankenberg was our best return trip. With reefed main, topsail, tow foresail, red inner jib and Jewitt outer, we carried a beam north-easterly all the way across. It took us fourteen hours, which included an hour hove to for fishing.

European Champion
and a Dutch Cruise
1997

In 1995 the VKSJ, which is the Dutch Classic or "Sharp" Yacht organisation, set up a European Challenge Cup, based on the best ten classic boat race results in European waters. At least one of those races had to be an offshore passage across the North Sea. So for most of us on the East Coast this meant Shotley Classics and the Dutch Classic Yacht Regatta at Hellevoetsluis. It is an interesting challenge because the waters sailed are so diverse. It is not like having a series in the Solent or the Blackwater, racing round the same cans every day. As in any points series, you need consistent performance to win. It is a good test of the versatility of a boat design and to a certain extent the crew. The boat needs to be nimble enough to race on narrow rivers, fast enough to make the best of the wide sheltered waters of the Dutch Inland Seas, and seaworthy enough to make a fast passage in open seas. The crew need to be crafty enough to work currents and back-eddies in estuary, river and sea, and have the stamina to handle the long passages, and in *Deva*'s case the big breakfasts!

In the first year of the Challenge Cup *Deva* actually came third, which was considered remarkable. Second was a Thirty Square *Korybant*, but the first was *Soma*, a Dutch Hillyard. She had an extra offshore race with double points to help her, and her skipper Hugo did very well in VKSJ races in Holland. My son and I went to collect the cup by a rather interesting route. I went to Manningtree station and asked for a single to Mistley, the next station on the Harwich branch line. Just as he was about to print the ticket I said "Ah! Could I have that via London, Brussels and Amsterdam?" We actually took the new Eurostar train under the new Channel Tunnel to Brussels, then changed to conventional rail to Amsterdam. We returned via the Hook-Harwich ferry, then got on a local train to Mistley and walked home.

In 1997 we weren't even thinking about the Challenge Cup when we entered Shotley Classic Boat Festival. We were having a difficult time with the marina. The marina manager had split the fleet, shoving most of them up to the vacant basin at the north end. Temporary facilities were provided, but the dreadful weather had made the ground very soft. The beer price had been jacked up by ten pence as well, and I was getting a lot of complaints.

I had a new crew for the week - Sarah Adie, from my sailing club. The boat she normally sailed on, the *Roker*, was not going to be there. David Shipley, Bob Farrow and Mandy Steer pomised to give a few days too. The first race was a straightforward race up the Stour via a few cans, with a port tack start off Shotley. Just as the gun was about to go, the bawley *Good Intent*, henceforth known as "Bad Intentions", decided to go on to the starboard tack down the line forcing the whole fleet to go about - except us. We managed to squeeze between her massive bowsprit and the committee boat *Stadats* as the gun fired and the smoke filled our cockpit, no watches, perfect timing, complete fluke! With only her local waters ahead of her, *Deva* was not going to do exactly badly. It was the last race we actually won at Shotley.

The next day, Saturday, should have seen boats racing offshore in the President's Race, but atrocious weather had set in, causing the committee to set a course up the Orwell and back. With the high tide well in, there were plenty of opportunities for boats to escape the constraints of the channel. The Hillyard *Bydand* made much ground by cutting corners in this way, as did *Deva* and the oyster police boat *Victoria*. Huge rain squalls dominated the race, and a dramatic windshift at the end of the race turned the last leg into a vicious beat. *Vashti* took line honours, but the Humber yawl *Snippet* won the Harwich Haven Cup on handicap, followed by the bawley *Bona* and *Deva*.

Surprise, surprise - it was neither downpour nor gale for Monday's cruise to the Walton Backwaters; the line of strong winds finished at Felixstowe, at least two cables away from our intended course. This day is really the best day for the open boat, with a picnic, a race round the islands and a passage race back home. The "Swallows & Amazons" Race, for this indeed is Arthur Ransome country, is entertaining for both participants and spectators as peaks of sails can be seen darting in and out of the many creeks and channels that form part of the five-mile course. The finish was quite a spectacle. The Thames Estuary One Design (TEOD) *Corsair* and gaff sloop *Murre* fought it out for line honours. *Corsair* took the gun, but the win also cost her rigging dearly; her mast failed on crossing the line. On handicap *Dipper* won from *Dabchick* and the yawl-rigged *Catherine Marie*. (*Corsair*'s mast was up and running the next day. Apparently her skipper epoxied a new scarf and slept with it in his sleeping bag overnight to help it cure in time!)

Next it was the turn of the big boats to have their "Pennyhole Bay Pursuit Race" for the Bona Trophy. Boats started in designated groups. There was a bit of a mix-up for the hotshots start, but all got away eventually, with a spanking north-north-westerly. The race is a challenge for both tactician and navigator, especially to locate the Armada. It is quite common for the whole fleet to go off out to sea in totally the wrong direction. After *Deva's* escapade a year or two back when she craftily went back to Stone Point and out of the Fisherman's Channel to pop up ahead of the others, we were being watched carefully.

However, *Victoria* sailed the best line across wind and tide to lead the fleet round the Armada. Beating up to the Cork Ledge mark was the next test of skill. In the early stages of the ebb the water tumbles off the back of the Cork sand, running into the deep water to the west rather like rainwater off a roof or road into a gutter. There was quite a lot of short tacking between *Victoria*, *Rainbow* and ourselves. We were all looking for a lee-bow or a better angle of tidal stream to work, and we were all local boats. We broke free of *Victoria* and started to close *Rainbow*. There was a lovely windshift to be had as *Rainbow* rounded Cork Ledge mark with *Deva* up her tail. We took the lead for the long reach to Landguard.

However, *Deva's* glory was to be short lived as *Bona* came storming through, crew deployed about the bowsprit bitts to keep the transom clear. The Hi-tech Spirit 47 *Ali Baba* and West Solent *Linette* went through to overtake *Bona* in turn, although she did hold off *Rising Hope*, *Sauntress* and *Eccelin*.

Two Rivers Race Day for some reason was always the most popular Shotley race. Unusually for June, the weather was dry, although the wind was fickle. It went round from a broad reach to a dead noser at the start. However badly one made a start, we all collected together up the Stour, awaiting the forecast south-westerly. As a light wind filled in, boats struggled in the shallows to stem the tide. With gaps in the wind the fleet spread out considerably, not, however, enough to prevent a minor altercation at the Bloody Point Mark which involved a '720' by *Deva* (two penalty turns in the boat) with much mirth from other competitors, and not a very good result for us. *Rising Hope*, extremely well sailed by Dutchman Van Dyke and co, won on handicap, second only to *Ali Baba* on line honours. The racers not unnaturally headed the bulk of the fleet, but marine heritage did have its moments as *Bona* and *Lutra* took second and third places.

Mistley Day was back to dark, dank and windy conditions. We were looking for a good result on our own river. After a brief run up the Orwell it was quite a slog for the smaller boats to beat out again against wind and tide. Crouch Mafia godfather Ray Austen in his Blackwater sloop *Phylla* challenged *Deva* early with some smashing close tacking and very nearly caught us out as we rounded Bloody Point, but, unlike us, he wasn't on his home waters. It was a magnificent, almost Wagnerian, reach up the Stour, with huge rainstorms and squalls. Apart from the out of sight hotshots, there were some great performances from *Gromit* (Heard 29), *Skandale* and *Snippet*. The Cornish Crabbers had their fun too, with a class race within a race won by *Die Schone Lau*. Once at Mistley, we moored against the quay and enjoyed a pub lunch at the Thorn Hotel with the many others who had come round by road. *Rising Hope* won the Thorn Trophy on handicap, followed by *Snippet*, *Scolopax* and *Deva*. The early beat against wind and tide in the Orwell had cost the smaller vessels dearly, but it was still a respectable placing for *Deva*.

Not to be dismayed by even worse weather and having cancelled the Deben cruise, the committee laid on even more races! For the "All in Classics", a course was set up the Orwell, to round a buoy which might be named on admiralty charts for those who can afford them, but is not named in actuality or in local pilot books. However most rounded successfully by process of elimination or dead reckoning -it was the buoy you missed while using the facilities below. *Telegraph* got into difficulty and was towed clear by *Bona*, and it was not a very good race for us either. With an element of sadness the 1997 Shotley racing finished when the converted dayboat *Betty* completed the All in Classics course in the afternoon gloom.

The major prizes of the festival were for points series. The Gaff Points Cup went deservedly to *Snippet*, with a very good second to *Bona*, and *Deva* in third place. In the over-all positions, which included the other classes, we were only twelfth, not a very good result, but not impossible to recover from for the European Cup.

Friday was scheduled for the Parade of Sail in support of the Nancy Oldfield Trust. TV was laid on, as were the OGA film crew. The rain was so heavy that it was difficult to see one end of the marina from the other. However, the last gun of the last Shotley event was fired "bang" on time as one hundred and fifty classic boats sailed up the Orwell, under the bridge into a very wet Ipswich Wet Dock for Sail Ipswich '97.

It was a marvellous sight to behold. Stars of the show were undoubtedly the tall ships. We had the French Navy topsail schooners *Belle Poule* and *Etoile* together with the Polish barquentines *Pogoria* and her sister ship. There were also a number of big ketches of different nationalities and local barges to give the display some bulk. Unfortunately the weather had prevented a large number of entrants from attending, so the Shotley classics were particularly welcome, their myriad of masts and flags making a very colourful presentation. On board there were lots of boat parties and receptions, whilst in the local hostelries impromptu groups of French, English and Polish crews burst into song. There was a tremendous atmosphere to be enjoyed by all.

All this would have been in vain if the sun had not shone miraculously for the public on Saturday. For the first time in days we were able to dry our gear, adding even more colour to the scene. There were all sorts of sideshows, bands and exhibitions both on the quayside and in warehouses. Classic boatmen wandered between shows, looking at the boats and just having the odd beer or two on board or in a hostelry. Brian meanwhile provided a major service to the festival by keeping up the public commentary as he had at Shotley, almost without a break.

The evening was party time, and we had Sarah's Fortieth Birthday Party on the Orwell Quay to the accompaniment of the "Zephyrs". At the party we awarded the Nancy Oldfield Cup for the Parade of Sail to the *Snark*. Single-handedly the little Deben Cherub had tacked up the length of the Orwell into the dock, exemplifying the spirit of the Old Gaffers. A huge firework display provided the grand finale to a wonderful day at Sail Ipswich.

The next major group of events was the East Coast Old Gaffers Race, the Tendring Coast Passage Race and the North Sea Classic Passage Race to Holland and Hellevoetsluis. Whilst the East Coast events were feasible for a small old gaffer, the thought of crossing the North Sea always filled me with anxiety. In moments of extreme stress on passage I have often said to myself "Never again!". But the vow, however intense, is always broken. Despite the ninety-year-old wood and nails which form the *Deva*, despite the lack of freeboard and open cockpit, despite the state of the skipper, it is "Just one more time".

After a mixed passage down the Wallet the day before, we entered West Mersea and were allocated a very convenient mooring next to *Paternoster*, a Norfolk (working) crabber we knew from Shotley. Sarah and Brian were waiting for us bright and early on the pontoon next morning. Unfortunately, there was still no sign of Eddie in *Merlyn III*. We thought that he must have gone to Brightlingsea by mistake. The plan had been for David to give him a hand in the race, but instead we put him to work cooking breakfast to set us up well for the race. Rolls were made up for the day. The sun was shining, the breeze was brisk from the north. I went ashore and advised that the long course should be set. What a spanking day for a sail! Few of the smacks were risking topsails, but with the human ballast aboard I thought we could set ours. We kept to the working jib, nevertheless, to avoid straining the mast.

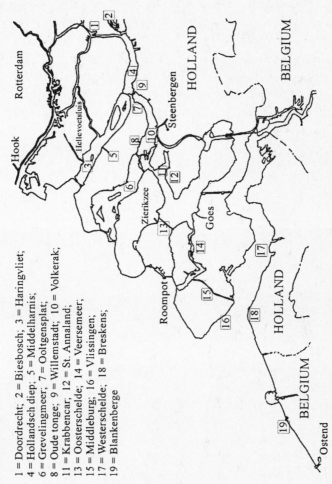

South Holland

1 = Doordrecht; 2 = Biesbosch; 3 = Haringvliet;
4 = Hollandsch diep; 5 = Middelharnis;
6 = Grevelingmeer; 7 = Ooltgensplat; 8 = Volkerak;
8 = Oude tonge; 9 = Willemstadt; 10 = Volkerak;
11 = Krabbencar; 12 = St. Annaland;
13 = Oosterschelde; 14 = Veersemeer;
15 = Middleburg; 16 = Vlissingen;
17 = Westerschelde; 18 = Breskens;
19 = Blankenberge

We selected one of the channel buoys as a timing marker for the start, and made a couple of practice runs; we sailed by the committee boat to ensure that the start party could identify us. The plan was to put Sarah on the tiller while the rest of us trimmed sheets for the reach. The line was heavily biased for a port hand start. There were about five square metres by the Nass where several score boats were planning to be at the same time. It was either start first or be squashed.

In the event we were line shy by about three seconds whilst Jonny James in *Cothele* was actually on the line but spilling wind. However, we were up to full speed with *Miranda* close astern, and briefly took the lead. With a beam reach to Mersea No 6 buoy, it was waterline length which counted, and some of the larger vessels managed to get by. This year we had a three-stage start, the small boats off first. With our size we should have sailed off with first group but as the one who had worked out the groups I had to be beyond reproach, so put *Deva* in a faster group.

Deva, as always, hated the run down to Bench Head, and watched her keen rival *Rainbow* set her chute and sail past. On rounding Bench Head, we caught up a number of tailenders, then found clear wind to beat to Inner Bench. We saw many make the mistake of not staying in the Colne Channel, where there was a lovely bit of flood to pull back our losses on the run with interest. A few beers had been opened by this time, and the crew were well into song. After another deadly run to Colne Bar we set off with relief on the reach back up the Blackwater estuary. The Jewitt was unfurled, so *Deva* was triple-headed forward of the mast and going like a train.

The hotshots then came through, magnificent sights all of them. *Deva*'s big sister *Laura* came through, her bow almost buried under a massive bow wave, a grim faced Gayle

Heard pressing her to the maximum. No singing or drinking on that ship, but at least we guaranteed having a good day out what ever the result whereas she had to win or weep. Other sailmakers were asked to pass to leeward if they wanted any more of my business. Some old friends of *Deva*, Mandy and Bob, waved to us from the mighty *Noorderzon*. We passed *Daisy Belle*, the smack on the next mooring at Mistley, with several locals aboard. Brian's brother Mal was crewing. He had heard about Brian's exploits on *Deva*, and thought incorrectly that *Daisy Belle* would have the same refreshment traditions. The sponsors' offer of a drink at the club could certainly not have been more timely.

The wind eased back and came aft, not to *Deva*'s liking. *Pelican* and *Rainbow*, lighter, faster boats which we had taken on the beat and held on the reach, were setting chutes and gaining rapidly. *Rainbow* slipped ahead at the Thirslet, but we managed to hold *Pelican*. Then came the downfall of the "Bradwell triangle", an area of the Blackwater where winds can do anything. As we rounded, *Pelican* and *Rainbow* put tacks into Bradwell and we chose the other tack. Had the wind gone a touch northerely we would have won. It went a touch to the south instead, and infuriatingly blew firm on the Bradwell side east-south-east while our sails flapped in calm. It was nobody's fault but mine. I could easily have chosen to track *Rainbow*. She might not have let us pass but we would have been close and our easier handicap would have given us a result. But, oh no, I thought I could do what we did at Inner Bench Head.

However, it was still judged to be a good sail as we crossed the line and turned towards the moorings. We had finished early in the afternoon, so afternoon tea was called for. Somehow a winebox was opened in the confusion. It certainly was very pleasant to be spread-eagled over the boat in the sun. We were suddenly awakened by a howl of pain as a man in a dinghy hit his head on the bowsprit. Why wasn't he looking where he was going? We turned and saw the object of his distraction. Sarah was dozing with her back on the deck and her bare legs up in the air, wrapped around the mainsheet. It was not a ladylike pose.

Having put Sarah ashore with the OGA files the next morning, we made our way to the line again for the start of the Tendring Coast Passage Race. The wind dropped to nothing just before the gun, leaving us to freewheel against the tide. We tried a bit of kedging, then we picked up a private breeze which took us to second place. *Mary Ritchie* stood out far to sea, well wide of the Colne Bar mark, to search for a sea breeze, whilst *Deva* and *Snippet* sneaked along the Clacton shore. *Mary Ritchie*'s tactics paid off, as she picked up a nice south-easterly, laying Frinton in one tack. By the time we made the Naze the breeze had picked up nicely, and all the boats romped into Harwich Harbour. We found that we had won on handicap. We spent the rest of the evening discussing the race across to Holland. Several Dutch boats had turned up. Margaret came along that night with her food for the journey, ferry tickets for the return of crew, my computer and one or two other essentials. The liferaft was loaded on board. There were several visits by incredulous Dutchmen, including one who had a Folkboat back home, and actually was impressed with the quart into pint pot design of our cabin.

The next morning we packed away another huge breakfast in readiness for the North Sea Race. In a little boat it can be very difficult to prepare food at sea. We then locked out of Shotley and made our way to the line off South Shelf. *Avola* was start boat. Although not terribly relevant on a race this long, we actually made a cracking start at 09.00 in the light north-east breeze.

The first mark was the South Cork, and there was a strong tide taking us down. The hotshots and almost everyone else drew away in the light northerly. However, it was clear that the current was taking the fleet well past to the south-west of the mark, so we gybed and reached across the back of the fleet. One by one the boats ahead realised the method in our madness and followed suit, but we had the "Bastard" drawing well and went up to second place.

When we rounded South Cork the wind dropped, so we headed to the north of our rhumb line. When the wind came it might be from the north-east. We had lunch in the calm and streamed the fishing gear. We are a sort of fishing boat after all! One or two competitors, including *Avola*, who should have known better, came too close for comfort, and were radioed to keep clear. The Racing Rules of Sailing do not appear to cover fishing gear. Does it contribute to boat length in situations such as rounding marks?

The wind started to pick up nicely from the north. We handed the "Bastard", and set Jewitt, small red and Huggett staysail. All these sails are relatively narrow high-cut sails which give much lift when sailing in a seaway. Large floppy headsails will tend to stop the bow rising, making the boat bore into the sea and heel over. The other advantage of this set-up is easy sail reduction. The long luffed Jewitt is on a furler, and can be put out of the way quite easily. Small red is only two thirds of the way along the bowsprit, and should not bury in big seas. Huggett is strong and pulls well, and is good up to a force 7 or 8. Handing the Jewitt and topsail brings the rig to a manageable profile for heavier weather, keeping most of the deckwork in the middle of the boat.

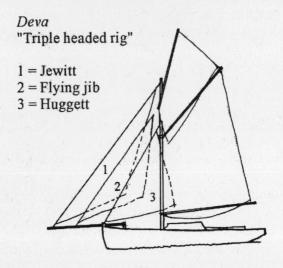

Deva
"Triple headed rig"

1 = Jewitt
2 = Flying jib
3 = Huggett

The wind was just what the boat needed for passage making. Our speed rarely dropped below 6 knots, and at times would register 7 and 8 for significant periods, far in excess of the theoretical hull speed. Many pooh-pooh such claims, but time and distance recordings do tend to back this up, never mind the GPS. Unfortunately, as most sailing on the East Coast is running or beating, it is rare that the boat can be set up for reaching as a long term project.

Sailing at speed in a seaway in such a small boat is not comfortable. We all had to keep to the weather side whether on deck or below, hanging on for grim death. The prepared rolls came in very useful, and the beer was refreshing in the sunshine. The other boats were clearly enjoying the conditions too, and unusually we could see several of our fleet for most of the day.

North Galloper came in sight at 1600, and we saw *Korybant* heading to the south. She should have been miles ahead at this stage; clearly we'd pulled the wind a lot earlier in the north. We saw *Mary Ritchie* to the north of us, appearing to sail in circles. I was concerned that Don might have lost something overboard. I radioed without success, but later understood that he had gone on starboard tack to put in a reef.

At 18.30 *Snippet* came abeam with a real bone in her teeth just after passing North Hinder Junction. We were starting to tire now, not quite having the concentration to keep the boat going at her best. The wind was also increasing, and that gave the bigger boats the chance to build up speed, whereas we could go no faster. *Sea Scamp* came through half an hour later, but, for goodness sake, she is an 8 Metre! For a little old fishing boat we had done incredibly well against these greyhounds of the sea.

Into the night we raced on. The seas were building but *Deva* kept ploughing on relentlessly, water sluicing down both side decks, phosphorescent wake streaming off into the blackness. We were really just hanging on, watching the miles clock away on the GPS as the boat almost sailed herself with three headsails, topsail and full main. She was possibly on the edge of stability, but we kept thinking that we would hang on just a little bit longer.

It is at times like these that I really believe the boat has a soul. She is taking us more than we are sailing her. Mile after mile the stem cuts through the sea, rising and falling rhythmically like the head of a horse galloping across the prairie. Eighty-five years old most of her nails and timbers may be, but we feel that she is in charge, looking after us as she has looked after so many in work and play over most of this century. Possibly it is to do with the state of mind and time of night, but I can almost sense the presence of such people. Perhaps they have left some of themselves aboard in a ghostly way; more likely it is *Deva*'s timbers talking to me. If flowers can talk to Prince Charles, why can't *Deva* have a chat with me?

It was such fine night for a sail that it was almost a pity to finish it. With boats all around us, we had plenty of confirmation that we were on course for the finish line, and at 02.42 we crossed, just astern of *Snippet*. We found out later that we had done incredibly well in the race. Because we had not used the engine as much as the others, we had suffered least on penalty. Our elapsed time adjusted for engine use put us halfway up the fleet and as we were the smallest boat by far our handicap gave us first place overall.

It is some years since I made the right choice of channel into the East Schelde, north or south. I had timed the race to catch the flood tide, rather than according to the North Sea Pilot recommendation, and it was sweeping in nicely. Why the hell did I choose the unlit south channel rather than the lit northern one? Probably it was just tiredness. Anyway we crept very gingerly through the channel under reduced sail, taking Decca readings at very short intervals. Just as the dark was lifting we sailed into Roompot Harbour, where we met most of the fleet. Shortly afterwards the lock was opened and we motored into the East Schelde and across to Roompot Marina. Berths had been arranged for us, and we took the opportunity to wash and shave. We also went to the local supermarket for more provisions. I had asked at a coffee bar if Dutch shops still shut on a Monday. The locals looked at me rather strangely as they gave me an answer. Then David pointed out that it was actually Tuesday. I was obviously suffering a mental eclipse or boat lag.

Whilst Brian had managed a couple of hours of sleep, there was no rest for the wicked as it was cast off and Steenbergen-ho. The tide was flooding again, and we set sail at 11.00hrs before running out of the harbour and up the Oosterschelde. We took it very gently, no topsail today! Technology moves on, and this year we had Brian's GPS plus my digital phone. It was amazing to receive a call from Sarah to find out how we had got on. She had planned to take the ferry over for the regatta, but family problems had prevented this.

It was an uneventful sail up the Oosterschelde, under the massive Zeeland bridge, then up towards the Krammersluis locks. There are many yachts on these waterways, which are really link routes to major sailing areas north and south. We tied alongside *Vashti*, the boat which took line honours in the North Sea Race. She was a lovely boat, a former ocean racer. We had a beer and a scout round with her skipper, the ebullient Dr Paul Wright, who was not a "pox-doctor" so he informed us. The lock here is always an ordeal for a long bowsprit and a boat that does not go astern. Following gin palaces with bow thrusters which stop and start on a sixpence is most disconcerting. They often wonder why the gel coat peeler, bowsprit, gets to lick its lips in such a situation at the sight of so many fibreglass backsides.

Out into the Volkerak we went, then across to Slikken van de Heen-oost. There is a canalised river which flows in here at Benedensas. It is not referred to on charts or in pilot books, but the canal extends several miles inland to Roosendal and Breda. After the M25 feeling of the Volkerak, it was lovely to cruise gently up a quiet canal. We turned off the main line and headed up a cut to Steenbergen. A little sign directed us "Classic Yachts" towards a staging. Being smaller than anyone else, we were sent right to the end to tie alongside a converted tug.

There was a briefing on one of the classic yachts, *White Heather*. We had been told originally that we were to have a civic reception. This was not to be so. The good burghers would give us free moorings for the night, but the main activity was to be round the pub. There would to be a band, herrings and beer. That is what I call a civic reception. My crew impressed the locals with their appetite for raw herrings and their consumption of the local brew. We had a lovely meal in the restaurant. I offered to pay for it with my 1000 guilder note or volunteer my crew for washing up. They found some change. Back in the bar we studied the landlady with interest. Every time she served a beer she cleaned off the froth with a knife, then wiped her rump with her hand. Her jeans became very damp and we fantasised. The band broke out into some old Cockney rhymes, and we sang in a big way. The local yacht club were so impressed that they gave us each a "moustachio" flag, a great honour apparently. Then there was dancing, and I met a lovely girl called Monique. The nice thing about Dutch girls is that you can have a decent conversation about boats and marine environment matters and learn something. Mentally I was still on Monday, although I had eaten at least six meals and seen two sunsets.

After a leisurely, if fragile, breakfast on the Wednesday morning, we had a look round the town, and bought some postcards and victuals. As we took our leave to sail to Willemstadt we saw that the landlady was staying on a boat opposite. I deliberately took the boat as close as I could, so that Brian could have a better look. She was not wearing her jeans. They were being washed. I asked her if she would like to serve us beers on the *Deva*, to get us to Willemstadt. She could borrow my jeans if she wanted. It was a very gentle drift up the Volkerak. A couple of hours later we were locking out of the big sluices into the Harringvliet, then turning into the old harbour at Willemstadt. The site was magnificent, with the harbour cleared of gin palaces. We had a nice meal ashore and a fairly quiet night after the "civic reception" of the night before.

The next day greeted us rather glumly without much wind for the Passage Race to Hellevoetsluis. The forecast wind, north 2/3, would have given a fine reach for us, but it was not blowing so that day. The start line had incredible bias on it. Why was everybody sailing from the other end, furthest from the next mark? Fools! Two minutes before the gun the water around us was buzzing with Dragons and 5.5 Metres thinking exactly the same. The gun went, they went, but we had a marvellous opportunity to take out 150 boats on port tack with all sorts of chaos. I chickened out and went with the flow, meekly. The rain came down, the wind went astern and dropped - a veritable private calm.

We experimented with a "blooper" system with an old spinnaker and the "Bastard" set together. This was all right until the bottle screw upon which the bearing out pole was fastened buckled, the pole going over the side in the process. We did quite a good "Man Overboard" drill in retrieving it. The sky cleared and we had a nice little romp over the line of Hellevoetsluis. I think that we were 15th out of about 65 finishers, which was not too bad in the circumstances. We moored in the harbour alongside *Snippet*, OGA member Kaas Koomen giving authoritative berthing instructions as *Deva*'s bowsprit searched for the glossiest and most worked upon topside paint job.

We had a proper civic reception in the sumptuous council offices. There was as much Pilsner and Dutch gin as could be consumed in the time frame. The time frame was favourably extended by the need to have speeches in two languages. We had a nice meal ashore and registered with the DCYR. Several old friends from two years previously were there. A marvellous octagonal fairground type structure had been set up. It was really a tent structure, but actually looked very solid, with fixed seating round the perimeter and timber columns and walls.

Friday was the first day of the regatta, but the wind was so strong that racing was cancelled. We shopped at the supermarket in the modern town, about a mile away. We "pigged out" at the restaurant on the waterfront for lunch. This used to be out of reach of my finances, but the strong pound in 1997, made life now very economical in Holland. After lunch, we thought we would blow the cobwebs away with a quick thrash to Stellendam and back. The wind moderated while we were out. We returned suitably refreshed.

Brian had to take the ferry back the next day, and one of the DCYR helpers, Keith, very kindly ran him back to the Hook. He managed to get back in time to crew with Jaqueline, another DC helper, and we hurried to the line. All the starting arrangements for the various classes were in a state of flux. Originally the plan was to start after the hotshots had finished, but they were taking too long. Unfortunately we could not read the class flags, and whilst keeping well clear of the line missed our signals. We started eight minutes late.

The course involved a beat out towards Stellendam, then a run back up the Harringvliet, then down past the entrance to Hellevoetsluis, almost repeating the circuit. It was either beating or running, with virtually no reaching. We tried, but not too seriously. *Mary Ritchie* and *Snippet* quickly took control of the race. *Snippet* was the current Shotley Gaff Rigger Champion, and *Mary Ritchie* has always been well sailed. It was not surprising that they showed the locals how to do it.

Having Keith and Jaqueline aboard was interesting. Keith was an Englishman who had settled in Holland, and actually understood the language. When he was telling Dutch jokes in English quite often a word in the punchline had no English equivalent, and when he was telling English jokes in Dutch the same thing would happen. It was hilarious.

The wind fell very light toward the finish, and the fleet stood still. On the last leg came a light wind on the beam. We set the "Bastard". Ungainly it might look, but, to the absolute amazement of Keith, Jaqueline and the Dutch boats nearby, the little boat ghosted right through the fleet. It was pure magic. Although *Mary Ritchie* and *Snippet* had already crossed the line to save their time on us, we still managed a third prize. It had been a fun sail, although we ran out of beer.

A rather nasty incident had happened in another race. Apparently the perpetrator was English and Ron Valent of the DCYR expected me to sort him out. He was threatening to kill a Dutchman, he had already rammed him; the police had been sent for. He was a big bloke too, and I recognised the name. I told Ron about the special presentation of haemorrhoid cream he had received at a rugby club AGM dinner. This was translated into Dutch. To cut a long story short, tempers did cool down, and the two skippers were drinking buddies by the end of the evening. The protest committee awarded them three tins of varnish which they had to divide between themselves, a very nice touch.

The last day of the regatta saw strong winds again. Don Garman gave me some of their beer, and Keith brought a case of Heineken aboard for us. This time our guest crew was Hannahe, a reporter from *Nautique*, a Dutch magazine equivalent of *Classic Boat* magazine. She had done a feature on one of the very big classics, now she wanted one at the other end of the scale. I pointed out we could not run to the twelve coats of varnish, but at least the timber treatment for houses and fences used on our brightwork was still Dutch! The interview had to be terminated when the helm was thrust into her hands while I set the sails. It was a "reef and topsail" day, which meant a reef in the main and re-fixing the topsail halliard. I had just finished doing that, when I saw the topsail lacing coming undone, requiring emergency treatment. Hannahe's knowledge of English or Anglo Saxon was greatly increased, though hardly improved.

We made for the line, checking our start times with instructions. It really was quite hairy as we reached up and down. David gave me running reports on the signals, and started counting from the five minute gun. I went up to the committee boat, put *Deva* on starboard tack, and beam reached at speed along the line with two minutes to go. The gun went; we hardened up just before the limit mark, shooting off to windward.

After a couple of minutes we looked around and thought "Where the hell are the others?". *Mary Ritchie* was way off the line; just one or two Bermudans were coming after us, some distance away. There was something of an inquisition. We must have read the instructions wrongly, but we could not see where. The trouble was that we were now so far away from the line that to go back would have made us last anyway. "Let's assume we had actually made a cracking start and keep going," I thought. "It's a nice day for a sail anyway."

Once we had rounded the windward mark and started the long run back the bigger boats started to catch us up. But they had to struggle, in contrast to us with beers in hand. Hannahe was fascinated at the contrast in the conduct of the two boats she had interviewed. The other boat had a big well-drilled crew, team colours, the lot. Both David and

I were official medical failures, and were just kitted out in T-shirt and shorts. The other boat spent eight months of the year being refitted under cover. *Deva* sailed twelve months a year sometimes trawling as well, and came out for a quick lick of paint between tides. I explained that after my last heart operation, which was only a year after the previous one, I realised that there would be "Only so many tides" which I could catch in the short time I might have. I could not risk wasting them with affected varnishing or fancy woodwork. *Deva* is kitted out to "fitness for purpose" standards only. Hannahe thought our boat was much more relaxing to sail on, for having beer and sandwiches whilst racing is frowned upon in some quarters.

I wish that the furling gear had been more fit for purpose, for the Jewitt decided to show itself at the wrong time as we came on to a short reaching leg. This required desperate action; I could not afford to let it run back on the traveller to foul the red jib. In the end we managed to lash it to the bowsprit. It did not look too good on the photographs, but that's racing. The photographers did not have anything to complain about though - we supplied them with beer as they took several photographs.

The beat went reasonably well for our little boat, although we did mess up a couple of tacks with a Hooker. *Mary Ritchie* got by but not by much, and we won the race easily on handicap. Unfortunately for *Deva*, there was no other boat to touch *Mary Ritchie*, with *Snippet* not racing, so despite her very bad start, she still came second. Her first on the Saturday and this second place were better than our third and first, so she won the series.

We had quite a long interview ashore, where we told Hannahe more about the boat and her history. There was quite a spread in the magazine, including photos of *Deva* and *Marie Ritchie*. The social in the evening was really great - the right kind of band, the right kind of people, the right price of beer. Prizegiving and speeches took quite a long time, partly because of the two languages. Brian Hammett gave a speech in Dutch, which went down very well. Then he did it in English so that they would understand!

The next day David went back on the ferry. Keith kindly took him to the Hook. Margaret arrived on the bus. I could not work out why the bus had the number it had or arrived when it did. It turned out that Margaret, and a party of English people crewing on the 8 Metres, had caught the bus to new Hellevoetsluis rather than the old place. However, Margaret ordered the bus to drive on. Nobody disobeys my wife, and the Brits were given a free private bus ride. The classic boats had mostly departed or gone into the marina, and modern boats were taking their place on the staging. Suddenly we felt rather small and old. I took Margaret to the posh restaurant at the waterfront, where we enjoyed a good meal at a reasonable price.

The next day we sailed for Dortse Biesbosch. The headsails were still in a bit of a mess from Sunday, the furling gear particularly. However, we set the lot in a very light air to see if everything worked. It was a very slow drift up the Harringvliet, and well before Hollands Diep we had reverted to the iron topsail. We anchored in the Zuid Maartensgat, the river that leads up to Dortse Biesbosch. It was very quiet, the sun was blisteringly hot. I went for a swim. Even then we were still so hot we spent much of the evening pouring buckets of water over each other. We set up the over-boom cover, with an oil lamp to attract the midges.

We awoke to find a police boat messing around a hundred metres astern, taking water samples, or so it appeared. I always feel guilty when I see a police boat. I worry that our boat does not comply in some way with the myriad of regulations. Anyway the police seemed not to be interested in us, so we made sail, or at least we tried to until I found that the Fox's pennant from the East Coast Old Gaffers Race had jammed in the peak halliard block. It took twenty minutes to shift it.

We sailed into the Amer in a rather greyish day, then into Noordgat van de Vissen for the Brabantse Biesbosch. The plan had been to sail up to the Biesbosch Museum via the Gat den Kleinen Hil. However, I kept running aground on a secret shoal, not marked in any way on the ground or in my chart. There are no navigation marks in the Biesbosch. The chart was confusing, using soundings in decimetres, which I am not used to. There must have been a way through, but I could not find a safe passage easily. There were no deeper routes to follow.

We aborted the visit and instead sailed up to Rietplaat Island, and anchored nearby. The chart was surprisingly inaccurate. There were many Dutch campers here, but not a German, Belgian or British boat to be seen. Some lads had made a very effective raft, and, setting a dinghy sail and skull and crossbones, she made a fitting sight for the locality, for here the Dutch Resistance hid during the German occupation. After lunch we began to make our way back to the Hollands Diep. The wind was foul, both in content and direction, and the marine juggernauts ploughed by. It was not a comfortable experience. We were glad to find shelter in Willemstadt.

Willemstadt had changed greatly since the Classic Boat Festival. Instead of the wood and varnish of the classic boats, we had the gleaming plastic of three-storey motor boats, not totally in keeping with the atmosphere of this historic harbour. Some might think that their wealthy occupants would be good for the local economy, but the strange thing is that their occupants do not come ashore much. They pose for the benefit of the public in a demonstration of opulence, but do not do much else. The landlord of one of the harbourside taverns confirmed this point. He said that he had far more business from the classic boat festival because the classic boats, being so uncomfortable, encouraged the crews to come ashore!

I had reported that we had had a good time at Steenbergen, and that made Margaret keen to go there. The weather was still quite foul, giving a rough beat down the Volkerak, rough not only with the wind but also with the wash of commercial shipping. We were glad to get away from the bustle of the big waterway and into the little canal and its beautifully peaceful world of reeds, coots, woods, and unspoilt countryside. We tied up in the same berth again, alongside the converted tug. It was much quieter without the classics, but still very friendly. We dined in the pub again, and had another marvellous meal. They seemed to remember me, however. When Margaret asked for a translation on the menu the waitress exclaimed "Why don't you ask him? - He knows the menu backwards!" As we were leaving, walking through the bar, "Jon, Jon, How are you?" came from a smoke filled corner, and Monique followed, looking just as glamorous as the last time. It did not go down well with "she who must be obeyed"!

The wind had dropped to virtually nothing, and it was a bit drizzly next day. We did some shopping and had a look round this excellent little town before leaving. Steenbergen was certainly the find of this trip. I also bought some stern gland packing from the local chandlery, having sketched out what I wanted. We had a leak from the gland, and I could not loosen the locknut.

We motored across the Volkerak and found the little channel up to Oode Tonge. For some reason very few yachts call in here, though there is plenty of space in the town harbour for visitors. It is very convenient for shops; a big supermarket is a stone's throw away; there are several bars and cafés. We went for a walk along the Moulindijk, and looked at the restored windmill. Margaret bought some shoes and some clogs. We also noted developers' plans for a Port Solent type complex, so perhaps Oode Tonge will change considerably in the future.

I took phone calls on the mobile, but found reception bad in the cabin and had to stand on deck. Crew arrangements had to be made for the passage back. In a couple of days Caroline was going to be bringing over a fellow villager's boat, the barge yacht *Sunlight*. Middleberg was the proposed rendezvous.

The next day we motored through the little channel again to the Volkerak, and went into the Krammersluis. A rope round the prop, stopped us from going astern, but luckily the bowsprit only went into the side of an inflatable dinghy on davits. We were able to unwind the prop to release the rope. We had a lovely sail on leaving the lock, turning off to go up the Krabben creek to St Phillipsland. These were tidal waters now, and we had the flood tide to take us up. I wished that I had time to look at the creek nearer low water, for there were several potential anchorages at the top end. Pilot information and charts were very sketchy.

Before the tide left we went downstream again into the marina at St Annaland, and we went for a walk to look at the fields and the windmill before settling in for drink in a town square café. The town square was the old fishing harbour until the 1950s.

It was a lovely sail down the Krabben creek into the Oosterschelde. My goodness, it was busy with nose-to-tail boats in both directions. We set full sail for the occasion, and swept down the estuary. An English boat we passed pretended we weren't there, but kept putting his engine on to minimise the disgrace. Many boats had to stop to wait for the Zeeland bridge to open, but not *Deva*. We sailed right up the canal to Zierikzee, but were rather worried by the number of power boats which were being badly driven with scant respect for vessels under sail. We had a lovely meal ashore at a restaurant which we discovered on our first Dutch holiday. We also had a pleasant chat with a Belgian family. Father was a rugby referee, and we had a long discussion about the game in the Netherlands and Belgium.

I had remembered our wedding anniversary, and did give Margaret something to hang up in the loo!

There was a spanking breeze to take us to the Goes canal entrance. Setting sail in the canal caused a certain element of panic in the "rush hour" traffic. An old gaff-rigged boat which has picked up speed is not something some modern boat owners are used to. We stormed under the Zeeland bridge again, then crossed the Oosterschelde to Sas van Goes. The jib furler fouled again, requiring some more attention. We slipped into the lock, and soon were chugging along the canal. There was a slight wait for the Ringbrug, and we had a little difficulty in keeping our distance from the stop-start gin palaces. Why can they not sail at a steady slow speed? Why do they stand on their brakes every five minutes? Designers of such vessels have a lot to answer for.

We went under the quaint lift bridge into the Town Harbour at Goes, thence into a mooring box. Our narrow bow makes it necessary to go in stern first, which is not easy with a quarter mounted prop. There tends to be a bit of panic! However, with a little help from the locals we managed.

We had a good walk round the town and did some shopping. There are some lovely buildings in Goes, old and modern. We had a drink and a bite to eat at a harbourside café. The opulence being demonstrated by the gin palaces was generally disgusting. Big slabs of plastic and chrome cheek by jowl, were hardly in keeping with Goes. Occasionally a waiter would bring a drink out. The most obscene expression of wealth yet was demonstrated by one of these power boats. Fido wanted to go ashore. His skipper pointed a remote control unit. A hydraulic deck lift took Fido down to water level, where a boatman in a 40hp Ridged Inflatable Boat (RIB) waited to take him ashore. When he reached shore, Fido just peed on the lamppost where the common dogs peed. The difference was that Fido had needed about £50,000 of kit and paid hands to get him to the same position.

So many boats were about that I kept the bowsprit run in for the short passage to the lock into Veersmeer. Having got through the Goes bridges all the gin palaces ahead slammed on their brakes. A large passenger ferry was backing up the canal. There was plenty of space for us, but they would not let us through. We found refuge in a winding basin; getting out again was difficult. We locked out safely into the Oosterschelde, then turned up the Zandkreek towards Veersemeer. The Zandkreeksluis/brug was ever unfriendly, still with the curmudgeonly bridge keeper. Having invited boats in, he drops the bridge down on their masts. When the chap in front suddenly slows down, how the hell can I get a move on?

In the Veersemeer we let the rat race get ahead while we set some sail. The waters were very busy, for it was the height of the holiday season. We found our little island again, and moored alongside the jetty. We had a swim, a little walk, ate and went to bed. We then noted that there were anglers with their rods out right by us. How embarrassing! What did they hear? What must they have thought about the invisible swell which set the mast swaying?

The holiday was drawing to a conclusion now. We sailed for Veere. As we approached the town we saw that the landing stage was no place for occupation in a moderate breeze. We therefore decided to lock into the Walcheren Canal, where we found a very convenient landing stage to tie up to. We went ashore to have a look at the town and some lunch. I also had a quick look round a museum and saw a model of what I think was a sailing icebreaker. After Veere we had a very gentle drift up the canal under staysail to Middleberg. The harbourmaster directed us to one of those horrible "box" berths, which was in a very tight position. In all the manoeuvring the propeller fell off. At first I thought the gearbox had gone on the engine. Then I went over the side to check. There was just a bare shaft.

The old harbour was very deep, with several feet of silt and slime at the bottom. In no way could we recover the prop. There was nothing to lift the boat out to fit the spare propeller I kept on board. We would have to go back to Veersemeer and get someone to tow us.

I do not know why the folding prop fell off. Because of the design, you cannot have a split pin to retain the special cylindrical nut. It is my suspicion that the nut broke, possibly because it was pitted with electrolysis. Certainly the edges were brittle when I checked it earlier in the year. I have since learnt my lesson and electrically bonded the engine and the shaft. Incidentally, this should have been done by the original installers, and the failure may have been responsible for the previous propeller problem, when *Deva* was marooned.

With delivery crew lined up, the setback was the last thing we wanted. By this time everyone had gone home. What could I do? Then I had the idea of fitting the prop under water. All I needed was a key to the shaft keyway. I thought about it all night. I rang Brian and told him of the problem. He would bring vice, file and brass.

Next morning I went to the chandlery. Amazingly they had keys for keyways. I had to guess the size from the prop, but bought two on spec. We were in business. I ran through the procedure with Margaret like a surgical operation. We heeled the boat over to lift the prop up a little, so that at least I could breathe. I was surgeon, seated on a sunken bosun's chair. Margaret was nurse. First she handed down the key, which I slotted in the keyway. Then she passed down two elastic bands to hold it in place. The propeller was lowered on a rope. With a bit of a fiddle and a feel I managed to slide the prop on. The hammer was lowered. It is quite difficult to hammer under water. The washer and the nut were sent down next, on thin thread. This was very critical. I bet the Dutch would not have 3/4 Whitworth nuts on sale. There was great relief when the first turn of the nut was made on the thread. With my feet on the dead wood I managed to get a good purchase on the

spanner to wind the nut on. We untied all the support ropes - it worked. The locals were very suspicious. Nobody had ever fitted a prop under water before. We started the engine gingerly in forward drive. There was no vibration, just a prop wash. I ran it for ten minutes, and checked the nut again. Still "OK".

Margaret went to catch her train. I went to the supermarket to stock up for the passage, then went to meet Brian. He was not amused when I told him that I had fixed the prop, and there was no need for the things he had lugged across the North Sea and half Holland. Never mind, we had a very nice meal in a back street restaurant called Le Mug, where coincidentally we met Brian's old skipper. We adjourned to his boat for a brandy or two.

Caroline arrived in the morning, and we stowed up ready to go. The bridge did not open till after 10.00. The bridges on the Walcheren canal were even more cantankerous than usual. Having no astern, we had to approach very gently, so we were not popular. A big ketch broke its gear box and had to be towed in. We went and fetched a tow for her, rather than risk our prop.

We did not lock out into the West Schelde until 12.50. There was hardly any wind, so we had to motor sail much of the way to Blankenberg. Where was the easterly 3-4 which had been promised? Blankenberg was very lively with the trams swishing by, an open air rock band and thousands of people. We had another nice meal, then tried out various clubs and establishments. The mooring was 24 guilders, quite expensive.

We set off for England at daybreak, only to run into thick fog. Fortunately we had the GPS. We put the "electric man" or tiller pilot into gear, and went slowly ahead, straining to work out the whereabouts of shipping. We did hear the bow wave of one ship. Eventually the fog became more patchy, but still without a suitable wind. After a few hours we trailed our mackerel line. Soon we had a bucket full of fish, despite the fact that we were eating them six at a time off the grill. We crossed the shipping lanes, still motor sailing, still without easterly 3-4. The fog came in again, and cleared again, and then we did have a slight breeze. We set the "Bastard", and had an hour's pure sailing! That propeller was working overtime.

We made a landfall before darkness, and found our way in round South Cork. We had considered stopping overnight at Shotley, but as the bar would be shut we carried on up to Mistley, mooring to Foster's pontoon at 00.30 Dutch time. It was not a spectacular crossing, but at least we were safe, and the little engine had only used three gallons since Middleberg!

It was not until the winter that I started to realise that something might be on regarding the European Cup. Ron Valent kept ringing me from Holland to ask questions about races. Unfortunately, he would not take our Tendring Coast Passage Race into account because only Old Gaffers had taken part, even though Bermudans were invited. Nor was he happy with the OGA handicap for the North Sea Race so we must have got him worried.

In the winter we went over to Amsterdam for the VKSJ prizegiving and social in the Amsterdam Rowing Club, taking our 3rd Prize Cup back with us. Again the journey was not what was planned. The Stena Discovery catamaran had her windscreen smashed by a wave and was taken out of service. We took the Eurostar again.

The Dutch were, as always, very pleasant to us. Ron Valent announced the first three in the European Points. They were all British! The lovely Humber yawl *Snippet* was third, the glistening 30 Square Metre *Korybant* was second, and the dirty little *Deva* was first! I learnt later that they had done the calculations in all sorts of different ways with VKSJ and OGA handicaps, but whatever they did *Deva* won by a big margin. It was as if she had jinxed the computer. I thanked the assembled gathering in Amsterdam with due humility.

Whilst everyone was nice to me, I just had a feeling that the cup was really meant for a glistening Twelve Metre with polished bronze winches, fifteen coats of varnish and uniformed crew in white trousers. It was not meant for an old fishing boat sailed by a medical reject. I felt that we had cheated somehow, and sensed that we had degraded the competition. The boating press in the UK were not impressed and the only spark of interest was from the Manningtree and Harwich Standard, and it was only a spark - imagine the difference if we had been European Champion in tiddlywinks or soccer!

I did of course christen the cup at the sailing club with all the crew who had participated. It was only on reflection that I appreciated what the boat had achieved. The boat had been sailed to the best of her ability most of the time, and she had delivered a consistent result in a range of conditions and seas. She was not a new rebuild like so many, and she was a boat which sailed the whole year round. Not only was she capable of ghosting round courses in a light wind, she was also capable of carrying full sail and topsail at hull speed-plus right across the North Sea with three crew perched on her weather rail, with a delivery of six or seven knots mile after mile, so she was very tough as well. She was not a stripped-out racer; she carried liferaft, victuals, the gear for three people, cruising gear, toilet, stove and sink. At nearly four tons displacement on eighteen feet waterline she was no lightweight. Her design must be a true credit to her simple builders. She may not be a winner of a concourse d'elegance or a feature on a prestigious Den Phillips nautical calendar, but underneath there is a very stout heart, and she rates with the best. She won a race for those of modest means and aspirations. She is their European Champion.

A New Partnership,
But What Future?

1997 - 2001

During a summer cruise with my wife, I had come across an unusual boat in a quiet creek by Skippers Island in the Walton Backwaters. She was masthead Bermudan rig, with stainless steel pulpit and push pit, looking very like an early sixties cruiser-racer. Closer inspection revealed that she had an elliptical counter and some rather hefty ironwork at the bow. This was no 60s yacht, it was a gentrified prawner. One of my winter day trips in *Deva* was to go out to Outer Ridge for a spot of fishing, then into the Walton Backwaters for a spot of lunch. Soon I had got to know the old boy, Evan Marshall, who lived on her. Indeed she was only registered at 26ft LOA, but he had lived on her for several years. Yes, she had been a prawner, built in 1937, and must have been one of the last as the yard at Arnside was shut shortly afterwards. I used to call on him for a cuppa and a yarn on a regular basis. He had been a merchant seaman and seen the world.

I was quite interested in the boat, the final development of the type. She carried beam further aft than a true sailing prawner, as she was built for an engine. She also had more depth aft, which enabled her to have an in-line engine and centre-line prop, a combination impossible to achieve in most nobby types; they must have a quarter installation like *Deva*. Her counter is not as pinched either, possibly for the same reason. However, she was certainly meant to sail, with an almost full outside ballast keel. She had the classic hollow garboards, but her bilges were slightly slacker than *Deva*'s. She also had a cheeky little sheer towards the bow, whereas most prawners are fairly straight sheered. She was registered as a yacht in 1948 in Portsmouth, strangely with Bermudan rig, as she was later shown in Lloyds register as a gaffer. If she had been laid up for the war in 1939, she had not spent much time fishing. However, I met a smacksman who had been interested in buying her when she was at Leigh in 1960, and he said that then she was "A proper little nobby". In fact a friend of his bought her and modernised her, so he himself ended up buying the Maldon smack *Joseph T.*

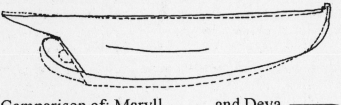

Comparison of: Maryll - - - - and Deva ————

The boat was called *Maryll*, which is Welsh for Mary. It is possible then that she may have been based at one of the North Wales ports when she was first commissioned. It is very difficult to find out. The building of nobbies, especially smaller ones, continued long after many other British coastal regions finished building working sailing vessels. The later ones were powered, often with the ubiquitous Stuart. A picture of the launch of the prawner *Ellen Mount* in 1934 shows that the rig was a little less extreme and the bowsprit much more modest. Some fisheries had a rule or a tradition that the catching had to be carried out under sail as a conservation measure, although power could be used on passage. Rule or not, this seemed to be practice when I first remember seeing working nobbies in the 1950s and 60s. Possibly this was also because many of the boats were powered by ex-army truck engines, which were very thirsty on fuel.

Crossfield's of Arnside shut their yard in 1938, so *Maryll* must have been one of their very last boats. The shipwright Cyril White, of Brightlingsea, worked there in his youth, and told me that they used up all the odd bits of timber to build her. However, they still must have taken some pride in building her, for the planking and the general fit of the frames is better than most I have seen on old fishing boat types.

Evan decided to move ashore. He was considering buying a narrow boat and living on the canals. He particularly wanted a dog. He had had one on *Maryll* until a year earlier, but did not think that it was right to keep a dog on board now. He did not want the hassle of selling the boat through agents, and offered her to me at a very reasonable price. This was a bit of a dilemma. I already had *Deva*, and had no intention of selling her. I knew that there would be very few people who would value her background, and restore her. She would just be bought by a bargain hunter, who would let her go to seed once she needed anything doing. Had she been an Essex smack, I would have been trampled in the rush. The merest fragment of an ex-registered smack or bawley will form the basis of a total rebuild or replica, such is the enthusiasm on the East Coast. Unfortunately this does not extend to other craft as a rule, although I do know of some smackies rebuilding a Shetland Zulu in Suffolk.

If I bought *Maryll*, would I still have time to sail *Deva*? I did not want to embark on a major project which would take all my leisure time. In the end I thought it was worth taking a chance. If it did not work out, I could always sell her again. So the deal was done, and Evan brought her up to Mistley Boatyard. When she came round *Deva* was sailing in the Stour, and we spotted *Maryll* ahead. *Deva* shot through her lee going to windward. Clearly some changes would have to be made.

Evan cleared up his belongings and made arrangements for his brother to pick him up. He left a lot of gear with the boat with the comment that he who travels lightest travels furthest. *Maryll* was mine! I looked about the cabin. She had a little bogey stove port side forward, two bunks, a gas cooker and a plastic sink. There was a toilet, but it was still in its packaging. There was a hanging locker to starboard for storage, and some lockers were under the side decks. Compared with *Deva* she was very spacious. Her keelson was thinner, but made of harder wood, and she had no ballast lying over it. Her slacker bilges gave her greater depth of hull. This was taken aft to enable her to carry a centre-line engine installation, rather than the un-handy quarter installation seen on most motorised nobby types. Her interior was mostly lined with softboard insulation, which concerned me rather.

I put her on *Deva*'s mooring, and had *Deva* lifted out for a brief refit for the classic boat festival. I could not wait to have a sail in *Maryll*. The first thing I noticed was that she was very much heavier on the helm. Her rudder blade was huge compared with *Deva*'s, possibly to make up for the propeller cut-out and the need to control steering at low speed for fishing under power. The Bermudan rig was unfamiliar, but it was a nice day, and I seemed to be able to work something out. I hoisted the main and the big genoa, and we were off. Without any instruments it was difficult to establish a comparison with *Deva*. Running seemed about the same, reaching seemed slower, beating I was not sure about. She certainly did not make the leeway *Deva* does. I expected the weather helm to be much better than with a gaff rig, but actually it was quite considerable in a moderate breeze. Still, she was an interesting boat to sail.

She had an engine, a Petter Mini 6 diesel, which was fine as a pure auxiliary, but not as a passage maker. Unfortunately the splice on the cap shrouds went, causing the stick to bend like a banana, so I had to down sails and motor very slowly all the way up the Stour. Back at the mooring, I examined the damage more closely. The splice was only a tiny clip thing held with a couple of screws. It certainly was not man enough for a masthead rig. A lot of work would be needed to bring the rig up to a sea-going condition. If I was eventually going to replace the rig with gaff, what was the point? So that was the last time *Maryll* sailed under Bermudan rig.

My thoughts were to restore *Maryll* to a working nobby format by taking off the cabin and just having a narrow cockpit. I could squeeze a couple of berths in the forepeak, and if there were more aboard we could use a cockpit tent. *Maryll* would be a fisher-racer, while *Deva* would be the cruiser. I did lots of drawings, and worked out on the boat how I would construct the project. Unfortunately my wife got to hear about my plans and asked how I could contemplate such an operation on the first boat I had had with a decent cabin! Furthermore I would be spending all this money to make something worth less than when I started. She had a point.

The trouble was that I would have two cruisers with very similar functions. I then thought of the option of running one boat in the summer, and one in the winter. *Maryll* would be the summer boat, as she had greater accommodation. Also I would be sailing less in the winter and therefore have more time to complete the alterations. When *Maryll* was completed I would berth her in Dutch waters for my "retirement", commuting over on the high speed ferry. *Deva* would then go back to a continuous commission basis in English waters. I would have a Dutch boat and an English boat.

Most people think it is utter madness to have one wooden boat, with all the maintenance and repair that are necessary. To have two is certifiable. However I have always believed that the difference between having one and having two is highly over-rated, depending on the standard aspired to. Once the hull of a strongly built wooden boat is up to a reasonable standard, the principal differences are the topsides and the brightwork. The Glass Re-inforced Polyester (GRP) boat owner of a new boat will save, although he has to spend several hours polishing and waxing. On an older boat one is likely to have to deal with osmosis, which can often involve the stripping of the gel coat, renewal and re-spraying, specialised and expensive work. The real problem with having two boats are that there is twice as much gear and equipment to maintain and twice the mooring and insurance costs.

The difficulty I had was that *Maryll* did need a lot of work on her, not the original bits, but the 60s work. I had an autumn, a winter and a spring to get her into useable condition. I planned to launch her for the 1998 Classics. From what I had seen on the mooring, she needed a new rudder, bullring or gammon iron and keel band on the bottom. On the topsides she needed new rubbing strakes. The cabin sides and cockpit coamings were too thin, and were too ugly. She needed a completely new rig, including spars, sails, standing and running rigging, bowsprit bitts and chainplates. Inside she needed a new engine, shaft and propeller. She needed to have the toilet fitted, electrics and two more berths in the cabin accommodation. There were of course plenty of other items which needed doing or replacing at a later date. I had a budget of £6,000.

When *Deva* returned from her bid for European Gold, work began in earnest. Sarah helped me to measure the boat, so that a rig could be designed. I had some detailed measurements from the Royal Mersey Rivers Class rules, which I scaled up proportionally for *Maryll*. I later found out that *Deva* is slightly squatter and fatter than the Rivers Class she gave birth to, so *Maryll* ended up a bit over-rigged.

I had quotes from three sailmakers - Heard & Clatworthy, Jeckells and James Lawrence. The first mentioned was slightly the lowest. However the firm broke up as, I was told, Gayle Heard was retiring. Sean Clatworthy did not want to take the job on. So the job went to James Lawrence of Brightlingsea.

Graham Pearson of Mistley Quay workshop supplied me with the timber for the gaff, boom and bowsprit, as well as that for the cabin sides and rubbing strakes. He also cut the corners off with his saw. It was really good timber. Timber for the mast I obtained at St Osyth Boatyard. Andy Harman had an old pitchpine beam from the Great Eastern Hotel at Clacton. He also let me use a corner of the shed, where the smack *ADC* was being built, for planing and finishing the mast.

Thus I had three work sites for the project - Clacton, Mistley Boatyard and my garage at home. This was quite important, as I had subcontracted some aspects of the work. The boatyard, which was really a shipyard, did the keel band and rudder, whilst Gerald Abbott installed the new engine. I was quite lucky to get the engine, a current model Yanmar 1GM10 like *Deva*'s. It came out of a larger boat where it was a bit undersized. Several used notes changed hands at a certain marine engineers, but at least it was a third of the price of a new one. I was also lucky that Gerald managed to sell the Petter for a very good price.

The installation was still going to be expensive with new bearers as well, but the budget was looking very good.

Of course, with such a project I did find slightly unexpected problems to solve. The top rubbing strake, not the original, was too small to cover the joint between the covering board on the deck and the top plank or strake of the hull. Water had got in behind, and there were areas of wet rot which needed chopping out in both the topstrake and the covering board. Some corruption was about to start behind the cabin insulation, but I caught this in the nick of time. Otherwise the hull seemed very good, which was a relief, especially as I had bought the boat before seeing her lifted out, without an independent survey.

I sanded the bottom to bare wood, and soaked the planking with linseed oil and Cuprinol before applying the primer paint. I often wonder why more people do not use linseed oil - it really does penetrate the timber and stabilises it. The cabin sides and cockpit coaming were cut out of quarter inch mahogany, and bonded in place with epoxy. They were then treated with linseed oil and mahogany stain. The ugly square windows were filled in, and new elliptical ones formed. The replacement rubbing strakes were a bit of a beast to bend and fit. I was screwing one of the last fastenings on the starboard side upper, and the force I was using on the brace and bit transferred its way down the ladder and it buckled under the strain. I went down with a hell of a crash and damaged my back. My wife, who had been bravely helping me, was not impressed! That did put me out of action for a while, and even now I have to be careful how I sit.

The spar making went very well, especially with the help of an electric plane. I cannot understand why people use aluminium poles so readily. *Deva*'s mast has lasted nearly a century so the reason cannot be rot. It is much easier to make fittings for a wooden mast which are really strong. Pete Osborne kindly towed my mast from St Osyth to Mistley on Eddie Williams's trailer. I fixed the running rigging on the mast and fitted the chainplates. They actually went in the original positions of the old gaff rig, and I used the same holes through the frames too. Moray McPhail, of Classic Marine, had done an excellent job. I rang up the sailmaker to see how things were going. I wanted to fix a date for fitting the standing rigging. Mark Butler did not believe we were ready for him. He had been down to Mistley to look at another boat, and thought that there was a lot more to go. He still did not believe me until the team fitting the shrouds reported back. Then it was panic at Brightlingsea, but they did deliver just on time.

David Shipley helped me with the launch, and we toasted *Maryll*'s rebirth to a gaffer in champagne. Gerald checked the engine, and it started first time. We were off! The first job was to go to the mooring, leave *Maryll* there and bring *Deva* back. The boat seemed to steer well, but I could not understand why the tiller appeared to have fifteen degrees helm on it. It could not just be the paddlewheel effect. We quickly transferred essential gear between the boats, and took *Deva* back to the shore to be craned out. Later, when the tide had ebbed, I waded through the mud out to *Maryll*. I was worried that the rudder had come adrift, but the reason became obvious when I looked under the counter. The rudder stock had been welded on at fifteen degrees to the blade!

With the Classic Boat Festival approaching, we did not have time to have the boat slipped for rectification. Structurally it was no problem; it just took a bit of getting used to. We bent the sails on, hoisted them, and cast off. Both Mark Butler and Gayle Heard thought I had got the centre of effort of the sail plan too far ahead of the centre of lateral resistance of the hull. Instead of wanting to weathercock into the wind, as a boat should, she might want to turn the other way. This could be dangerous in a squall, as the wind could not be spilled out of the sail. However, the nobby does not behave in the same way as ordinary boats. It is something to do with the asymmetrical shape of the hull when she heels, the shape of the bow and stern waves and the leverage of the rig. Trial and error over twenty years had designed *Deva's* rig, and *Maryll's* was drawing on that experience. *Maryll* actually balanced very well for a gaffer, which was a relief.

Laden with beer and large portions of pig, Shippers and I were racing up the coast to Southwold at the start of the East Coast Classics. When we had been up to the Lowestoft Fish Fayre and Smack Race a year earlier, we had called in at Southwold for a pit stop and found it very pleasant, so when Adele and John Buckley of the local boatyard, Harbour Marine Services, thought of staging a smack and classic boat rally I immediately offered the OGA services and added it as a header to the East Coast Classics. Unfortunately Lowestoft and Maritime Ipswich clashed. Boats would have the choice of sailing south to Ipswich after the rally or north to Lowestoft.

A good brisk south-westerly pushed us along. The bawlies *Bona* and *Good Intent* were sailing with us, when I noticed the other bawley, *Blackbird*, steaming up behind. I thought it a waste to use the engine just to get to the pub earlier in such a fine sailing breeze. *Blackbird* came past us as if we were standing still, and I could not see any sign of an exhaust. What I did see were multicoloured stripes of anti-fouling. Apparently she was being used as a test bed for the different types of paint, and, whatever it was, it was making her shift. She also overtook the larger, more heavily rigged boats. She was clear winner of the passage race.

After the usual jollifications we had a race off the town, sponsored by the local brewery, Adnams. It was a very good turnout, as every entrant had been promised a case of Broadside strong ale. I have never seen a prizegiving like it. There was a huge mountain of beer cases, and watching all the skippers and crews swaying back to their boats in the dusk clutching cases of ale was very amusing. As I watched the sunrise from the bar I thought what a beautiful place Southwold was. It is totally different from the Essex coast. The light is different, the sea is different and the town is something special - delightfully crazy, with breweries and a lighthouse in its midst, and some lovely buildings and beautifully laid out greens. If only Walton and Clacton were like it.

Adnams were also sponsoring the passage race to Harwich, so *Maryll* was really laden down with beer cases up to the cabin ceiling. It was nice to be able to present them at Ipswich in sight of the Tolly Cobbold Brewery, who had refused to support us! Mandy and Bob had just finished fitting out *Polly*, and she looked a real picture. Mandy was supervising the rigging of the boat, when I approached her from behind with a photographer from *Classic Boat* magazine, saying "Mandy, look natural". She gave me an even worse look when I arrived half an hour later with the Mayor of Ipswich, but we did award her the Concourse Prize! During Maritime Ipswich I unexpectedly had to do an interview with a rather refined lady from Radio 3. I managed to get her onto *Boadicea*. This vessel, an Essex smack, is probably the oldest sailing vessel in commission, having been built in about 1808. She has been rebuilt a few times since then, but her shape and form is that of Nelson's day. She has been in the same Mersea family for generations, and is now owned by Reuben Frost, who was on board with his dog and family on that occasion.

The Classics Week was based at Suffolk Yacht Harbour, Levington. Shotley Marina had suddenly told us at the eleventh hour that they did not want to host the festival. Not only the Yacht Harbour, which was managed by a sympathetic chap who had a West Solent, but also the Haven Ports Yacht Club came to our rescue. Brian Tower provided a huge army tent, whilst Pete "the Knife" Elliston and Don Windley organised the entertainment from amongst us. The change in format from the more commercial approach of Shotley appeared to go down very well with the entrants. The grand finale of the classics was on the last day, just as were packing up. A tornado came through, and the tent levitated fifty feet in the air and attempted to fly over some woods. It was quite a display!

The racing in the classics was a little disappointing for the *Maryll*. Although she balanced well enough, there was something wrong with her windward performance. Coming out of a tack, she seemed to take a long time to get going. There wasn't any drive in her; she felt dead in the water. Sarah, who was crewing on another boat, the Zeeschow *Roker*, said rather unkindly that I should have a poster on her saying "My other boat's the *Deva*!". I felt sure that the trouble was something to do with the staysail, but I could not be specific. The sailmaker came out with me after the classics and adjusted the lead of the sheet, but could not really see anything wrong.

The East Coast Old Gaffers Race at Mersea was a tough race, with plenty of water coming on board. When we were racing from Bench Head to the line we called down for more ale. Instead of the beer coming up, we had a question - "How much longer is the race going to last?". We shouted down "Pass the beer up Shippers, don't mess around". Then we looked below and saw the lee bunk under water. Shippers dived under water to get some bottles. We just about made the line before the ship became dangerous. We hove to and pumped her out. We unclogged the electric bilge pump. Later that night she nearly filled up again, as the stern gland nut had come loose.

In August that year we sailed to Portsmouth for the International Festival of the Sea (IFOS). We had quite a dusting getting down Channel, but the boat proved that she could do it. Even if she was not much of a racer she was inherently a good sea boat, capable of making passages. This is particularly critical in the Channel, where there are several tidal gates to work, and a boat speed of about five to six knots is advantageous. We met up with the smack *Ellen* at Dover. Jane Rule had insisted that *Ellen* was only 26ft long, and she only paid the same as we did. We also sailed down in company with the 50ft Boston Smack *Telegraph*. She had no engine and had headwinds to face. Whereas we could get to a port every night, they had to sit it out at sea, although once a strong blow made them seek shelter in Rye Harbour. To enter such a narrow unknown harbour under sail in a blow took some courage.

Our knowledge of the South Coast was limited. We had on board a 1943 English Channel Handbook, which basically said "Keep the Hun on the left". It is a pretty monotonous coastline compared with our East Coast rivers area. We went into Brighton Marina with the waves crashing over the breakwater. Where do people go for a day's sail round there? We went aboard *Noorderzon*, which was also on her way to IFOS. Even she had had a dusting.

From Brighton we made the holy waters of the Solent in one hit. I was surprised to see that few boats were coming in and out of the Solent. We could hear chatter on the VHF and called up the IFOS guardship, which was a naval vessel. We could hear them. Yachts next to the guardship could hear us. But could the dear old RN. Our name confused them not much Welsh spoken there obviously, but eventually after much delay we were told to proceed to the guardship and await instructions. More delay. We radioed them again. "We still can't see you," this pompous voice replied. "We are half a cable off your port quarter," we said. It worries me that the RN is so vulnerable to a stealth prawner, which is apparently invisible to its radar, VHF, sonar and the eyesight of its lookouts!

By the time that we had approval to enter, the tide had gone and we had a fearsome ebb to face. I was appalled at the management of the harbour and the ill manners of all the power boats and naval vessels. Speed limits were totally ignored. The Solent was not in the same league as Harwich. We berthed in the usual dirty dock reserved for traditional vessels on these occasions. The usual overpriced beer in plastic glasses and fast food on polystyrene plates were on sale. The usual blocked portaloos were laid on for us. That is the way which seems to be for us at big public festivals which everybody goes to.

It was some relief that we escaped the IFOS for the Solent Old Gaffers Race, which was to start from Cowes. Caroline Peeke, ex-Stour SC came down to help Shippers and myself in the race. We had a gentle sail to the Mecca of yachting, which I thought was a bit like an up-market Brightlingsea. We moored alongside some pontoons on piles out in the river. I was pleasantly surprised that the mooring cost was reasonable. We pumped up the inflatable and went ashore. The sailing club there was a very friendly place, and we were absolutely delighted to see that Adnams Ale was on sale. It really made us feel at home! We had a hog roast to devour, and good company to talk to. It was a bit more refined than the East Coast, no Estuary drawl to be heard, but these were the Old Gaffers on the Solent. Whereas on the East Coast there is the tradition of smacks, barges and Maurice Griffiths, the chaps on the Solent have to "gaff" in a much more hostile environment than we do. The OGA on the Solent might be smaller in number than on the East Coast, but they stick together better than we do.

With the entry swollen because of IFOS, about eighty boats were on the line and it was a beautiful sight. It was slightly different from an East Coast Old Gaffers Race. There were not the twenty or thirty smacks with their fidded topmasts, long bowsprits, straight stems and counter sterns. However, there were many more beautiful gaff yachts. *Partridge* and *Marigold* were two prime examples. *Bonita*, a Crossfield yacht with clipper bow and prawner hull, was of particular interest to me. Built about 1880, she must have been one of the very first hulls to demonstrate the classic prawner shape. She was owned by Mike Beckett, one of three brothers to have gaffers. George Beckett, the vice president of the Solent Area, was sailing *Young Alert*.

The start was just a drift with the tide eastwards, not a breath of wind. Shippers pointed at a mark which drifted by, and asked if that was a turning mark. We looked at the chart - nobody else seemed to be turning. Then we noticed a couple of boats close the shore and anchor. We checked the bearing and position; yes, it was the mark. However, we were quite a way out in twelve fathoms of water. Our competitors would not have thought that any East Coast Muddy would have carried more than ten feet of chain, but we also had *Deva*'s chain on board. Anchoring was no problem!

We dropped the headsails and over the side went the "lunch hook", as they call anchors in the Solent. We rigged the black ball to show that we were at anchor, and laid the table in the cockpit for a magnificent lunch. Then we really started to pull through the fleet, who were being swept away by the tide. Three courses, wine and coffee later, we washed dishes and put everything away. A dainty little breeze picked up and we weighed anchor. We followed Dick Dawson in *Lone Wolf* and rounded the next mark, and then it was a short run home. We had an old spinnaker on board, but I noticed in the rules that the Solent OGA did not allow balloon spinnakers. However, the boat seemed to do pretty well. I was quite pleased that she compared well with the Falmouth oyster dredgers, which have a frightening reputation. Open boats with huge sail plans, they are very keenly sailed in the West Country. We also got the edge on *Ziska*, a 37ft prawner. This was the prawner that in 1970 my dad and I had very nearly bought in Plymouth, but, although she had been reasonably sound and fairly priced, I had not been able to bear parting with my beloved *Deva*! I had a look at *Ziska* in Portsmouth. Ashley, her skipper, was a shipwright, and he had fitted her out for blue water cruising. She was quite different from when I had seen her last. Her bowsprit was offset the stem, she had bulwarks, she was flush decked and had a steering thwart aft across the bulwarks. It was as if someone had converted her to an Essex smack. I went below and was amazed at the spaciousness. I then realised that the iron keelson she used to have was no longer there. Of course, most boats do not have the prawner's raised keelson, so he could not see the point. She already had a ballast keel anyway. Possibly the exposed drying moorings in the North-West made a keelson more necessary, and certainly a keelson spreads the mast loadings along the boat. However, Ashley has sailed *Ziska* across the Atlantic, without an engine, without any trouble. The proof of the pudding is in the eating.

We had a very pleasant surprise at the prizegiving. We had won the Edgar Marsh Trophy and the Freda Trophy, and come second in class - all through having a decent lunch!

Maryll was laid up that autumn and *Deva* was launched for the winter. *Maryll* needed a lot more work on her still. The cockpit seats needed raising to limit the amount of green water we took over the side. The berths needed doing, and I fitted a heater. *Deva* sailed out of Titchmarsh Marina at Walton for the winter months.

In the following year I managed to get *Maryll* to sail better. The trouble had been all in the staysail. Because of my unhappiness about the staysail, Mark offered to replace it with new one or re-cut the old Bermudan genoa to become a tow-foresail. Mandy had given me *Polly's* staysail, which she had in turn off the smack *Lizzie Annie*, so I went for the tow-foresail, as that way it was three sails for the price of one. We launched just in time for the East Coast Classics. Our first port of call was Shotley to pick up Alice. Alice had come all the way from Scotland. Originally she had intended to cruise her own boat to Southwold. We had met "on the Net", which was the subject of a bit of leg pulling. Alice was used to racing proper boats. She was also very clever, with PhD and string of other letters after her name. However, she did not seem to mind us two old fogies, and indeed she was very useful.

We raced up to Southwold with a following wind, so it was not until the Sole Bay Race, with a Manningtree lass called Lucy also on board, that we had our first chance to go to windward. With the north wind and tidal set a great deal of beating was involved. Instead of the working staysail, we set the tow-foresail. The start was on the run, and all hell was let loose as the committee decided to move the mark to deeper water just as several smacks were about to round it. Eventually we turned and came on the wind, and the boat began to drive as she had not done all the previous season. I could not work out why *Vashti* was going one way, and the rest of the fleet were going the other. Then I realised that it was a difference of windward ability. *Maryll* was sailing closer to *Vashti's* course, and started to gain on the rest of the fleet. Probably the length of the sea was a factor in our being beaten over the water by only *Vashti*, a red hot late 50s ocean racer with Mylar/Kevlar Tapedrive sails.

When we returned to Ipswich and Levington we had new competition in the form of *Airlie*. At thirty feet and only six feet beam, she had a beautiful clipper bow and counter stern. Looking every bit a Victorian gentleman's yacht, she was the result of a design competition in a yachting magazine. She was actually faster than *Maryll*, but sometimes we could get a tactical edge on her for part of a race. She was a very good vessel to watch and learn from as her skipper Robert Berk really knew how to sail her. Being a longer vessel, she had a slightly worse handicap rating than *Maryll*, so if we could keep near her we had no need to worry about the rest. After the race to Mistley, we took on Molly from Amsterdam. Molly had a Deben Cherub, *Sea Nymph*, which she looked after immaculately, as they do in Holland. She showed me photos of restoration work on the keel which put my bodging to shame. She also was very interested in Shippers' technical views on Vire Marine engines, taking copious notes in Dutch whilst speaking in English.

The really big event of the year 1999 was meant to be Europe Week. This had last been held in Britain in 1910, and for some reason the European Classic Yacht Union which is based in Norway wanted to hold it again in the UK. They looked at a number of sites on the South and East Coasts. The OGA World Secretary asked if I could help them over the East Coast. With West Mersea Yacht Club we suggested that they might want to stage it here. WMYC had their centenary, we had the East Coast Old Gaffers Race. Furthermore we could have it back-to-back with the Dutch Classic Yacht Regatta at Hellevoetsluis, linked with our North Sea Classic Passage Race. There was talk by the ECYU of huge sponsorship deals, crews being put up in hotels, special buses, gala dinners. How was the local economy of Mersea Island going to cope?

Unfortunately it was only talk. There was no sponsorship. ECYU were now not interested. The trouble was that we had already announced it. The ECYU might be able to hide from the flak in Norway, but we could not. So West Mersea YC and the OGA decided to go it alone. The Yacht Club were having centenary celebrations, which could be the Europe finale as well. We were going to be there for Gaffers Race anyway. So plan B, a more modest, realistic event was laid on. WMYC went to Hamburg to drum up support for the event.

However, the publicity and the coverage we were able to get were very limited. There seemed be a conspiracy by the yachting press as well as the ordinary media to keep it under wraps. After all the work we had put in to save the event, and various reputations, it was a sad situation indeed.

The actual sailing event was very good. Despite the best negative efforts of the press, word did get round in local pub and club eventually. After starting slowly entries poured in at the eleventh hour. Admittedly the foreign representation was limited to a few Dutch and a solitary Norwegian Eight Metre, which had been shipped over to publicise Europe Week 2000! Thank goodness our own people supported us; we had two hundred boats taking part in various events during the week.

The winds were generally quite brisk, giving exciting sailing. In our class we were up against the local racing smacks like *Charlotte Ellen*, *Peace*, *Dorothy* and *Boadicea*, who knew the waters and the marks much better than we did. However *Maryll*'s new-found windward ability helped, even if the smacks flew away from her on the run, and we were doing quite well in the points series, nailing up firsts and seconds. Unfortunately we blew a race we should have won easily. *Maryll* made a flying start out in clear wind to windward, leaving the smacks floundering. Then we noticed them rounding a mark half a mile astern. We could not work it out, because we were definitely sailing the course shown on the committee boat when we had sailed past. We heard some chat on the radio. They had changed the course on the five minute gun, so we ended up being second in the series by a point.

After the racing they had all the celebrations, including air displays and fireworks. I was stuck in the computer room - a glitch in the spreadsheet had made a mess of all the Old Gaffers Race results. Time and time again we reworked the results. Eventually we had some sort of answer which was vaguely acceptable.

On the Sunday we had a sail past. Brian, Shippers and the lovely Swedish Lena Reekie took the *Maryll* round. Lena had signed on for the voyage to Holland. I was on the yacht club balcony with the top brass, including the Lord Lieutenant of Essex, the Acting Commodore Richard Taylor and Mrs. Sue Taylor herself. Sue was our very efficient and effective OGA representative at West Mersea. Most Islanders lived in trepidation of her, and did exactly as she told them. The Lord Lieutenant was to take the salute; my humble role was to help with the commentary. I saw *Maryll* come by with all her bunting up. There were one or two "trophies" amongst the flags. His Lordship did not know that he was saluting some of Lucy's apparel.

Almost straight after the sail past we had to start the race to Holland. Sue took a yacht out to the line as start boat, with *Maryll* in hot pursuit. There seemed to be general panic amongst the other competitors, who seemed far less ready than we were. We made a perfect start alone, and wondered where the others were. A lot of chatter on the radio made me look at the instructions. WMYC had prepared the general race programme with start times. I had prepared and dished out to the competitors the sailing instructions for that particular race. The start times did not match! After quite a bit of debate we worked out that we were in the wrong. You start a race later than advertised, but certainly not earlier; the sailing instructions took precedence. Oh dear, what a mess! And we were sinking too.

I could not work out why we kept getting water over the floorboards. The boat was close hauled on the starboard tack, but not taking any waves in the cockpit. Why wasn't the electric bilge pump dealing with it? Shippers looked under the floorboards, fished out the bilge pump and found that, far from removing the water, it was siphoning it in! We tried stuffing something into the outlet, but under water it would not stay in. We turned about on the other tack, and headed back for Mersea.

A lot of banter from other boats about Holland being the other way did not help my temper. Eventually I threw all the rubbish out of the counter, stuck my head in and drilled a small hole in the bilge pump pipe. I was not sure whether I would get a squirt of water coming in or break the siphon. If it were the former we would have to go in for repairs and retire. With great relief I heard the hiss of the siphon breaking. We crossed the line at Mersea, went about and restarted.

We missed the tide at North East Gunfleet, and a Dante's Inferno of a thunderstorm broke on us when we rounded. A veritable waterfall poured from the cockpit down the companionway, all rainwater and hail. During this time one of the Dutch boats, *Fifth Symphony*, went aground on a sandbank. Paul Wright on *Vashti* heard the calls to the lifeboat, and because he had a Dutch crew he acted as a relay vessel to get over the language problem. *Symphony* was towed off, and continued her passage to Holland under power. Meanwhile *Maryll* picked up a fair wind, and soon we reached the killing grounds for the mackerel. Brian was trolling off the counter, Shippers was cooking the catch, I was eating, the boat steered itself, and we were offshore racing! It seemed a very fair arrangement to me; it took eight minutes for a fish to be processed from the sea to my stomach.

I went below for a snooze, and woke up later wondering why Brian could not steer the boat in the building seas. It was now blowing a force five on the quarter, and we were under full sail. I said to Brian "Look, you anticipate where she is going to swing, and give her a little twitch on the helm before it happens." "You bloody take her then, she needs a reef in," he said, which is quite something for Brian to say. I took her and swore to myself, and ate considerable quantities of humble pie. We saw *Snippet* in the distance, but no one else on the passage. The seas continued to build with the wind, and by the time we approached the Dutch coast they were getting very steep, nasty and breaking. Although it was terrifying to look astern, *Maryll* rose to every occasion. We had to put in a couple of dangerous gybes whilst looking for the line, and some more as we pushed up the entrance channel against the ebb. We really were shattered when we locked into the Oosterschelde, and I went up the wrong channel. By the time we found our way out again and got into Zierekzee, with a stray piece of rope round our prop, it was dark.

Maryll had been no *Deva*, but she had actually made the best elapsed time of the gaffers, and came fourth on handicap. We had a reasonable Hellevoetsluis, making a couple of splendid starts with highly risky "Port tack flyers". We had Molly "Mallone" aboard, and it was quite something to see the shock on competing Dutch skippers' faces at the stream of Netherlands invective coming from underneath the sails of a British boat. With Brian shouting "Hold your course" from the bows as we crossed the line of foaming bowsprits, it was total confusion. Our main concern was to keep a watch on the top British boats, *Mary Ritchie* and *Snippet*. If we could keep them within reach, with our better handicap we would win. Unfortunately I did not watch a certain Belgian boat, which slipped ahead of us near the end of the first race. We tacked in her wake, and tacked again to cross the line on starboard, knowing full well that she would have to go port tack to cross. The skipper got the shock of his life when he saw what our game was, and went out of control. I tacked again to avoid a collision, but he still grazed us before dropping astern to let us take the line. I did not protest, but drank all his beer instead, satisfied with our victory. However, I found out later that the handicappers were not satisfied, for, although the Belgian was a bigger boat, she had a better handicap. *Maryll* did win the next race, but on the final day's two very short races gambles on windshifts did not quite pay off. *Maryll* had to make do with second place in the series, and third prize in the European Challenge Cup. The boat in many ways was technically faster than *Deva*, but she lacked her luck and mysterious magic.

On the trip back to England I found out why the pundits do not recommend having a skinfull before setting sail. Jim and Brian came over on the ferry to help me get the boat back. Jim's dad, who lives in Germany, gave them a lift from the Hook to Middleberg. We had a bit of a "Lads night out" at a pub called the Mug, which had a whole range of traditional beers on offer as well as good food. Unfortunately we did not have a day spare to recover and had to set out straight away. The sea was very greasy and we all felt very ill. Eventually we made Mistley Quay, and the engine promptly failed. There was a defect in the head casting which allowed water to go into the cylinder. I had to sail from the quay to the mooring after unloading.

Later that year *Maryll* won her class at the Swale Match, and the Maldon Town Regatta and OGA Anniversary Rally. They were very easy wins for the fastest boat. We also went to the Laying Up Race on the Blackwater, beating down the Wallet against a seven. The race was cancelled when we arrived at West Mersea, something to do with a force nine. We sailed the course up to Maldon, and I suppose it was a two-reef breeze.

In October *Maryll* was laid up and *Deva* launched. There is something strange about getting in a "fresh" boat when everyone else's boat is either laying up or looking worn out. By this time I had a new member of crew, Barbara. Several years previously I had put my name down for crew with an agency, Crewseekers. I had very little interest. Who wants to sail on the grubby East Coast in an antiquated little wooden boat when there are all these proper yachts to sail on in respectable waters like the Solent and beyond?

Barbara's reason for choosing *Deva* out of all the respectable vessels was that she was the only one in commission in the winter. We had exchanged email addresses, and I had sent her a picture of the boat. However, neither knew what the other looked like. We agreed a rendezvous at Mistley Quay, but there was no agreement about me wearing a white carnation. I looked around at the various people on the quay for somebody who looked like the person I had spoken to on the phone. Feeding the swans was a woman in her late thirties, with a hair-do that Cher would have killed for. Couldn't be she. She must have decided not to come - must have come to her senses. I started unloading the inflatable, and this woman nervously approached me.

Barbara is a very unusual and interesting person. She is a leading geneticist from Cambridge – has given talks to international conferences in Miami and that type of thing. She rode bicycles and horses; she went diving; she was an ultra distance runner - ran across Wales in one go. Her "ex" had a cruiser at Maldon, so she had some experience of the East Coast. The first sail in *Maryll* started in nice weather. It was only a short sail on the tide. Off Parkeston, as we turned to come back, a storm blew up, but she did not seem to mind. This impressed me even more than the hair. However, regular sailing partners have to be able to relate socially. She had already made some remark about Northerners being thick, without realising that I was one! Barbara clearly came from a higher socio-economic standing than mine - Cambridge is a bit more up market and cultured than Manningtree. Also her intellect was far in excess of mine. I took her to the Stour Sailing Club to see how she would get on with my friends there. The Stour Sailing Club is quite unusual in that its membership is mostly local, and drawn from a very wide social base. The factory worker drinks with the farmer. The fisherman drinks with the yachtsman. You do not stand on ceremony without getting taken down a peg. Barbara seemed to get on very well with them, and within the hour had been given a nickname, DNA! I took her to Pontet's. Graham Pontet is an artist and interior designer, highly cultured, who lives in a Japanese interior. It is a totally unexpected atmosphere, and somehow it encourages conversation and brainstorming, lubricated with a continuous flow of wine. I've left there in an evening and wondered why everyone was off to work, then realised that it was 7.30 in the morning! Pontet was very impressed with Barbara's background, and called her "Cambridge".

After the culture of Cambridge, goodness knows what she thought of the madness of Manningtree. But then she had to face the Old Gaffers. We had decided to move our AGM from Maldon to Woolverstone. Maldon were charging us a lot of money, and the facilities were limited. For Woolverstone we arranged more of a party, with a gaffers rally and shanty band. We set off from Walton, in company with the Bawley *Bona*. Shippers could not come, but Tessa Mackenzie said she would come for the trip, as her smack was laid up. Tessa is a lovely girl with salt in her veins and she has a lovely sister, and is actually a very powerful woman holding down an important job. Later Barbara confided that it was unusual that there were so many powerful, attractive women with gaffers and classic yachts. Apparently in the modern GRP navy it is all testosterone and machismo. Sure, the skippers do have "wifeys" or "gurlies", but they are just appendages or decorative items. I had never appreciated this before, but I must know more people with modern boats than with old boats, but none with women owners. I said to Barbara that it must be because girls like pretty things, and gaffers are prettier. That was the first of many politically incorrect statements to be made by me.

The sail up to Woolverstone was interesting, not just because I had two attractive ladies as crew. On the beat to Harwich Harbour *Deva* had actually overtaken *Bona*, but once we came into smoother water and fairer wind *Bona* began to catch us rapidly, but not quite enough. We tied up alongside *Bona* after she had berthed. The AGM was a great do. Lots of people attended, we had a good meeting and some welcome new blood and new women on the committee. I "came to" next day to find the marina moving by. *Bona* was under way, with *Deva* still tied on. A cup of coffee was passed over. Barbara used the luxury facilities. I had a stroll round the deck. The interesting thing was that *Deva* was being towed at higher than hull speed by a boat that she had overtaken previously. Ian, *Bona*'s skipper, concluded that having *Deva* alongside must have changed or broken the natural wave formation properties of *Bona*'s hull, so reducing resistance and increasing speed. Therefore, could he borrow *Deva* to tie alongside for the next smack race?

The winter sails of the last year of the twentieth century were marvellous. Whatever the weather, Barbara would drive over in her BMW, and we would set out from Walton. The clouds would part, the wind blow a fair breeze, we would have a delightful sail in *Deva* on our own North Sea, sharing it with no other. We would come back to land and people would say "You haven't been out in this?". *Deva* could really work her magic. Once there was a blizzard on land, yet we were fine out at sea, quite warm as well, for the open sea had yet to cool down. The bird life in the Backwaters was incredible, and the seals so friendly. When returning from a trip up the Orwell we found a chap stranded with two dogs on the banks at High Hill. We called out the lifeboat and stood by, just in case the tide came in too quickly. The seals arrived and did all sorts of tricks to amuse the dogs.

That winter passed all too quickly. Suddenly the waters were no longer exclusively ours. The bawley *Good Intent* (Bad Intentions!) came alongside one Sunday lunch time. Spring was back again. We had to share the East Coast with other boats. It was then that Barbara appreciated how tied up I was with the OGA and event organisation. There were events throughout the summer, and she did not want to race. I tried to explain that old gaffers races were not like proper yacht racing, but more of a rally, and that the "après gaff" social really was good fun. She came to a couple of events, and seemed to like the company. But it wasn't quite the same. It was not what she had signed up to. Suddenly there were lots of others coming on the boat, people had to be fitted in whom I had promised sails to. I was no longer the same host - mind on OGA business, no time for my friends.

Thus Barbara did not come to the East Coast Classics, which really were a new departure from the old Shotley festivals. Because nobody could host us for any length of time, we decided to have a roving festival, racing and socialising from place to place. Virtually every day was totally different in style and format. We started with a weekend at Walton, guests at the Walton and Frinton Yacht Club. We had arranged to berth the big boats in the pond, and for the little boats to have a race round the islands on the Saturday and a picnic on the Sunday. It was real Swallows and Amazons stuff, very well organised by Tessa. Alice came down from Scotland and joined me, Shippers and Dave Hart. Next day was a pursuit race to Mistley Quay, where we lunched heartily in the Thorn, then dropped down to Wrabness for a superb barbeque and international cabaret act, arranged by Don and Ali of *Good Intent*. Tuesday was a race up to Pin Mill and lunch at the Butt and Oyster, before going to Levington and the Haven Ports Yacht Club for a social. Wednesday was a nice 04.00 start for the passage race up to Southwold. At Southwold we had a regatta day, and vast quantities of the local brew. Having barely recovered from that, we were off, racing to Lowestoft. We finished the week with a smack race off the front and a display at the Fish Fayre. The social at the Royal Norfolk and Suffolk Yacht Club went on through the night. The club steward dressed up as Father Christmas. Mario Price came straight from a gig to play us through to sunrise. It was great fun, and a very nice way of taking a holiday on the East Coast, which was far more satisfying than a Cowes Week type of regatta, where there is nothing but serious racing round the same boring cans.

Although the weather was not entirely to *Maryll's* satisfaction, we came top equal with *Bona* in the Points Series. Consistent reasonable placing had paid off.

Barbara did start coming again, and we planned to go on the OGA cruise to Belgium and Holland straight after the Old Gaffers Race. Shippers could not come, but Brian was willing. We had a nice sail down to West Mersea, but then things started to go wrong. As usual I got tied up with OGA business, and I neglected my friends again. We had a dreadful old gaffers race, and after a row with me Barbara left us at Levington. Perhaps she did the right thing, because we had a rough passage to Holland. The weather was fairly bad when we started off but was forecast to moderate. The seas were especially big with the north wind, and we lowered the mainsail, just going under tow foresail and jib. For some reason we have a perfect slot with those sails on a beam reach, and *Maryll* was still doing over six and a half knots. The forecast was revised upwards, but we were past the point of no return. By the Shipwash, the high speed ferry came by at forty knots and swamped us. It was going to be a wet passage! The seas grew and grew, and it was getting very difficult to dodge the breaking crests. We found to our horror that the pumps were not working to capacity. Because the water kept sloshing up the side of the cabin when we rolled, the electric pump kept switching off. And the big hand pump's inlet pipe was too restricted. This had never been a problem in ordinary cruising before, but because we were taking so much water from spindrift and the wave crests breaking over us Brian had to pump almost continuously. My life was in his hands. We had to slow down so we did not make an entry to Flushing before daybreak. We made a successful landfall after negotiating an unlit half tide channel, and then saw *Vashti* just astern. *Woodstock* was a couple of miles behind her, but the rest of the fleet had not made it.

On returning from Holland we brought with us a Mussel Pot from Middleharniss, for the wedding of Pete the Knife and Sarah on a barge at Maldon. Shippers and I decided to sail to the wedding to deliver the present. I was quite surprised to get a text message on my mobile phone from Barbara asking if she could have a sail from Brightlingsea. I think she wanted to see if her ex's boat was still about, and make a return to Maldon. At Maldon, *Good Intent*, *Bona*, *Roker* and *Letitia* were moored up. As soon as Sarah was married she went for a sail on *Bona* in her wedding outfit!

Barbara had one more sail with me at the Walton and Wolverstone Rally, although we hadn't really made it up. I was due to go for a hernia operation which was going to put me out of action for several weeks. Perhaps, I thought, we had better forget about sailing in the winter. Barbara was terribly upset. I immediately took back what I had said, but it was too late. She has never forgiven me.

It was the first time that anyone had fallen out with me on the boat. I have often fallen out with women on land, because I always say the wrong thing, but never on the boat. I was very upset, because I thought so much of her. But on reflection I can see where I went wrong. Basically she was the first regular crew I have ever had, who would be on board every time the boat went out. I have lots of friends who come out regularly for specific events, but it is not quite the same. A regular crew is part of a partnership, and a skipper has appropriate responsibilities and duty of care and respect. The skipper needs to consult crew on all aspects of the boat, and how it is going to be used, almost as if it is a marriage. It is a very special relationship on a small boat. You are cooped up in a space smaller than most rooms. There is almost no privacy, and if that is not bad enough you are constantly in dangerous situations. In a land marriage a wife or partner can say "I am not doing the washing up" and storm out. It is upsetting, but not life threatening. In a crew you trust your life to someone else.

I failed on those counts. I took her for granted. I did not show respect or support when we had others on board. I was a bad manager. Managing a small boat is a lot more difficult than people think. It is more than seamanship skills; it is more than navigation; it is more than maintenance. I have only recently found that out. It is one of the big mistakes I have made on a boat. I only wish that Barbara would forgive me.

The hernia operation left me too weak to fit *Deva* out for the winter, so I kept *Maryll* in commission. Unfortunately an oil pipe on the engine fractured, and the bottom end of the engine was ruined, so she had to be lifted out. *Deva* had to be fitted out at the worst time of the year in the snow, rain and frost. She has a new Brunton state of the art two-blade folding propeller, which she is trying out for the firm. Some new sails are on order, including a replacement for the "Bastard". I will fit out *Maryll* for the Classics and Holland, to see if she can emulate *Deva*'s 1997 season. I have some ideas on mast rake and ballasting which I would like to try out. At the moment she is trimmed to the builder's scribed waterline, but I am not sure that that is the best for performance. *Deva* is about six inches down at the stern, and she sails better for it. She rides up on her lee bow wave, and digs the heel of her keel in. I am sure that is how these shoal draft boats can sail to windward, and keep a grip of the sea. If they stall, of course they just slide to leeward, unlike a modern yacht or deep-drafted vessel.

After the Dutch regatta *Maryll* will stay in Dutch waters for a year at Durgerdam on the Ijsellmeer, while *Deva* is stationed on the East Coast. That will be my retirement, if I make it.

So that is about it forty-odd years on. It is strange to think of someone looking down from a certain newly launched White Star liner at the little *Deva* in the Mersey in 1912 and saying "I wouldn't fancy my chances in that!". It is amazing to think of the huge changes in society she has seen since then, from Empire to globalisation, and of the types of people who have sailed in her, from lords to labourers. She has gone from a world of steam and sail to one of oil and satellite. Who would have thought that one day such a little boat would be sailing the North Sea aided by Global Positioning sytems, electronic fish finders, VHF radio, mobile phone and text messaging?

Even under my stewardship she has seen much. The last of her working sisters bringing their catch through the Rock Channel; the thriving days of Liverpool as a sea town; the death of London Docks; the rise of the Haven Ports; the decline in the fishing industry; the rise in interest in traditional boats; the plasticisation of the yachting industry.

Thirty years ago *Deva* was sailed by four young men to London up a Thames which was still a workaday river. In 2001 she was sailed to London from Walton by three old men in the winter in a north-east 5-7. The River Thames had changed beyond recognition. Gone were nearly all the warehouses and factories. In their place, lining the river, were row upon on row of frightfully expensive flats, some of which were of questionable architectural taste, a Millennium Dome and Canary Wharf, all shouting "Smell our wealth because that is the nearest you will ever get to it", as poor *Deva*'s sails slatted in their lee. But little *Deva* in her dotage still had a trick up her sleeve, sailing amongst the city millionaires, winning their cup in the London Frostbite Race, the first gaff rigger, and probably the last, to do so! Where did she find the seven knots sailing to windward, slicing through the lee's of bigger modern Jenneau and Beneteau yachts, normally far faster than she? Her spirit is often beaten but never broken!

She has witnessed the trials and tribulations of my own life from being a young man with the world ahead of him to being an ageing person in inevitable decline. I see people who go through life without really understanding that there is a beginning and end to it. The years of exploitation in their work are only matched by commercial exploitation of their leisure. Like many of life's under-achievers, I am sometimes bitter and often depressed. But, man and boy, sad or happy, the sweet little *Deva* has been there for me, giving as much pleasure and adventure as any millionaire's yacht in the Caribbean. That is one bit of my life I did get right.

Deva 1912

1 = Counter; 2 = Horse; 3,6,8,9 = Nogs
4 = Thoft; 5 = Pin rail; 7 = Mooring post

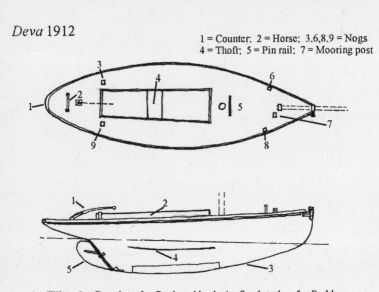

1 = Tiller; 2 = Coaming; 3 = Rockered keel; 4 = Sand strake; 5 = Rudder

Deva 1984 - Conversion

1 = Stern hatch; 2 = Nog:
3 = Pin rail;
4 = Bowsprit bitts;
5 = Twin stern rollers
6 = nogs reinstated; 7 = Nog
8 = Eliptical cockpit coaming

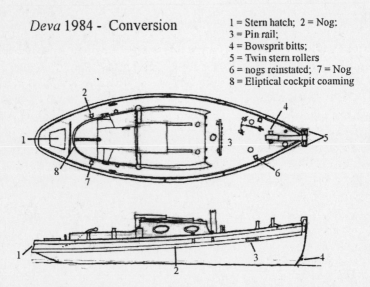

1 = Stern rebuilt; 2 = Rubbing strake; 3 = Bowsprit shroud fitting; 4 = Bobstay fitting

APPENDIX I

Deva And *Maryll* - The Boats

As with many small boats of her era, it is very difficult to establish a detailed picture of *Deva's* earlier years. After all, there were two world wars which devastated the very fabric of society. Registered fishing smacks such as those found on the East Coast were very carefully kept under the eye of the authorities, especially so where there were oyster fisheries, which were, and still are, very heavily regulated in the ownership of layings. The local constabulary had their own boats, fast little centreboard cutters like *Victoria*. They used to patrol the dredging smacks, watching out for poachers. With yachts a good reference document is the Lloyds Register of Yachts. Even in the humble North-West, where much of the yachting was in working men's sailing clubs, as opposed to gentlemen's yacht clubs, it was common practice to pay for an entry in Lloyds.

Deva first appeared in Lloyds in 1914, owners N.F. Hall and J.F. Jellico. Whether they made it through the Great War is uncertain, for in 1919 she reappears as belonging to Captain Bond at Liverpool. In 1923 he sold her to W. Furwood, who in turn sold her to the young Earl of Derby in 1926. In the late 1930s Lord Derby lent *Deva* to the Royal Navy for the training of midshipmen. She was attached to *HMS Eaglet*, and I had a very interesting letter from Robin Board who had suffered her discomforts in his formative years. Apparently they used to deliberately set the topsail badly, because Captain Elgood, the officer in charge, would invariably make them set it twice anyway. Not much changes! From 1939 onwards *Deva* has been in the hands of mere commoners. Mr Davidson kept her until 1952, and she goes out of the register. I think that I was about thirteen when I saw her at Winsford, and I guess that Harry bought her in 1959, so there is a seven year gap at this time, and there is a two year gap at the beginning. When Harry bought her in the late 1950s he redecked her and converted her to a cruiser with a full width cabin top.

Maryll first appears in official registers in 1950 registered as a British ship in Portsmouth owned by Donald Water Charters, a charter agent of Leigh on Sea. She appears in Lloyds in 1953, when the owner was registered as Holiday Boats Ltd. In 1964 Lloyds has her as owned by D.W. Charters, but there is every reason to suppose there is a link between the two owners. Bearing in mind that we know that she was still in basic nobby format, a half decker, it is possible that she was used to take people out day sailing and fishing in the early post-war period. British Registry documents describe her as a Bermudan sloop, but I think that was a mistake, because Lloyds show her as gaff and there are witnesses too. In December 1966 she was bought at Leigh-on-Sea by Arthur Davies, of Chelmondiston, who converted her to masthead Bermuda rig and put the big cabin on her. The present owner of the Maldon smack *Joseph T* also wanted to buy her, but was beaten by Arthur. He did however give Arthur a pair of cabin doors, which are still there. At some stage she was based at Heybridge Basin; shipwright Colin Swindale, who owns the Boston Smack *Telegraph*, surveyed her there when she was sold to S.G. Macpherson, of Maldon, in June 1981, the last entry. She drops out of the Lloyds register in 1974. I believe that Evan Marshall bought her in about 1989 at Pin Mill.

Maryll's first thirteen years are therefore still a mystery. Looking at her ex 2" planked deck, which is not built to the same standard as the original hull, I could speculate that she was laid up during the war years and allowed to suffer, re-decked with poor timber after the war, then brought to Portsmouth.

Deva's design and hull shape are very typical of the "advanced" design of prawners in the pre-First World War era. She is almost hard chine at her mid section, so sharp is the turn at the bilge. She was 23ft LOA, 7ft 3" on the beam and 18ft on the waterline, and she drew 2ft 9ins in theory. A model of a larger Dee Shrimper in the Merseyside Maritime Museum has almost her exact lines. Her ends are quite "pinched in", and, with the shallow depth of hull, there is typically very little volume in her - hence the need to have a quarter mounted propeller; it would be impossible to put an in-line engine in her. She has hollow garboards and quite a narrow counter. This means that when she heels to a breeze her steering characteristics change considerably until she settles down, Balancing on the lee bow wave up forward and with her keel, rudder and stern wave aft, she then becomes well behaved!

She has pitchpine planking just over an inch thick, spiked to frames made out of double 1¾ inch oak spaced at about 1ft 10" centres. There are steamed ribs in between the sawn oak frames which are copper clenched. At the "chine" there is a sand strake of oak. The oak keel is about 9" wide by 3", with an iron external ballast keel. There is a pitchpine keelson about 9" by 5" which goes over the top of the floors. Towards the stern she has a transom or tuck, an almost unique feature of the nobby, perhaps a throw-back to the days when the old style nobbies of the 1860s had transom sterns. The rudder post is contained in a wooden trunk.

The fact that so much of her original structure has survived for the best part of a century must be due to regular maintenance and regular use for most of her life. Surveyors reckon that an iron-fastened ship needs refastening every thirty years. Apart from the keel bolts, which Freddie

Smeeth, of Dedham, did as his last job before his death in 1978, *Deva's* fastenings are mostly original.

Pundits, of whom there are many, often speculate about how the prawner or nobby would have developed had it not been for the complete motorisation of working boats. Well, I think that they ought to study *Maryll*. Although at first glance she still has the common low freeboard, elliptical counter stern and rockered keel of the Edwardian era, there are significant design differences. A lot of the extremes have been ironed out. When she heels, there is not a huge increase in weather helm, because the hull is not heavily asymmetrical. When she motors, she does not dig her stern, because she carries some volume in her aft sections. This also enables her to carry an engine in line, instead of stuck out through the quarter. In contrast to *Deva*, who carries shaped pigs of internal ballast and a relatively small external ballast keel, *Maryll* only has a little trimming ballast and a big outside ballast keel. In her construction, *Maryll* has an elm keelson 9"x 3", and all sawn frames. The beam shelf arrangement up forward is slightly different, with a second shelf to take the strains of the bowsprit bitts and possibly the nogs originally. Aft she does not have the "tuck" or false transom, and her rudder post is in an iron tube. Whether she was built like that or not, I do not know. Generally speaking, she is heavily framed, and she really impressed the experienced surveyor who looked her over for insurance purposes. He could not believe the size of the breast hook on such a small boat, for instance!

One of the problems of researching these boats is that there was much less contemporary recording of practices, customs and variations of the type than of, say, the Essex smacks. There are very few "original" sources, and I have seen Edgar Marsh's prose repeated several times. There is a lot going on now. Nick Miller and L. J. Lloyd have done a tremendous amount of excellent work on the few remains left. I hear that there is even someone taking a degree in the subject. I wish that they had been around when I studied the hundreds of nobbies which were about when I was a lad. I wish that they had seen the variety within the theme. Nobbies were not as standardised as the pundits make out; I can remember that quite clearly. I looked at a lot of nobbies long before I saw *Deva*. They were a common boat for a large area from Wales to Scotland. But even I cannot remember what they were like as full sailing boats, racing regularly at regattas. I believe that stopped long before my time, whereas there always were a few smacks or smack yachts kept in racing trim in Essex for regattas at Mersea and elsewhere. People like Marsh were not around to see the nobbies at their sailing zenith, and based a lot of their opinions on the sailing and setting on the auxiliary sail/motor era. The nobby sailors did not have the experience of the Essex smacksmen crewing on the big yachts, so tow foresails and spinnakers would have been a bit of a worry to them. However, the nobby had a big powerful classic gaff cutter rig, and generally well cut sails. Many of the nobby restorations you see today are rigged on memories based on the auxillary/motor sailing era of the 1920s and 30s. The only one I have seen which demonstrates the true power of the nobby as a sailing machine is Gayle Heard's *Laura*. Significantly when she went to the Liverpool Nobby Race from Tollesbury she left the locals standing on every point of sailing.

One aspect of the traditional nobby rig which I have disagreed with is the headsail configuration. Photos of the old nobby races seem to indicate a big jib and standard staysail. For a fine-bowed boat with most of its buoyancy aft of amidships I think this is wrong. On both *Deva* and *Maryll* I have a fairly high cut jib with a long luff and not much overlap at the forestay. I would rather put the beef into the staysail, as a tow foresail. Interestingly Gayle Heard did this as well with his big green tow foresail, which he swears by in virtually all weathers. He will reef the main and set a small jib, but the green'un stays up. He claims the drive of the rig is in that sail. For light winds we have the "Bastard" set from the bowsprit. High performance dinghies are doing the same now.

Typical Nobby Sail Plan 1912

1 = Flying jib
2 = Staysail
3 = Mainsail
4 = Topsail

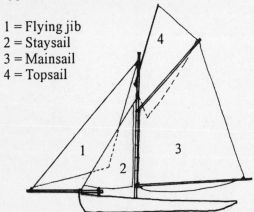

However, when I went on a pilgrimage to Arnside a few years ago there were hardly any nobbies about. It is not surprising, I suppose, when they were only built to last ten years or so in the days of sail. It really was more amazing that so many found commercial use up till relatively recently. I remember that when I first saw them they were all motorised, but still very much sailing boats to look at. The sailing mast was still there, with a gaff main, and a staysail was often set too. The deck layout was fairly original, although the rail/bulwarks were often built up more - no longer did they sail lee gunwale under the whole time. At the stem the gammon iron had often been removed and a second bow roller fitted, unless the vessel had a centre line bowsprit and already had two bow rollers like *Maryll*. Then in the 1960s wheelhouses started to be fitted at the forward end of the cockpit, but sufficiently low for a small sail to be set above. Eventually the sail was dispensed with in the 1970s and 80s, and the wheel houses grew bigger. At the same time the beautiful counter often had surgery - cheaper to cut it off square than repair it. So the last commercial nobbies in the 1990s were not the elegant "yachts" of the Edwardian era. Although enthusiasm is not lacking, sadly, few in the North-West have had the huge resources needed to rebuild them to their former glory, and to do what has been done in Essex with restoration of the local smacks.

Approximate Lines of *Deva*

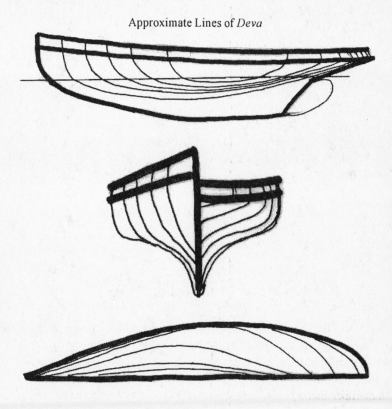

Deva – The Rig

One of the advantages of having owned *Deva* for such a long time is that I have had time to experiment with matters like the rig. Also, having raced her for such a long time too in similar company, I can verify such experiments on performance. People marvel or shudder at the amount of running rigging she has, and possibly a modern high performance rig might give a better result. However, within the confines of a reasonably traditional rig design, she has evolved a rig which is both seaworthy and efficient. There are plenty of faster boats, but at her size they very rarely have to displace four tons, they do not have a diesel engine to drag, they do not have the cruising kit of four berths, they do not have a heavy shoal hull to motivate.

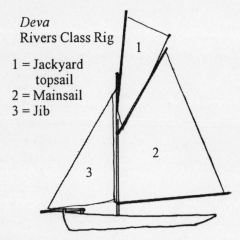

Deva
Rivers Class Rig

1 = Jackyard
      topsail
2 = Mainsail
3 = Jib

The mainsail

When Harry had her first, he had a high peaked gaff, about 15 degrees, but he re-cut the sail to 40 degrees. He claimed that it set better. The first "new" mainsail I had for *Deva* was a direct copy of this, and the three new mains I have had since have maintained the same gaff angle, so that I could use the same topsail. When I re-rigged *Maryll*, I followed advice from pundits, and increased the peak to 30 degrees. It does not seem to work as well. There is not the same drive.

To ease weather helm I took three feet off the boom/foot of the sail, from fifteen feet to twelve, about the same as the luff and the head, which gives nearly vertical leech, not as much as on a barge or a bawley, but similar. With a mainsheet horse wider than standard, this has not increased the "sag" of the gaff, as might be expected. The first short footed mainsail had a zipper flattening reef along the foot, copying practice in modern boats of the time. Subsequently I decided to have a loose footed main, which avoids this complication, but the value of flattening or bellying the main was not lost on me; I always fiddle with the clew outhaul now. To help with single-handing, I lead the peak and throat halliards aft to the cockpit. A convenient sheet winch enables the peak and throat to be tensioned for changing conditions.

So, unlike many who just adjust the set of the sail with the mainsheet, I ensure that *Deva*'s main is constantly adjusted in flatness and peak as well. The proportions of the sail enable the maximum benefit to be gained from this facility. It also enables her to hold a full main longer than would be the case normally. She will often carry a full main when bigger smacks are reefed.

The topsail

The topsail on most gaff boats is a bit of an afterthought, even in the minds of sailmakers and designers, but not so for the bawleyman or the bargeman. It is particularly relevant to a small boat, because the wind is constantly disturbed by the waves at low level. On the basis of experience, I will not let a sailmaker measure for a topsail unless the main is set, and I am there to set the main too! Invariably they do not give the peak enough "grunt" for windward sailing in a firm breeze. On *Deva* we often set the topsail over a reefed or even double reefed main, so it needs to be reasonably flat and made out of good stuff.

Deva's topsail is a simple "yard" headed topsail - not a "jackyard" which she had in the Rivers Class, which had a jackyard on the foot to extend it past the higher peaked mainsail. The position of attachment of the halliard to the yard is very critical to the set. The halliard is made fast first, then the down haul is made fast, sometimes with a wagoner's hitch, because it must be firm. Only then is the sheet made up. Some of the old sailing books used to recommend over peaking the main, making fast the sheet, then easing the peak halliard to flatten the sail. I think they were wrong, or not bothered about sailing properly. The main needs to be individually adjusted, and so does the topsail.

I do not know why, but the topsail on *Deva* makes an impression far greater than its size would suggest. It seems to work with the mainsail as one, extending the leading edge of the rig and enhancing the drive of both canvases. The profile is actually not dissimilar to the modern fully battened, heavily roached mainsails seen on ultra high performance racers and catamarans, so almost always it is set when racing, in most wind conditions. I will reef the main before losing the topsail. *Maryll*'s topsail is just a kite for light winds, and of limited use, developing less power. This I believe to be due to the shape. The sailmaker made the mainsail to the recommended optimum shape, and the topsail was just designed to fill in the gap, as per normal practice on a conventional gaff cutter. The topsail on a bawley, with its relatively low peaked gaff, is a different beast altogether, and *Deva*'s relatively vertical mainsail leech and wide topsail is more related to the bawley profile than to conventional gaff cutters.

Headsails

Gaff cutters have been going for hundreds of years, but we have to make it complicated on *Deva*! Traditionally prawners had large jibs off long unstayed bowsprits, which had to be changed for smaller ones as wind increased. This is no joke on a fine bow plunging through a sea; no wonder they gave up bowsprits when engines came in! So when I was offered a "skinny" or narrow long luffed jib off the wreck of the YW 4 Tonner *Painted Lady*, I broke with tradition. This was set on a Wykeham Martin furling gear from the masthead, and actually was better for going to windward in moderate conditions. In due course I managed to blow this out, and a sailmaker called Jewitt rebuilt it for me, hence its name. With only minimal overlap with the staysail, it enabled the staysail to be set to optimal shape. However, in stronger winds I still needed a small jib. Rather than take the Jewitt off, I ran out a second inner bowsprit traveller for a small red jib set off the four part "fish tackle". There are occasions when both jibs are set, particularly on open water on a beam or close reach. Should the wind pick up, the Jewitt is furled, leaving *Deva* with a snug headsail configuration, without the need for any one to go up forward.

The "Bastard"

Many gaff cutters set a really light weather jib from the end of the bowsprit, sheeted right aft. This is sometimes known as a balloon jib or bowsprit spinnaker. The bedsheet which was originally discarded from *Sheila*, then from *Tarka*, and given to *Deva* was none of these. I think it was a fairly flat spinnaker set with the tack to the foot of the mast, set to one side of the rig, rather than in front of it. As its true parentage was in doubt it was named "Bastard". I set it on the inside traveller, so it can be dispensed with or set with the Jewitt still pulling and balancing the boat. Obviously a fairly large sail is bound to assist a boat in light winds, but this particular sail is magic. Often is the time when all around stop, yet *Deva* keeps a-going. In many ways it is like the asymmetrical kite seen on many high performance racing dinghies with retractable bowsprits. For a dead run, however, the tack can be boomed out to weather to catch the wind. *Maryll* now has this arrangement, and that has also proved successful. She has a tri-radial head to induce some more shape in the sail.

The Staysail

On too many gaff cutters the staysail is just a sail used in heaving to for dredging and helping the bow round in a tack. Old photos of nobbies racing and most East Coast smacks show that this is the case. However, many West Country and Solent boats paid a lot more attention to their staysails, and recognised their importance to the overall efficiency of the rig. Similarly many of the traditional Dutch craft have efficient staysail arrangements, with some overlap of the mainsail to create a wind slot. On *Deva* we have an overlapping staysail, like a smack's tow foresail, but cut like a Bermudan boat's genoa to go to windward. It is called a Light Weather Staysail, but actually it is used in winds up to a force six or even seven in certain situations. For running in a stiff breeze we "bloop" with a second old staysail of the same shape, by hoisting the second sail tacked to the stem head directly opposite the first sail. The two sails share the forestay and billow out like a low slung bra. *Maryll* has a similar staysail made from an old genoa, and for some reason this generates an incredible slot with the flying jib on a beam reach. Dropping the whole mainsail only loses half a knot. I have done almost an entire passage across the North Sea in heavy weather under big staysail and jib. Alternatively this means that the gaff mainsail is pretty useless in certain wind strengths and directions. Anything is possible. Sailmaking must be a lottery, not a science! Some sailmakers are luckier than others.

For stronger breezes in heavier seas where the bow might be pressed down, we have a working staysail of smaller size on *Deva*. This is an amateur-made sail called the Huggett, after its maker. It was cut with a hollow luff, which means it still holds a good shape when the forestay stretches in the breeze. It is higher cut than normal, so it uses the same sheeting position as the larger staysail. On *Maryll*'s new working staysail it did not work. I do not know why; it was a normal shaped staysail. A hand-me-down from *Lizzie Annie* via *Polly* actually worked a lot better; again I do not know why.

Storm Sails

I have never been out in a force ten storm in *Deva*; I hope I never will. I think that I would just run under bare poles. I do have a spitfire jib and a storm staysail with reef points, but I have hardly ever used them. Huggett on his own is fine in winds of forty knots. I do not have a trysail, but the double reefed main can be bisected with the balance reef. This can work by either eliminating most of the luff and setting the gaff vertical, or by tying the reef to the head of the sail so that a trysail is formed with a gaff to its head, a boom to its foot, and a mast to its luff. With wood all round, the sail is unlikely to flap itself to shreds on the leech. It has to be bad weather indeed for this to be done. This is probably a good rig for motoring into the wind. Often it is blowing old boots down the Wallet, and I have to get to Mersea. I wait for the ebb tide to go on the ebb so that the water flattens. I set the balance reef, and diesel my way through.

Other Sails
In gaffer races all sorts of unofficial sails are set - sometimes borrowed, sometimes set in an unusual way. Most are not worth the effort, but pacify the crew. We often set a water sail, which is normally a small headsail not in use elsewhere, underneath the boom. We have been known to set one under the spinnaker boom.

Running Rigging
In the years throughout which I have had the boat I have seen the transfer from natural fibres such as manila, hemp, cotton and sisal to man-made fibres. The best natural fibres were a lot better than their man-made equivalents, although they were weaker and prone to rot. However, they were so much easier to splice in the difficult conditions you find at sea that it would almost be easier to put in a two-tuck short splice to a hawser than tie a suitable knot, and you could get away with two tucks rather than the four needed nowadays for most slippery synthetic ropes. There are some hemp look-alikes on the market which almost feel like the real thing, but the way they are laid up is different. The problem comes when a load goes on, such as on a flying jib halliard. The whole tackle can become horribly twisted and jam up, which can be very embarrassing. The outer flying jib (Jewitt) halliard on *Deva* is a single part and thus comes back aft to a winch. The inner flying jib halliard, which is really the fish tackle, is only used for small or light-wind sails which do not have heavy loading. *Deva* has a mixture of rope types which has evolved over the years with various hand-me-downs and reel-end bargains. There are three-strand polyester, three-strand polyester-hemp and various braided lines for sheets, red for the jib, green for the Jewitt, blue for the staysail. The fashion police would arrest me on the spot if they caught me, but they don't because the system works. For a confused crew it is no good shouting "Pull the other one!" in a crisis, much better to say "Pull the red one!" On halliards there is a little more time to indicate the correct rope.

For standing rigging I have gone for stainless steel. Good old galvanised is not what it used to be. I remember as a student "half-hitching" a mizzen mast off a derelict sailing barge in Cubits Dock on the Thames, which was about to be filled in. The wire shrouds off that, which must have been fifty years old when I stole them, are still good stuff today, but new galvanised shrouds have rotted away in a matter of ten years. Keeping an old boat going for a lifetime is difficult enough, without worrying about shrouds rusting through. Even worse, the after shrouds have polythene tube round them to prevent chafe on the mainsail. It's a fair cop, fashion police!

Running Rigging on *Deva*

Port Side Halliards

1 = Outer jib halliard - Jewitt; 2 = Port topping lift; 3 = Lazy jack;
4 = Tack downhaul to winch in Cockpit;
5 = Jewitt halliard to winch in cockpit; 6 = Fixed; 7 = Hardener;
8 = To pinrail; 9 = Staysail halliard; 10 = Inner jib halliard or 'Fish tackle'

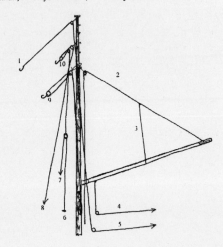

Rigging Starboard Side

1 = Peak; 2 = Topsail halliard;
3 = Starboard topping lift;
4 = Throat; 5 = Peak;
6 = Taken to winch aft;
7 = Topsail sheet;
8 = Topsail downhaul;
9 = Throat

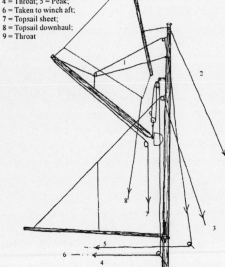

316

APPENDIX III

Adaptations for advancing years and infirmity

One issue in operating a boat is declining strength. In my case it came early with the ticker problem. Small sails, and plenty of them, are much easier to manage. When I first had my problem I did discuss the issue of "pully-hauly" with medical advisers. Much of the rope work of sweating in sheets and halliards is a matter of the technique of using the body weight. Concerning anchoring, I did discuss the use of a horizontal acting anchor winch to wind the chain in. Apparently this is just the wrong movement, so probably a gaff cutter with small headsails is a lot better than the modern equivalent with large genoas which need a huge amount of sheet winching. That applies also to in-mast reefing or anything else which needs a lot of winding.

However, I do have to admit to having winches on *Deva*. Even small sails can be difficult to haul in during breezy weather. The constraints of a small cockpit make it difficult to apply body weight techniques rather than enfeebled muscles. The winches are also used for halliard adjustment. The peak and throat halliards are led aft to a "modern" arrangement of halliard brakes and winch. Most of the rope can be pulled in with bodyweight, leaning back. However, the final "tweaking" is done easily with a winch. This is not just an advantage for the physically disadvantaged; it also enables the mainsail shape to be adjusted to varying wind situations for optimum performance. The Jewitt or outer jib halliard can also be tightened in this way. People sometimes remark on *Deva's* apparent speed; part of the answer is that we work hard at it in terms of constant adjustment, whereas others just set the main halliards and leave them.

Winches are not always feasible or affordable, but rope tackles or "handy-billies" can often be as useful. I have them on *Maryll* for the flying jib in the form of "hardeners". The main part of the sail is hoisted with a single whip and made fast. Then the hardener is drawn down giving a four-to-one purchase. On *Deva* the inner jib is a double purchase, but the halliard is two-ended. One end is made fast after hoisting the main part of the sail, the other goes to a "hardener" tackle. I also use this halliard as a fish tackle for lifting the beam trawl/cod end out. On *Maryll* I have "tack tackles" on the staysail and the mainsail.

An understandable observation might be "I don't know how you handle all that string". However, "All that string" means that I have better mechanical advantage in terms of the various pulley systems, and smaller loads to lift at that, with smaller sails. Some people think *Deva's* crew must have to be very tough because *Deva* can go out in weathers which keep many boats on their moorings, or because *Deva* can make longer passages than many vessels of her size would normally make. We might be hardy, but it is medically impossible for me to be tough. Circumstances make the disadvantaged adapt, if the attitude is right.

The use of a reliable engine, which starts easily, is part of the strategy. Although I have sailed in and out of some very restricted places, and some very difficult situations as well, I do not mind admitting to using the engine to get me out of trouble. I am not the only one concerned. If I am behind my E.T.A., people on shore may worry because of my medical condition (albeit unnecessarily in my opinion), and emergency services may be called out. On a race it is not so bad, because others are nearby, but when cruising I am often out of sight of everything so the engine comes in to play to ensure that I catch a tide or maintain a scheduled speed. The GPS is also an aid in this area, because on a given set of circumstances it can predict a time of arrival. Contact with the shore is important. People sneer at mobile phones, but they do have their place in putting people's minds at ease, and I have used them in emergency situations in preference to VHF. The VHF is obviously more useful out at sea, when the mobile is out of range. However, satellite phone technology is moving ahead all the time, and this position might change.

Managing weight generally needs to be looked at carefully. A two gallon, ten litre can is liftable in one hand and transportable, and two can be carried short distances. One gallon cans are very much easier, but the payload is a lot less. Why people keep buying huge five or ten gallon cans I do not know. The strain of lifting such weights in confined spaces or situations found on boats is very dangerous.

The ergonomics of sailing a boat need to be looked at very carefully. A wide cockpit which looks very comfortable in harbour with a nice table in the middle for the drinks can also be a very dangerous place out at sea for the less than nimble as they are thrown about great distances. A small cockpit, in which you can wedge yourself, with a handy shelf for the drinks in arm's reach, is far safer. It is the same in cabins. A wide open plan saloon may look fine at a boatshow, but being thrown in it in a seaway is like being thrown across a room into a wall. Weakness means lack of grip. Only a strong person can hold his own weight for any time. It is thus far better to put up with a cramped cabin where you cannot be thrown any distance.

Transfer from a dinghy or tender is often a critical operation. On *Deva* or *Maryll*, with their very low freeboards, it is possible to almost roll over from the tender to the boat, without standing up. In choppy conditions this is useful. One of the difficulties of getting out of a dinghy is actually going from the sitting position to standing, especially as the agility goes in the legs. Unable to balance properly, the person then causes instability in the dinghy. Consideration might be given to having a sort of anti-roll bar in a rigid dinghy so that people can haul themselves up without getting in a wobble. This would be difficult in an inflatable, but with low freeboard on *Deva* we can just kneel on the side of the dinghy and move our body weight over. Falling over the side is something most of us are terrified of. Apart from the shock to a feeble constitution, it is incredibly difficult even for a fit person to heave someone aboard. Obviously, the lower the freeboard the better. Boats which were designed to facilitate bringing in trawl nets by hand are going to be easier than vessels with high freeboard, but even climbing aboard a nobby is difficult. That is one of the reasons for fitting bobstays to the bowsprits of both boats. Traditionally nobbies did not have bobstays because they interfered with the nets, but using a bobstay is the easiest way to get back on board. You hold the chain or the bowsprit, put one foot at the stem fitting at waterline level, roll the bodyweight over, at top dead centre make a grab for the bowsprit, and you are now standing up. Rolling on the bowsprit itself, you can then easily get the legs on to the foredeck and grab the forestay, and you are safe and sound.

You do not have to do much research to note that a high proportion of people sailing are in their fifties or older. They might feel young at heart, but their bodies are well past their original design life. I worry when I see some of the boats which are marketed to them. The salesman looks to appeal to the older person's desire for comfort. Headroom, space and gadgets are all brought into play without consideration for seaworthiness and safety. Perhaps that salesman and his wife ought to be anchored off a lee shore in a full gale and made to sail their way off. The typical high freeboard boat with guard rails, big cabin, big cockpit, in-mast furling may appear to be the ideal boat for the middle-aged. But I would feel safer in my low freeboard gaff cutters with all their complicated but repairable string and wood.

APPENDIX IV

Engine Installation

Although *Deva* is a sailing boat, engines have featured very heavily in her life in terms of crisis and expense. However, I doubt whether she could have achieved as much without one. Apart from the increased ability to make passages, she has nearly always managed to get where she was going to, and on schedule. Bearing in mind that there is often an Old Gaffers Race to organise as well as everything else, this is very important! Her first engine was a Stuart four horse power two stroke engine P5MC, driving a folding propeller via a centrifugal clutch. Four horse power propelling four tons of boat sounds rather minimal by today's standards of even auxiliary power, but, having such good lines, *Deva* could get up to five knots with a three bladed propeller with a fair wind and smooth water. With the folder she would achieve about four knots. A subsequent doubling of horse power has not brought a doubling of speed, but it has enabled her to punch a head sea or tide much better.

As in many of her working sisters, the shaft is offset, coming out on the quarter. Some say that working nobbies always had the prop on the starboard side because they traditionally shot the trawl to port. I am not sure about this; I have seen working nobbies with installations port or starboard, or even twin screw. In terms of efficiency the side at which the propeller comes out is to do with the hand of the prop or which way it revolves. However, with a side mounted prop, there is no doubt that you are better shooting nets to the other side!

Deva's second engine was an eight horse power Stuart P55RME, which had a gearbox, a drive for a dynamo and a starting motor. The shaft was increased in diameter from ¾" to 1", but the same petrol tank was retained. The exhaust was a dry, having been through a big brass silencer. The route of the pipe was a problem on such a low freeboard boat, but eventually this was solved. The performance of the engine, when it worked, was incredible. The maintenance and repair were generally within my limited grasp. However, the first trip across the North Sea demonstrated to me the problems of carrying enough fuel. The engine would consume about one gallon of two-stroke mixture per hour, four times more than the equivalent diesel.

Rather reluctantly, I had a new Yanmar 1GM10 nine horse power professionally installed, with a steel frame which fitted on the old Stuart bearers. One of the ergonomic problems of replacing a two stroke marine engine with a modern four stroke diesel is the oil sump. Normally this is positioned below the out-put shaft from the gearbox which connects with the propeller shaft. This is of no matter in a modern plastic boat, or in most yachts, where the depth of the bilge can be used, but on *Deva*, with her massive keelson running nearly full length, there is no space. The Yanmar is one of the very few engines which can fit, similarly on *Maryll*.

Another problem of replacing the Stuart was the rotation of the propeller. The Stuart had a left-handed propeller, whereas the Yanmar and most other engines have a right-handed propeller. This does not matter when going ahead, but when going astern it is a real beast because of the adverse paddlewheel effect coupled with the offset shaft. Rather than being pulled astern, the boat is pulled sideways, which makes her almost impossible to manoeuvre in close quarters, say in a marina or a Dutch "box". This is quite a disadvantage, as we tend to back or go astern into berths to avoid problems with clambering over the bowsprit when going ashore.

The Yanmar has generally been very reliable, although not quite as powerful as the lower rated Stuart. It also is very economical on fuel. Where it does fall down is in the cost of servicing and spare parts. Engine mounts are about £400 a set (2001), about three times more costly than standard ones, for instance, and these only last a few years. There are mild steel external oil pipes which rust out of sight, particularly one which dives behind the starter motor - on *Maryll* this actually split and drained the oil from the engine, making a complete rebuild necessary. These pipes need to be replaced every five years. Whereas the Stuart needed relatively little in running replacements, the Yanmar needs much in terms of fuel filters, mounts, impellers, anodes and pipes, about £200 worth a season on average. The convenience comes at a price.

Another problem of modern engines and their modern electrical systems is that electrolysis and electrical bonding has to be taken much more seriously. The engine has a small anode, which needs regular replacement. This needs linking to the propshaft, and the seacocks and the engine itself need linking to an external anode. This was not done by the professional installers, and I learnt my lesson when my propeller fell off in Middleberg harbour.

The propeller itself causes problems when sailing, especially when set out on the quarter. Tremendous drag is experienced, and the helm is affected. I tried a geared folding two blade propeller. The performance under power went down, but the sailing benefited, so *Deva* has had a folding propeller for a long time. However, these are subject to wear, and the resulting vibration can cause things to become undone, as I have found out to my cost.

Recently I fitted a new two blade "Brunton" self-pitching propeller. These are expensive compared with fixed propellers or some of the more basic folders. Nevertheless I have been very favourably impressed to date. The design, by Bruntons Propellers Ltd of Clacton, is very clever. The blade is shaped in such a way that it swivels to match engine speed and conditions, effectively continuously adjusting the coarseness of the pitch. In layman's terms the propeller always has the best grip on the water, whether the boat is going slow or fast, or whether the sea is rough or smooth. Additionally, when astern is engaged the prop blades swing right round, so it performs as well astern as it does ahead - it really does grip better than anything else in an emergency stop.

When sailing, to lock the propeller in sailing position or stop it from revolving, forward gear, rather than the normal astern, is engaged. If it is allowed to revolve, the propeller does grip very heavily on the water, seemingly more heavily than the fixed three blader. When the propeller is folded or swivelled in sailing position, drag is, of course, very much less than with a fixed bladed prop, and compared with a conventional folding propeller it is nearly as little. Under power I have been very impressed to date. When motor sailing, or motoring with some sail drawing, the propeller adjusts to give the maximum benefit as the sail contribution varies. In lumpy or pitching seas it does not lose its grip, even at low speed. At full power the boat is about three quarters of a knot faster than with a fixed three blade propeller, going from 5.7 knots to 6.5 knots or even a little higher. As interesting as well is the fact that the engine no longer produces black smoke under full load, proving that the self pitching is working.

It really is a beautiful piece of design, and beautifully made too.

What's In A Name?

Boats of *Deva*'s generic type tended to be called "nobbies" in the south of their area from Liverpool or Southport down to mid Wales. From Fleetwood or Morecambe upwards they tended be called "prawners" or "sprawners". Sometimes there would be references to activity, for instance "shrimpers", "trawlers", "ferries". There were not today's fashion policemen to keep a watch on the situation, and there were a lot of local variations in terms and expressions.

Marine historians and other experts either refer to "Lancashire nobby" or "Morecambe Bay Prawners", both of which are technically wrong for obvious geographical reasons. When I came south, however, I had to start using the latter expression, because nobody knew what a nobby was. Nobody is quite sure where the word "nobby" came from. There is a Scottish term "nabbie" which I think means catcher (of fish?), which has the English derivative "nab". However, as the Scottish and Cumbrian boat owners did not refer to their boats as nabbies or nobbies, I am not sure of this. I tend to support L. Lloyd's theory advanced in his book "The Lancashire Nobby", which suggests that the term nobby is an aesthetic one, meaning posh or stylish, such as suggested in the English Dictionary. Compared with their forerunners or any other regional inshore craft, they were very stylish. These were the latest racing yacht design in outline, modified for local waters with more beam and less draft. They would have been very posh-looking boats.

This would tie up with my experience when the old longshoremen and local seamen would always refer to my boat as a "nobby", thinking of it as a compliment, which they did not always give to *Deva*'s butchered sisters with their cut down rigs and hen house superstructures. My firm recollection is that "nobby" was a generic term for a visual style of boat. You could have "fishing nobbies", "pilot nobbies", "nobby yachts".

Thirty-five years later on I get the feeling that the term "nobby" is used generally for ex-registered fishing vessels, as an alternative to "prawner" or smack. Nowadays, with virtually all the remaining fishing nobbies converted to yachts by people who were not around when they were commonplace working vessels, the application of the term is likely to have changed.

Maintenance and Repair

To maintain an old wooden boat is a labour of love, two boats even more so. However, it is not nearly as bad as the pundits make out. If I consider where the time and the money goes, only a relatively small proportion of the total goes on the "old wooden bit". Engines, rigging, electrical equipment, cabin fittings, gadgets and anti-fouling paint are much the same whatever the hull material. True, a wooden boat cannot be neglected, but the main difference is the annual lick of paint on the topsides and varnish/bright work. A fibreglass hull is not maintenance free - it needs lots of polishing which can take nearly as much time as painting. As virtually every other yacht station has an "Osmosis Centre", fibreglass boats appear to need the gel coat stripping off and replacing, plus a full spray job. This is very expensive. The old working smacks had very limited maintenance, and worked for half a century or more.

Although the skill of professional shipwrights is far more than any amateur can ever dream of, even those of modest "DIY" ability round the house can tackle a surprising number of jobs. I am hopeless round the house, but even I have managed to undertake substantial works on both boats. I have been lucky in that *Deva*'s hull was exceptionally strongly constructed by her builders, not to a particularly high standard, but very robust in performance. If something needs replacing or repairing, at least there is something sound to graft on to. There have also been technical developments, especially in tools and glues, which make possible many repairs in situ. Most operational damage can be overcome by graving pieces or grafts of timber glued to the original, saving the replacement of a plank. Ribs or frames can be replaced or doubled with timber of the same section laminated out of lots of thin pieces glued together in situ. If the boat is structurally sound and reasonably well maintained, keeping her going is not a great issue.

The problem comes with hidden corruption. Invariably there are nooks and crannies in any boat which harbour leaks or broken joints and potential rot. Most of these are where the deck joins the hull. Similarly cabin linings and unventilated lockers are ideal breeding grounds for trouble. The best preventative measure is to use the boat. Movement of air caused by habitation, motion in a seaway and exposure to the wind will help limit condensation, and a good dousing in saltwater acts as a mild antiseptic against fungi.

Some of these problems are caused by bad design detailing. On prawners one of the worst features is the practice of putting wooden blocking between the heads of frames before putting the deck or cover boarding on. Hidden by the beam clamp or shelf which goes right up to the underside of the deck, water can seep between the top strake of the hull and the deck planking and lodge undetected in this blocking for years. By the time it is found, the ends of the frames are rotting, the top of the topstrake is vulnerable, the deck plank is attacked from underneath, the ends of the deck beams rot, and there is a pig of a mess to sort out. On *Deva* I found several cases when raising her topsides, but overcame the problem by extending the frames and putting a second beam clamp in a bit higher which has a clear gap above it for ventilation.

The counter stern is another vulnerable area. The practice of putting in a "tuck" or dummy transom effectively cut out much needed ventilation. Although this did have two ventilation holes in, there was no through draft. On *Deva* one of the first things we did was to put a mushroom ventilator in the deck of the counter, but in her current design there are now a hatch and big hole from the cockpit. On *Maryll* there is no tuck, and hopefully no problem, because it is impossible to get at the far end to check.

In general painting there are really no short cuts. It is a matter of doing the minimum, but doing it regularly. Most paintwork only lasts a season. More coats can be put on to make it last two seasons; however, it does go eventually, and the repair work is much greater. Often I manage with a one-coat finish, using undercoat and top coat mixed. This does not have the same gloss level, but it does degrade gently without lifting, leaving an easy substrate for the next year.

Over the years I have tried most treatments or finishes for timber in the hope of finding a system which can be applied in poor conditions, is aesthetically pleasing, lasts, and is easily maintainable. I do not think there is a perfect solution. As for brightwork or varnish, the most vain of yacht finishes on a wooden boat, the short answer is not to have any. Generally paint lasts much longer. However, there are compromises which I have discovered and which may be of interest.

The mast takes a lot of abuse, and stays erected for years at a time. Conventional varnishes are pretty well shot at after a couple of years, water gets behind, peeling varnish out of sight, and corruption begins. On *Deva*'s mast I applied three coats of a mixture of linseed oil and pine-coloured Cuprinol. This could be applied in fairly adverse conditions and allowed to soak in for a couple of weeks. I then applied a base coat of Sikkens HLS woodstain and two coats of Sikkens Filter 7 topcoat. Where the gaff jaws wear I applied glass cloth and epoxy as a hard surface prior to linseed, and put the Sikkens over the top after it had cured. That mast is still pretty good after nearly five years out in the open.

Other spars have had Sikkens wood stain treatment. Where they get a lot of bashing, such as the topsail yard, I apply a couple of coats of varnish over the top. This is not full varnish, but let down with white spirit by about 30%.

Cabin and cockpit sides have had linseed oil and mahogany-coloured stain preservative mixture applied, and allowed to soak in. Varnish about 50% diluted with white spirit is applied in about three coats. That does not give a gloss finish, but more of a sheen. However the maintenance is easy and not too weather critical - just one or two coats applied when convenient.

My theory is that the linseed oil will soak in better than anything else, and stabilise the wood. The preservative or Cuprinol will be drawn in with the linseed, and provide preservation and some ultraviolet protection. On the mast the Sikkens stain system gives additional ultraviolet protection and provides a water repellent surface. The system is breathable, so moisture in the timber can escape without lifting the surface. The down side of stain systems is that eventually they cloud the timber grain with annually or bi-annually repeated maintenance coats. Using the linseed to stabilise the timber puts off the maintenance for a few years more.

The use of very diluted varnish provides a little better protection and binding of the timber surface fibres than a stain. It is water repellent, but not a vapour barrier, so timber would move if it were not for the inner linseed oil base. It is less likely to lift with moisture in the timber than if it were used neat, but by the same token it will not give the ultraviolet protection, so again the colouring in the stain within the linseed oil base provides the protection.

For the toe rail or gunwale, I use a straight forward Sikkens stain system. The grain is lost with annual maintenance, but it is not very nice looking timber, and it gets a good bashing in a season's use anyway.

The hull on *Deva* is sheathed in nylon cloth and epoxy. For many years a "Cascover" system, which uses a nylon cloth and polyester resin, has done nearly the same job. With carvel planking, the system has to be able to stretch with the movement of the timber, and the nylon and epoxy are very flexible. In the USA many of the wooden workboats are sheathed in epoxy and Versatex, which is a polypropylene cloth, to resist abrasion and ease maintenance, and again this does the same job. This sheathing has been on now for over fifteen years, and has not caused any problems to *Deva*'s timber. It is not a structural skin in any way, and will not strengthen a weak hull. The system is not to be confused with the fibreglass cloth and polyester resin system, which can have serious bonding and differential movement problems, leading to rot, especially when applied to suspect hulls as a last resort. The nylon-epoxy coat gives a stable surface for paint, and very little making-good to blisters and lifting paint is needed. I would also have used it on my decks had I realised the benefits. Unfortunately being under cover and having reasonably warm conditions are needed for application. This is difficult as both my vessels are permanently outside.

Maryll's hull was burnt off and sanded below the water line, and treated with linseed oil; then eventually three coats of International Metallic Pink Primer were applied, followed by anti-fouling.

Anti-fouling paint for the bottom is a vexed question. Environmental concerns mean that much of the anti-foul sold is not greatly effective. In my case, with a drying out mooring, it gets rubbed off as well. I tend to use Hard Racing Copper because of this. Launching in April or May means that the little devils of barnacles are at their most active, and they have made their mark by August. I therefore tend to anti-foul in early June, and then the paint will last through to the following March.

APPENDIX VI

Old Gaffers Association (OGA)

The OGA was formed in September 1963 at Maldon Little Ship Club in Essex, England, by enthusiasts from the East Coast and Solent areas. Both groups had been staging races for old gaff rigged vessels, as little was being done for them by established yachting clubs. Gaff rig had become virtually obsolete due to fashion and rating rules, and one of the prime aims of the new organisation was to ensure that gaff rig did not die out altogether. The movement was even more successful than the founders expected, causing many gaff rigged vessels to be lavishly restored and a number of new gaff rigged boats to be built. Since that time, the OGA has expanded in to most of the coastal regions of Britain and Ireland, mainland Europe, the Antipodes and America. With a membership of 1,400, it is probably one of the largest organisations of its kind. There is a huge variety of boats owned by members, including smacks and other ex working vessels, cruisers and racers, both large and small.

Having achieved its primary aims, the agenda for the OGA has moved on. It maintains a central register for its vessels, lobbies on potential legislative issues in UK and Europe, and is a founder member of Heritage Afloat. It produces a quarterly journal, the Gaffers Log, and maintains a website. It also has strong links with other organisations, such as the Dutch VKSJ and the Colne Smack Preservation Society.

Each area has its own committee, which is responsible for staging events of various kinds. Activities have grown considerably in the last fifteen years, particularly in the Solent, Northern Ireland, North Wales and East Coast. On the East Coast, for instance, a typical year's programme would include meetings at Foulness, Burnham and Manningtree in May, the East Coast Classics (about 10-14 days calling at Southwold, Lowestoft, Orford, Deben, Levington, Ipswich, Mistley, Wrabness, Walton, Brightlingsea etc) in June, whilst in July there might be East Coast Race, the North Sea Race and Dutch Classics at Hellevoetsluis. August is fairly clear to allow participation in the growing number of non-OGA events and regattas such as Mersea Week, with just a Bank Holiday Rally, the last race is the Maldon Town Regatta and OGA Anniversary in September, with a party, rally and AGM at Woolverstone in November.

A special weekend is staged in the Walton Backwaters for open boats and fans of Arthur Ransome's "Secret Waters".

A development in recent years is the participation of classic Bermuda rigged yachts, who faced the same problems as gaff did forty years ago.

They generally race in a separate class for different prizes, but sail the same course and go to the same party afterwards!

Membership in 2001 is typically £15.00 per year, applications being made to the Membership Secretary, Adrian Sharpe, 7 Rathmore Close, Winchcome, Cheltenham, Glos. GL54 5YX.

GLOSSARY of TERMS

Abaft	Behind e.g. Abaft the beam
Aft	Towards the stern, or rear of the ship
Amidships	Middle of the ship
Ballast	Heavy material to assist stability e.g. Pigs of ballast; ballast keel
Barque	3 or more masts; square rigged on all but aftermast
Beam	Width of the ship at widest point
Beam ends	Gunwale at maximum Beam
Beam trawl	Trawl net held open by beam of wood, iron etc.
Beat	Sailing up wind as hard as possible
Bermudan rig	3-sided mainsail, luff to mast
Bilges	Bottom of boat inside
Bitts	Support posts e.g. Bowsprit bitts
Black fish	Fish caught by unlicensed vessels
Blue water cruising	Cruising across oceans
Bluff-bowed	Full / unstreamlined bow
Bogie	Wheeled device for carrying loads
Bow	Front of boat / forward end of the ship
Bow thruster	Motor in the bows to push bows round when manoeuvering
Broach	Uncontrollable swerve caused by following sea in strong winds
Bulwark	'wall' round edge of boat
Careened	Keeled right over normally so that work can be done on ship's bottom
Carlines	Longitudinal structural member supporting the underside of the deck fixed to the top of the frames or ribs of the boat
Cleats	Device for tying lines, sheets etc.
Close fetch	Course close to the wind
Coamings	Vertical boards to stop water on deck going down hatches, cockpit etc.
Coaster	Ship carrying cargoes along the coast
Cod's head	Bow shaped like a cod's head
Cotton caulking	Cotton rope/string set between plank seams to prevent water coming in
Counter	Overhanging stern
Cuddy	Little cab for shelter, normally not fully enclosed
Cutter	Single-masted vessel with 2 or more headsails
Davits	Craning device for lifting dinghies or tenders out of the water
Draft	Depth required by vessel to float
Ebb	Out-going tide
Elsan	Chemical toilet
Eye of the wind	Where the wind is coming from
Feather the mainsail	Let the mainsail out so that wind goes either side of it, to avoid strain
Fenders	Inflatable spheres to prevent damage when vessels come alongside
Fidded	Section mast which can be lowered – held up by wedge device called fid
Fin keel	Leeway moderating Device
Flashes	Lakes
Forestay	Line running from the bow of boat to the upper part of the mast - to pull the mast forward. A forestay that attaches slightly below the top of the mast can be used to help control the bend of the mast. The most forward stay on boat is also called the headstay

Freeboard	The distance between the top of the hull and the waterline
Full and bye	Sailing as close to the wind as possible with every sail full
Gaff	A spar which is bent to the head of a fore and aft sail
Gaff rig	4-sided sail supported by gaff
Garboards	Planks next to the keel
Gat	Gap e.g. In sand banks
Genniker	Hybrid genoa jib and spinnaker
Gunter	Gaff set near vertical
Grown frames	Ribs cut from timber so that grain follows the curve of the rib or frame
Gunwale	Pronounced gunnel. Rail around the edge of a boat at deck level. Originally where guns fired through. Smaller versions are called toe rails
Gybe	Changing set of mainsail
Halliard	Rope for hoisting sails
Hawser	Large diameter rope, such as a tug would use for towing ships
Headway	Forward motion
Heels	When a ship leans to one side
Hemp warp	Rope for mooring etc. Made out of hemp fibres
Hollow entry	Where the stern cuts into the water, naval architural term, less buoyant than a full bow but more efficient
Horn timber	Structural member, usually supporting stern
Hulked	Laid up, awaiting dismantling
Iroko	Species of timber
Jib	Triangular sail attached to the headstay. A jib that extends aft of the mast is known as a genoa.
Jib topsail	A small jib set high on the headstay of a double headsail rig
Kedged	Haul off using a light anchor e.g. to kedge off a mud bank to pull off
Keel	Flat surface built into the bottom of boat to reduce the leeway caused by the wind pushing against the side of the boat
Keel hauling	Form of torture – guilty party is hauled under the keel
Keelson	Beam attached to top of the floors to add strength to keel on wooden boat
Keruing	Species of timber
Knockdown	When the force of the wind on the sails turns the hull of the boat onto her beam ends so that the mast goes from a vertical to a horizontal position
Lanyard	Thin line, normally rove several times round giving flexible but strong binding e.g. for shrouds
Lay through	Able to take a straight course through
Lee bow wave	Wave where the boat cuts through, lee side
Leeward	The direction the wind is going downwind
Leeway	Sideways movement of a boat away from the wind, usually unwanted. Keels & other devices help prevent a boat from having excessive leeway
Lengths man	Man who looks after length of canal or railway track
Loa	Length over all
Luff	Leading edge of sail
Luffing	Pointing the boat into the wind - sail flapping
Mackerel stern	Fine-lined stern like mackerel
Mainsail	Principle sail of ship
Matelots	Blue collar workers on ship
Midship frames	'ribs' in the middle section of the boat
Mizzen	Aftermast mast on yawl, ketch, 3-masted vessel

Navigation (as canal)	Originally stream or river made officially navigable with locks, towpath & civil engineering works. Often used for entirely man-made canals suitable for navigation; rather than drainage purposes
Otterboards	Boards at the head of a trawl net that keep the mouth of net open
Packet port	Ferry port, originally for mail ships – mail packet
Pantiles	Roof tiles of a specific wavy Section – clay
Picking up way	Starting to move in the right direction
Pig	Heavy weight of iron or lead, used to ballast or trim vessels for stability
Pitching	Dipping and reaving motion of boat at sea
Pitchpole	When the bow of boat dives into the sea so far that the boat turns turtle bow down upside down & surfaces having made a complete circle
Point of plane	The point where boat starts to skim over water instead of sailing through
Port	Left side of the ship
Port tack	Wind across the port side
Prow	Stern, bow
Ream it out	Scrape out furring, corrosion etc. From tube, pipe etc.
Reefing	Reducing the amount of sail area
Revictualling	Re-stocking on food and drink
Rhumb line	Navigation term – planned line on chart/course
Rockered keels	Curved in fore and aft direction, so it rocks
Sailing trim	All gear stowed away and lashed down so the boat can sail, also with all necessary gear aboard
Sail-loft	Loft to keep or make sails
Saltings	Marshes which are flooded by the sea on occasions
Scandalise	To take the power out of the mainsail by rucking the peak or hoisting the tack, thus taking the power out of the top half of sail
Scarph	Special joint for timber of same section, so that one tapers into the other
Shakes	Longitudinal cracks in timber caused by drying out
Sheer	Upward curve of the deck
Skiff	Open boat
Slip the cable	'let go' the cable
Sloop	A single masted boat with one sail before the mast and a fore and aft mainsail after the mast
Sluicing tide	Fast moving tidal current
Snout	Nose/bow
Snub (against cable)	Jerk to halt against cable
Spars	Poles for holding up sails etc. E.g. Mast, boom, jackyard, club
Spindrift	Fine spray/ mist blown off sea surface in extreme conditions
Spinnaker	Light weather balloon shaped reaching / running sail
Spoon bow	Bow rounded like a spoon, without fore foot
Sprit rig	A spar reaching diagonally from the mast to the upper outer end of a four sided fore and aft sail
Square rigger	Vessel with predominantly square sails
Starboard	Right side of the ship
Steerage	The term meant "the cheapest passenger quarters", 3rd class
Step the mast	Erect the mast
Stern	Rear of the ship
Stevedore	Docker for unloading cargo from ships
Strop	Rope or leather device used on blocks and spars

Tabernacle	The housing in which the heel of a lowered mast sits
Tacking	Working a vessel to windward by sailing alternatively close hauled with the wind on the starboard side and close hauled with the wind on the port side; to alter course through the wind when beating to windward
Tender	A small vessel e.g. a yacht's dinghy, used to attend on her parent vessel
Thwart	Toft, or seat/plank going across boat
Topgallants	The sail set on the topgallant yard in square rigged ships
Topside	The part of the ship above water
Topstrake	The top plank of a boat
Tow-foresail	Overlapping staysail
Transom	The stern planking of a square-sterned vessel
Traveller	Deice enabling headsail to travel up and down bowsprit
Trawling nogs	Posts from which warps can be tied in fishing practice
Warp	A rope by which anything is hauled along
Wear ship	To go round stern to wind from starboard tack to port tack and vice versa
Weather a mark	To pass safely to windward
Windward	The direction the wind is coming from, up wind.
Yard arms	Outer end of a yard, especially of a square-sail yard

List of Illustrations,
Maps and Drawings

About The Author

Jonathan Wainwright was born in 1946 to parents Betty and Bill, and has a sister Gillian. He grew up in the Merseyside Village of Hale, then in Lancashire, and went to school in Liverpool. He studied to be an Architect in London, and on qualifying in 1971 married Margaret Heywood and went to live in Bury St. Edmunds in East Anglia, before moving nearer to the coast where he now lives, in Mistley, Manningtree. He has two grown up children, Andrew and Elizabeth.

He started sailing dinghies when he was eleven, and has been sailing his present boat *Deva* for thirty-eight years! He also has another boat *Maryll*, which he restored recently, and currently keeps in Holland. In association with his sailing, he is an active member of the Old Gaffers Association, which maintains a register of gaff rigged boats and lays on several events for gaff and classic craft.

His career took a nose-dive when he was struck by coronary heart disease at only forty years old, and was forced to retire from mainstream work at forty-seven. However, he still operates as a sole practitioner architect at Mistley Quay.

This is his first book on sailing related matters, although he has had a book *Computers in Architectural Practice*, of which he was co-author, published in 1972.